SOUTH BRISTOL

Totterdown, Windmill Hill, Bedminster, Southville & Ashton

THROUGH TIME

Will Musgrave

AMBERLEY PUBLISHING

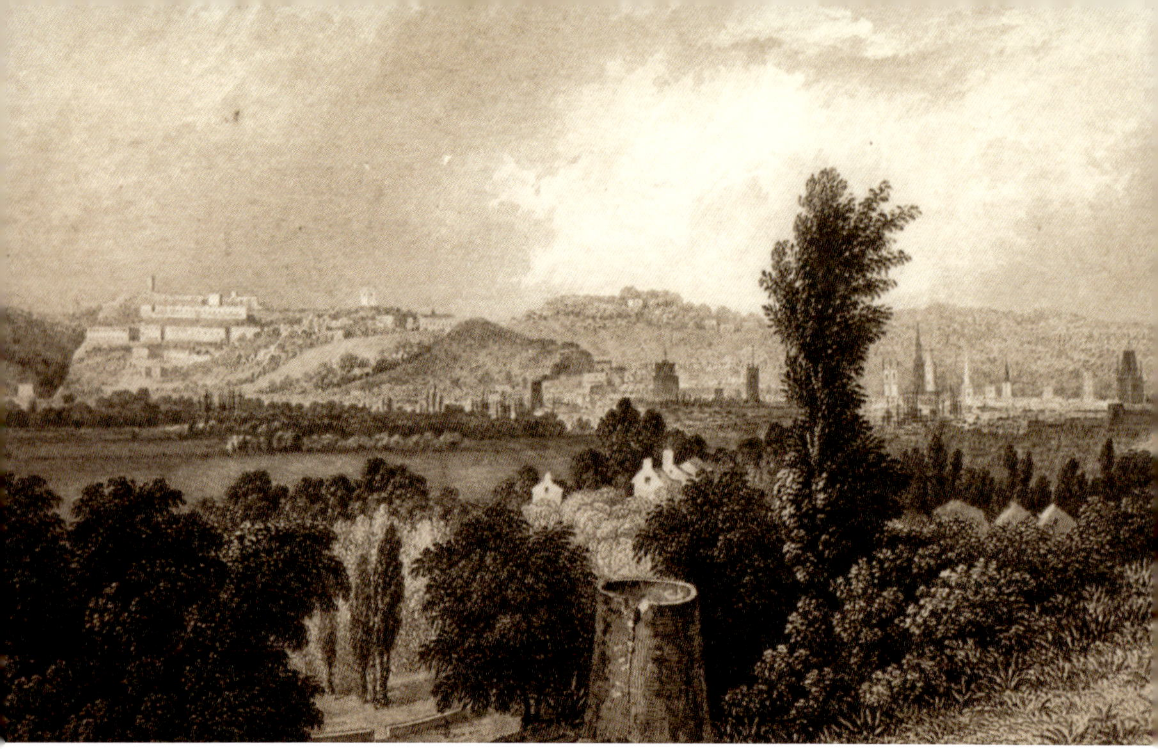

A view from Bedminster Down, across Ashton, towards Bristol, *c*. 1828.

First published 2013

Amberley Publishing
The Hill, Stroud, Gloucestershire, GL5 4EP
www.amberley-books.com

ISBN 978 1 4456 1927 9 (print)
ISBN 978 1 4456 1933 0 (ebook)

British Library Cataloguing in Publication Data.
A catalogue record for this book is available from the British Library.

Typesetting by Amberley Publishing.
Printed in Great Britain.

Introduction

For many visitors to Bristol, their first impression of the history of the city is invariably shaped by the Georgian terraces of Clifton, the medieval maze of the streets in the centre of the city and Brunel's numerous engineering works. However, if they stopped during their pilgrimage across the suspension bridge and looked south, they would see one of the most important and oldest parts of the city. The land that lies stretched out south of the River Avon from Ashton, through Southville, Bedminster, Totterdown and as far as Brislington, was once known as the Royal Manor of Bedminster, and was recorded in the Domesday Book. In the twelfth century it passed into the hands of Robert Fitzharding and became part of the Berkeley estate. At the time, Bedminster was a rural community separated from Bristol by the River Avon. Despite its small size, Bedminster held some influence in the district – St John's church predated St Mary Redcliffe and consequently became its mother church (along with Abbots Leigh). During this period, Robert Berkeley built a hospice for travellers to Bristol, called St Catherine's Hostel, which stood at what is now the top end of East Street.

For the next few centuries Bedminster continued to be a small market town, surrounded by fertile fields and orchards watered by the Malago stream. In 1605, the Smyth family of Ashton Court bought the Manor of Bedminster (they retained ownership until the nineteenth century). During the English Civil War, Prince Rupert burned Bedminster at the second siege of Bristol to prevent the attackers finding shelter outside the city. Forty years later the neighbourhood suffered further misfortune when it was the first part of Bristol to be struck by an outbreak of plague, probably a recurrence of the bubonic plague that had ravished London in the mid-1660s. The population slowly recovered, but by the turn of the seventeenth century the area was still primarily agricultural, with some small industries such as brickworks and rope-making, also providing employment. It was the discovery of rich coal seams in the 1740s that was to changed the face of South Bristol. Landowner Jarrit Smyth brought in a surveyor from Kingswood and in 1748 mining began at South Liberty Lane in Ashton Vale. By the nineteenth century there were eighteen coal pits in Bedminster and Ashton, providing fuel for numerous local tanneries, dockyards, smelting operations, and glass, soap, paper, glue, brass and copper manufacturers. This growth in industry also created a rural migration when poor workers from Somerset and South Wales moved to the city in search of employment. By 1850, the coal pits were employing up to 50 per cent of the male population. The population as a whole grew from just 3,000 in 1801 to 78,000 in 1884. This enormous influx of people into a relatively small area resulted in cramped, unhygienic living conditions. Slums grew up as families were forced to share small terraced houses, which often lacked the most rudimentary sanitary amenities. The smell of open sewers, discarded rubbish and the detritus from the tanneries, butchers, slaughterhouses and glue factories was inescapable in the small streets, tiny courtyards and back alleys, and public health suffered accordingly. The sewage system, where it existed, was woefully inadequate. Often the effluent from dozens of houses and shops would flow into an open drain that eventually found its way to the River Avon. Sewers and cesspits frequently overran, and a clean water supply was literally a pipe dream (prior to 1850 there were only four public pumps or wells). Cholera epidemics broke out in 1832, 1849 and 1886. Another source of ill health came from the noxious discharges from metal and alkali manufacturing industries, potteries and chemical processing plants. These chemicals mixed with the choking fumes of coal smoke to create a toxic cloud.

Nevertheless, the population continued to grow throughout the nineteenth century and the attraction of reliable factory work meant that many families were prepared to put up with the deprivations. In 1886 and 1887, two large factories were built: W. D. & H. O. Wills Tobacco and E. S. & A. Robinson. Both companies offered relatively good working conditions and the attraction of continuous employment in a clean and safe environment. There were even opportunities for girls and women – although Wills did have a rule that they left upon marriage. Between 1902 and 1940, Wills extended in East Street until it occupied not only the large site behind the existing original façade but spread over the site of what is now the Asda supermarket and car park. Factories 2, 3 and 4 were built in 1904 to 1906 in the North Street and Raleigh Road sites. They were employers who realised the importance of having a satisfied and loyal workforce. Their benevolence went beyond the workplace; they funded sports clubs, recreational facilities, churches and other amenities in the area. Robinson's expanded their factory at the southern end of East Street by adding extra storeys.

During this time, a number of churches, public houses, shops and businesses were built to cater for the workers. Between 1854 and 1900, eleven churches and fourteen chapels were erected for the spiritual well-being of the populace, while their physical health was improved by the establishment of two public parks: Victoria Park at Windmill Hill and Greville Smyth Park at Ashton Gate. The old pictures of North Street and East Street show them as prosperous and busy high streets. But behind these shopping streets, the overcrowded, insanitary terraces still lurked. Bristol City Council built 15,000 houses between 1919 and 1939 to help alleviate the city's housing problem (new housing estates were created in nearby Knowle and Filwood Park). Many of the slums were also cleared in the 1930s.

South Bristol was particularly badly hit by the Blitz attacks of the Second World War. It suffered a large number of civilian casualties and lost many streets and prominent buildings. In the post-war years, heavy industry disappeared or relocated to the rural areas in the south, while town planning created new estates in Withywood and Hartcliffe. Several decades of decline followed, not helped by poor central planning and a lack of investment. Despite these external problems, South Bristol retained its community spirit. Today, a new generation of people are moving to the area, attracted to the pleasant terraced houses, parks, shops, and the unique character of the area.

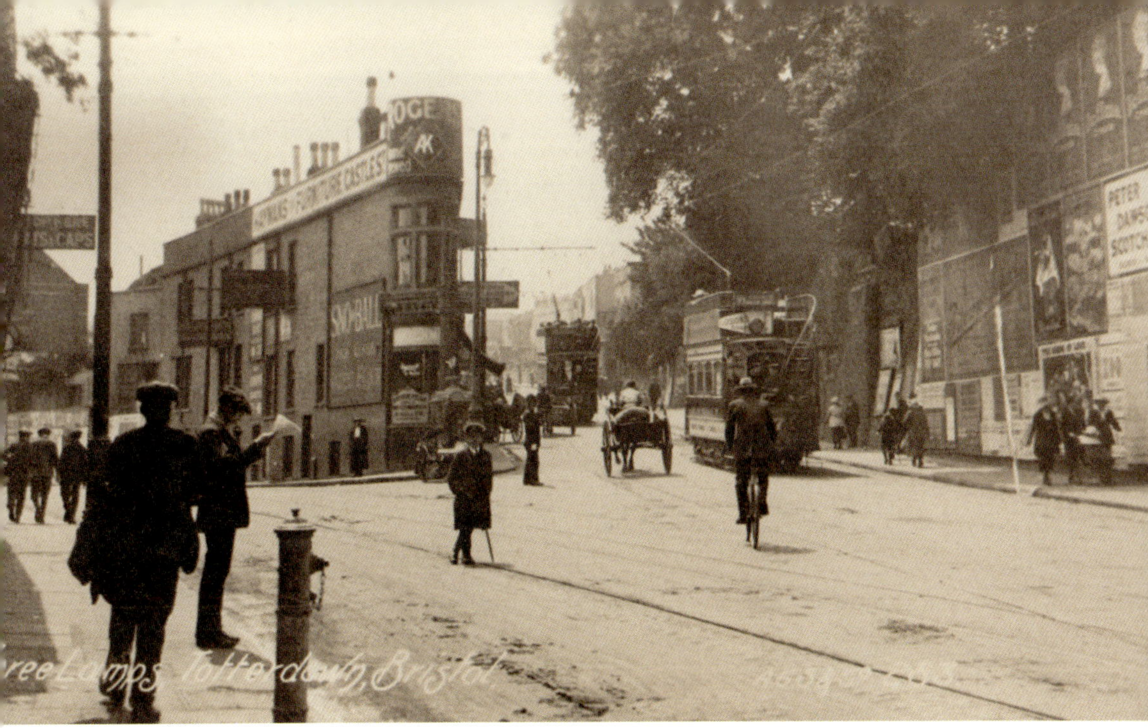

Three Lamps Junction, Totterdown, Early 1900s

Standing at the junction of Bath Road (A4) and Wells Road (A37), this fine cast-iron openwork fingerpost directs people leaving Bristol and has been doing so since 1830. It was temporarily removed in 1973, when much of the surrounding area was laid bare for the proposed Outer Circuit Road and other road improvements, most of which were later abandoned. Over 500 houses and small shops were removed in this exercise, causing much distress at the time. Now with trees, landscaped open spaces and modern housing, it is hard to imagine the packed streets.

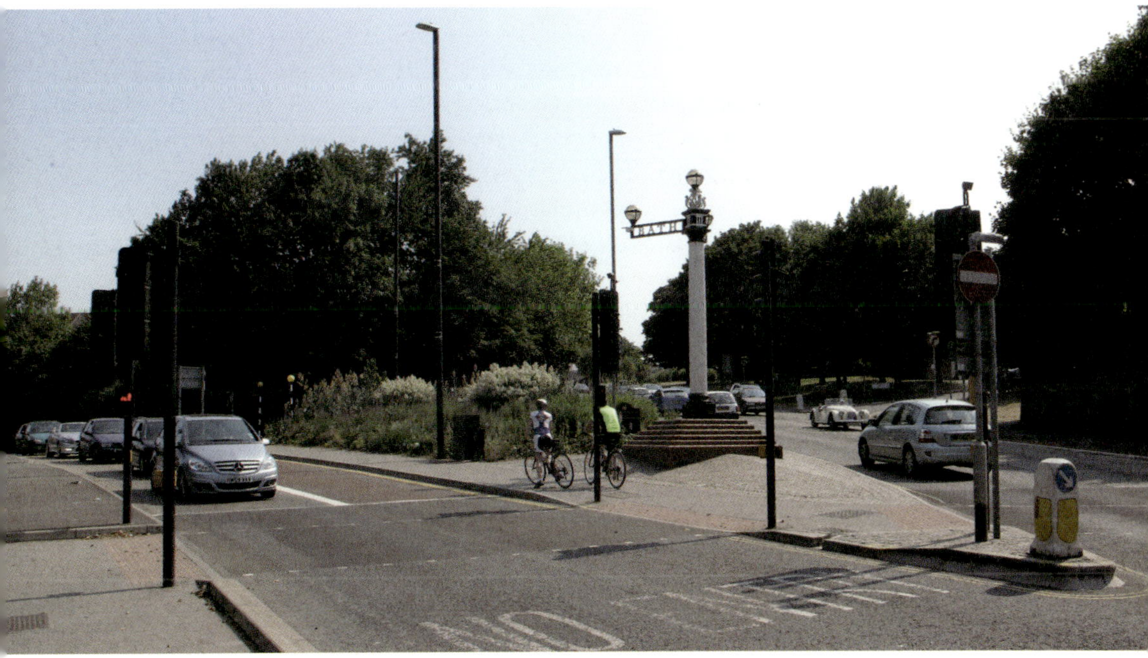

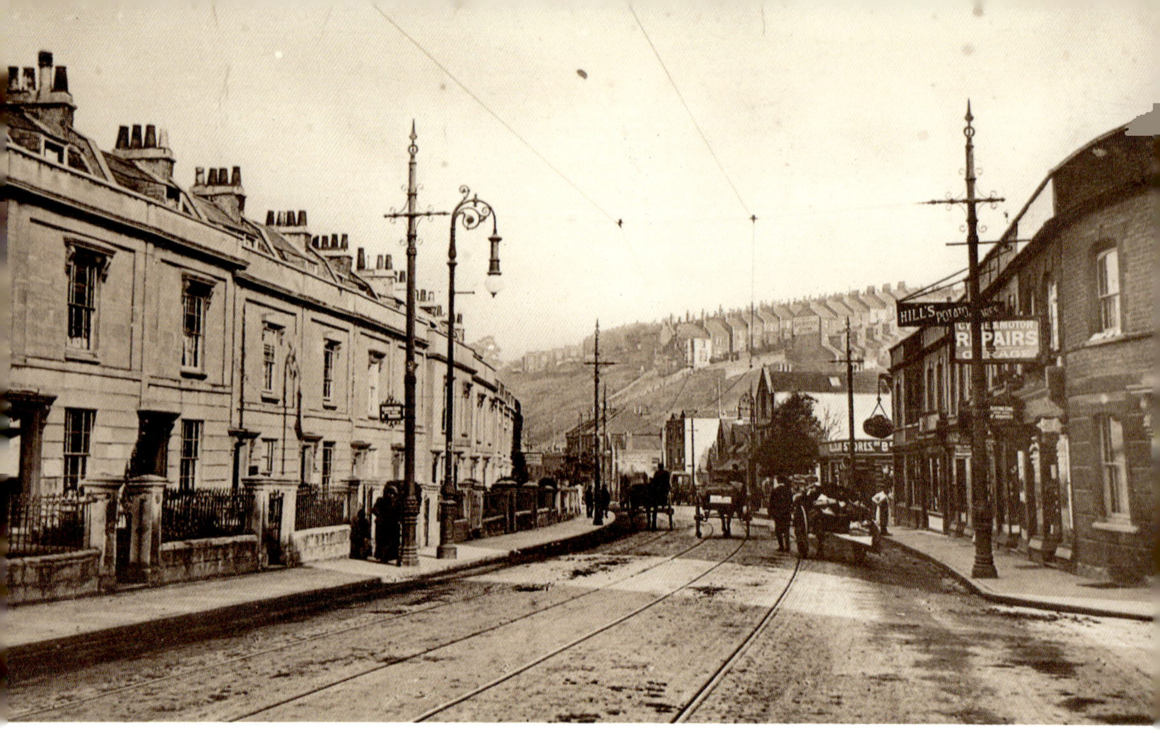

Bath Road, Early 1900s

If it was not for the terraced houses on the hill in the distance, one would never know these pictures were taken from almost the same place. This is Bath Road (A4) looking towards Totterdown. The housing and small shops were levelled to make way for this wide, two-lane stretch of road. Gone are the ornate lampposts and tram poles, and a bus replaces the horse-drawn vehicles. By coincidence, Bristol Direct Motors is on land that would have been behind the old Cycle and Motor Repairers Garage.

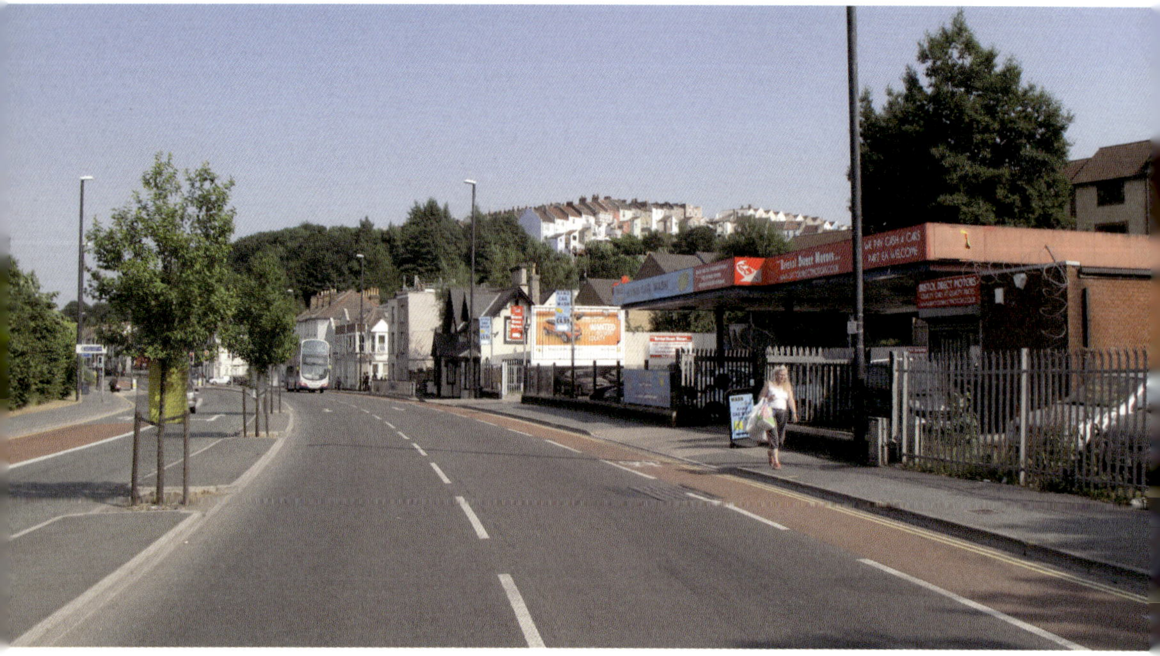

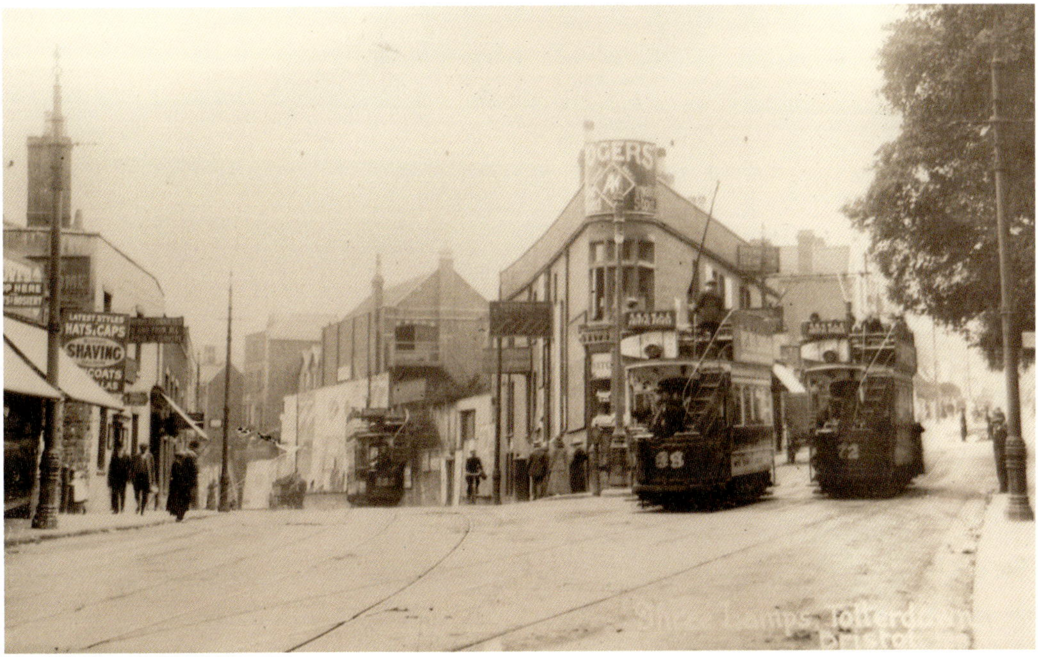

Three Lamps Junction, Totterdown, Early 1900s

This southwards view is of the fingerpost. The tram on the left is going off towards the tram depot in Brislington, and the other two trams are on Wells Road. These pictures clearly show the significant widening of the roads, which culminated with the present system in the early 1980s and the installation of new traffic lights. Many people will remember the long tailback of traffic in the rush hours before these improvements.

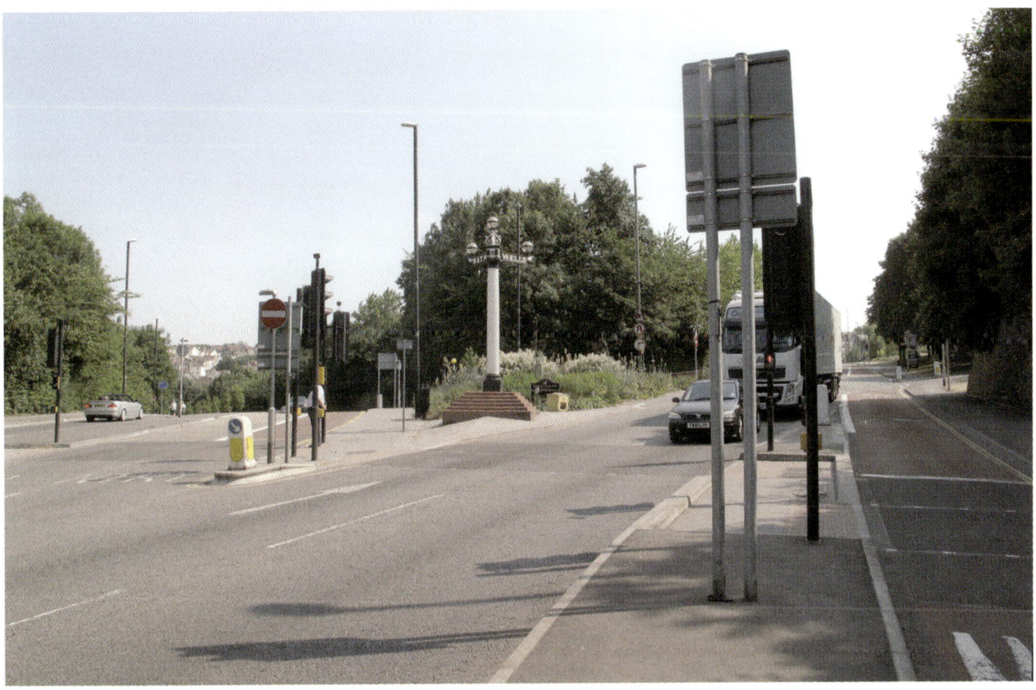

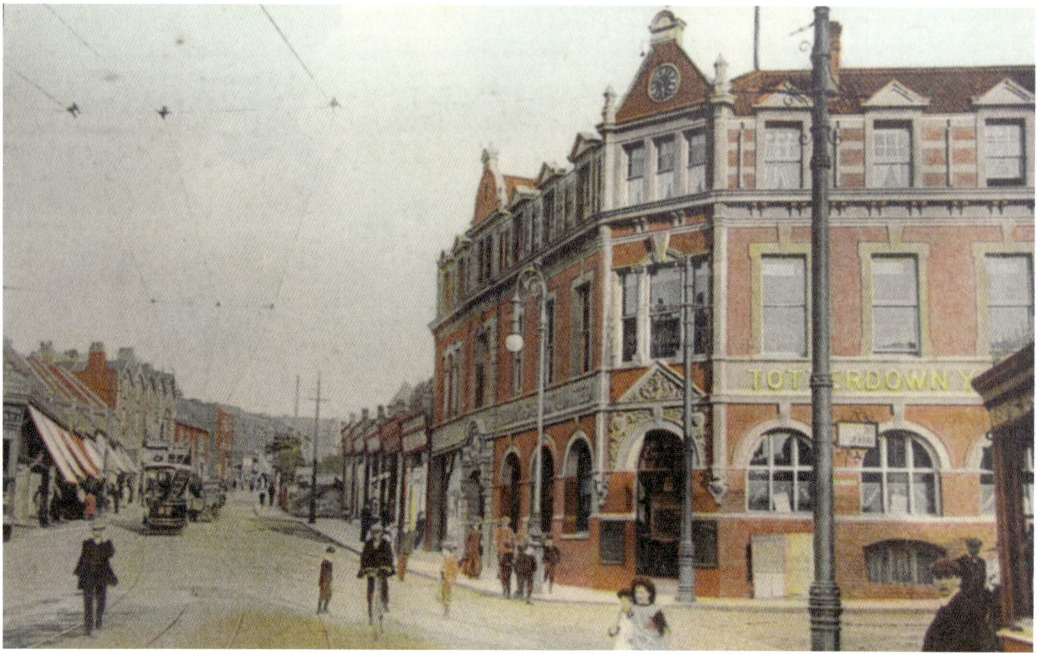

The YMCA, Totterdown, Postcard Dated 27 May 1910

Standing on a bend in Wells Road, just above Three Lamps Junction, is one of the few survivors of the demolition. Outside it remains virtually unchanged, from the clock at the top to the ornate entrance and the carved lettering above the windows. Originally, it was built as a Lloyds Bank. In 1900, it changed hands and became a building for the Young Men's Christian Association (YMCA). Inside it has recently been developed, with nine flats, a gym, a beauty salon and a cafe/wine bar, whose owner's aim is to foster a community spirit.

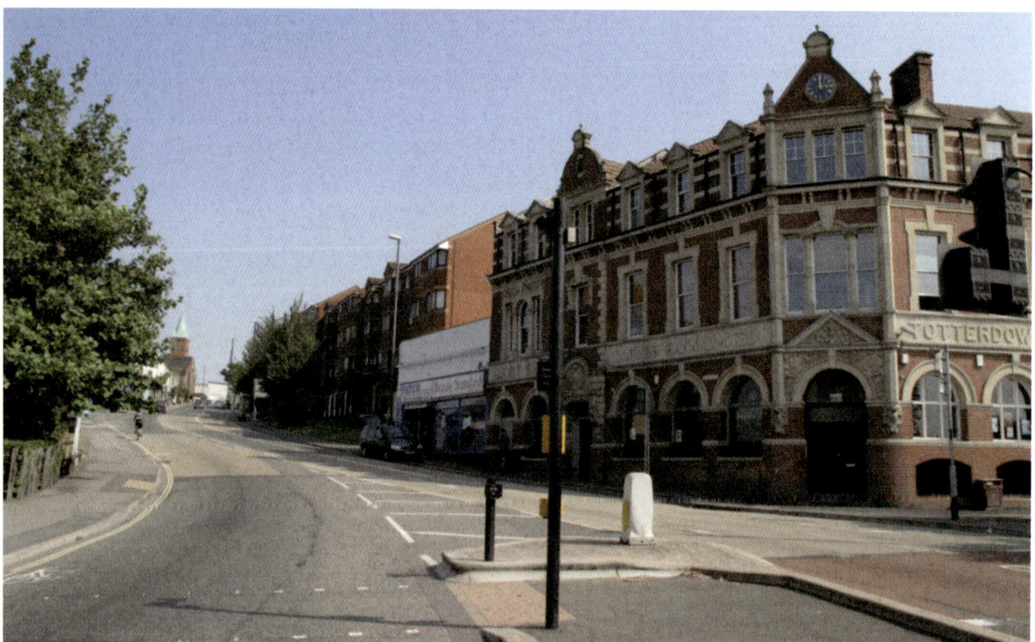

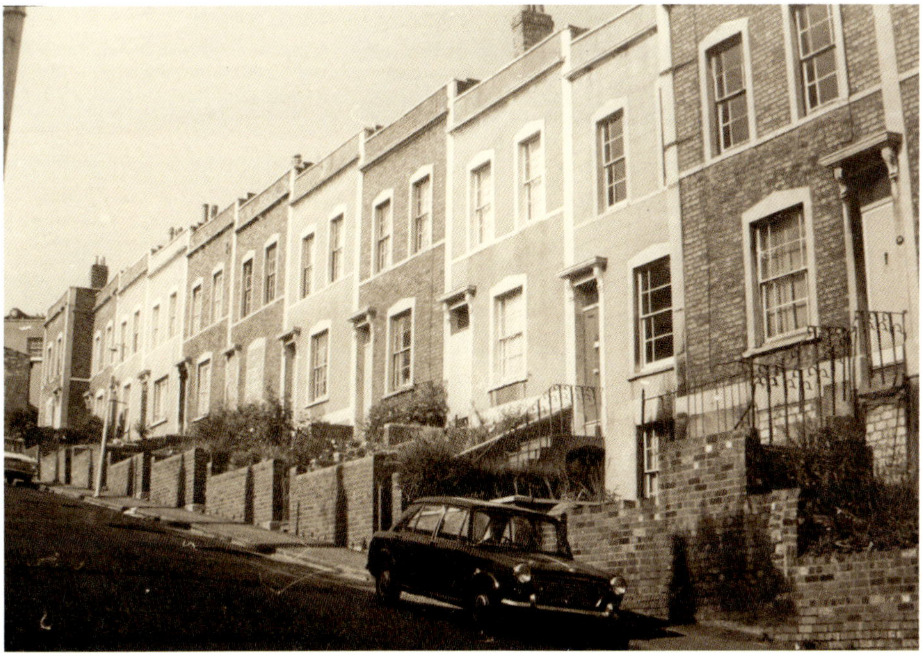

Angers Road, Totterdown, 1970

Angers Road links Wells Road and Bath Road around 200 metres from Three Lamps Junction. It owes its rather unusual name to a farmer, John Anjor, who leased the land in the 1870s, when the terraced houses were built. In 1973, the local authorities demolished the housing (550 houses and small shops) to make way for an interchange between the A37 and A4 and the proposed Outer Circuit Road. The latter was never built and the land is now a small, planned estate of grouped houses, with front and back gardens and hard standing for cars.

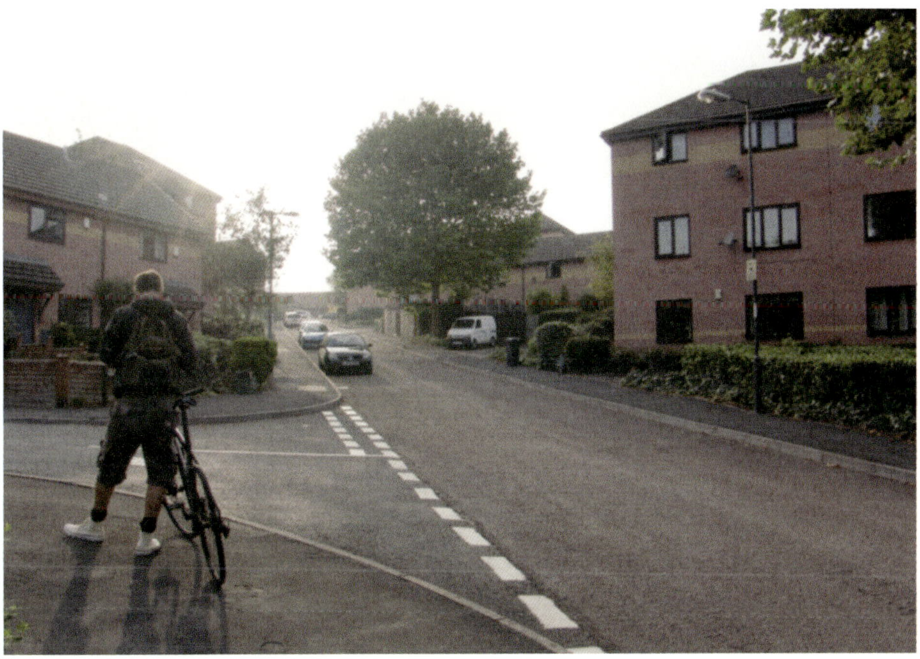

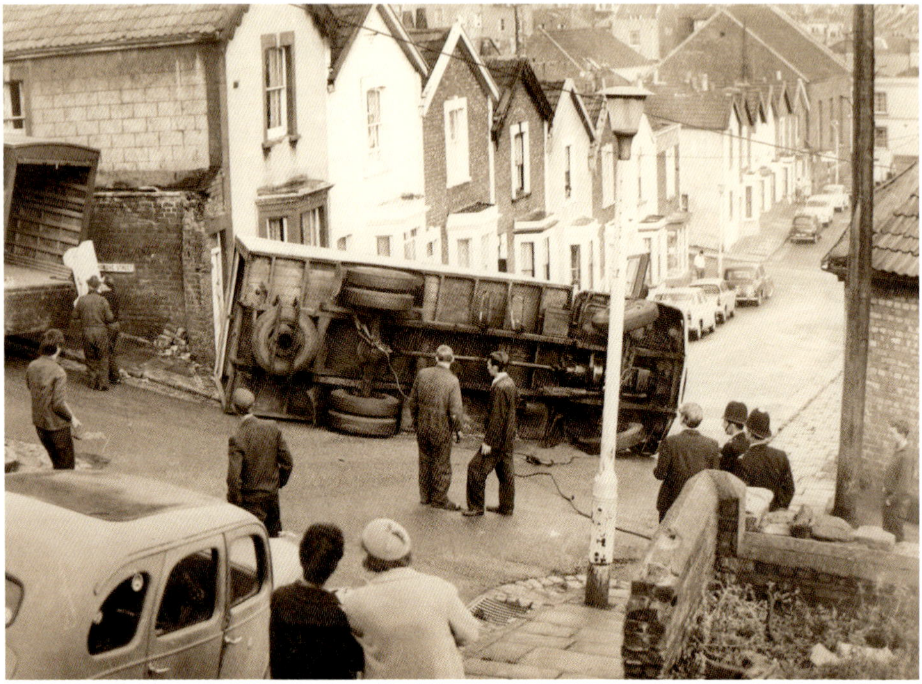

Stanley Hill, Totterdown, 1970

Beyond the interesting road accident, which is clearly absorbing those in the picture, this intersection with Highgrove Street is a good place to stand to get an idea of the changes in the recent history of Totterdown. In both pictures on the right are what are described on maps as 'works'. On the left, the housing differs. Here is where the demolition for the aborted road scheme ended and the new housing commenced; the street going up behind the pictures retains the original terrace housing.

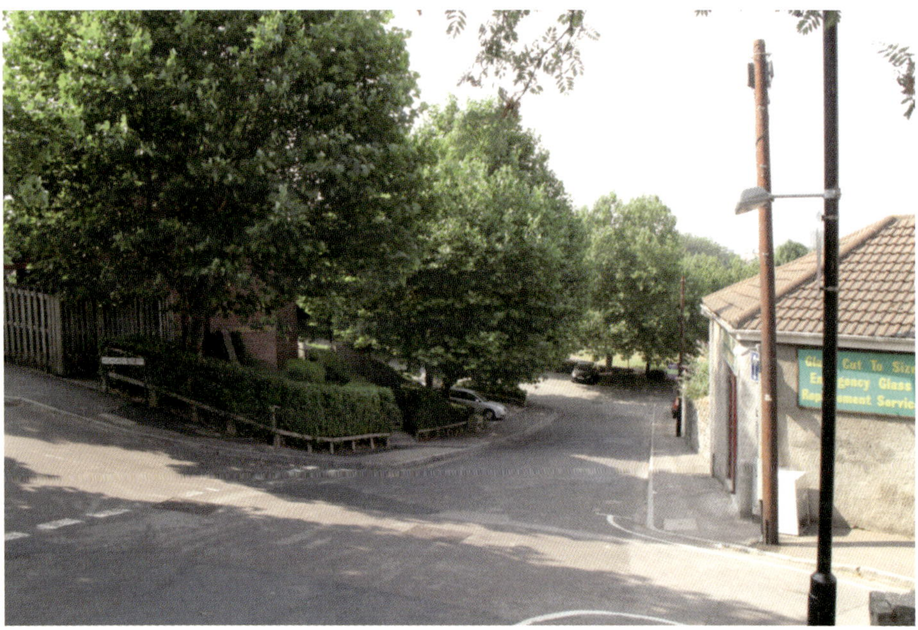

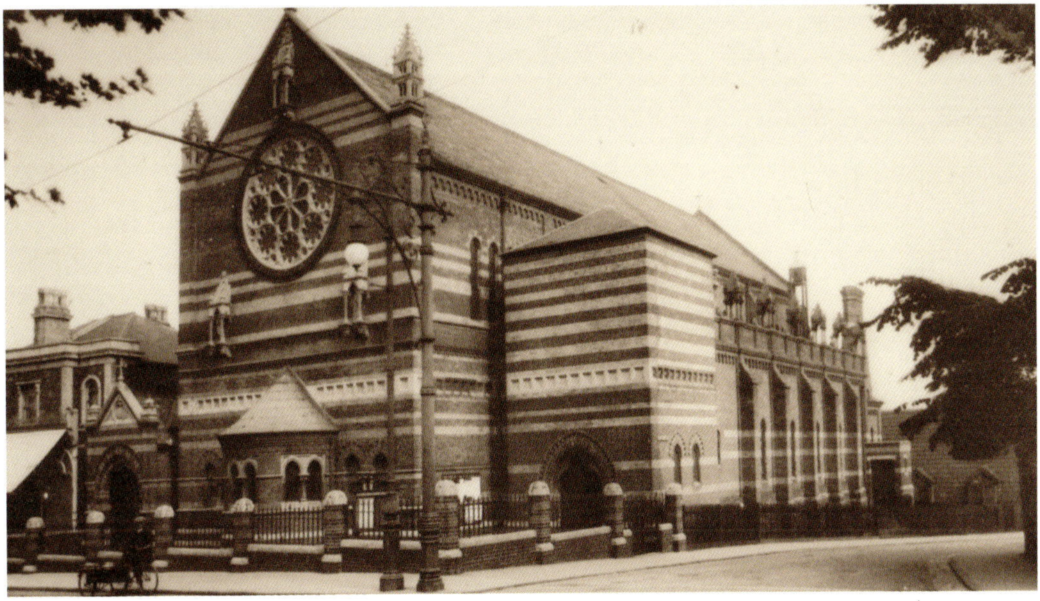

Church of the Holy Nativity, Totterdown, Early 1900s

Standing on Wells Road, the church of the Holy Nativity was first dedicated in 1871 to serve the growing population of Totterdown and Knowle. The architect was William Venn Gough, who also designed Cabot Tower, Colston's Girls' School and nearby St Aldhelm's church. Gough is noted for his ornate exteriors (some of his buildings have been rather unkindly compared to Liquorice Allsorts). The church suffered a direct hit by an incendiary bomb in the Blitz, but unlike other churches in Bristol it survived the attack and was rebuilt.

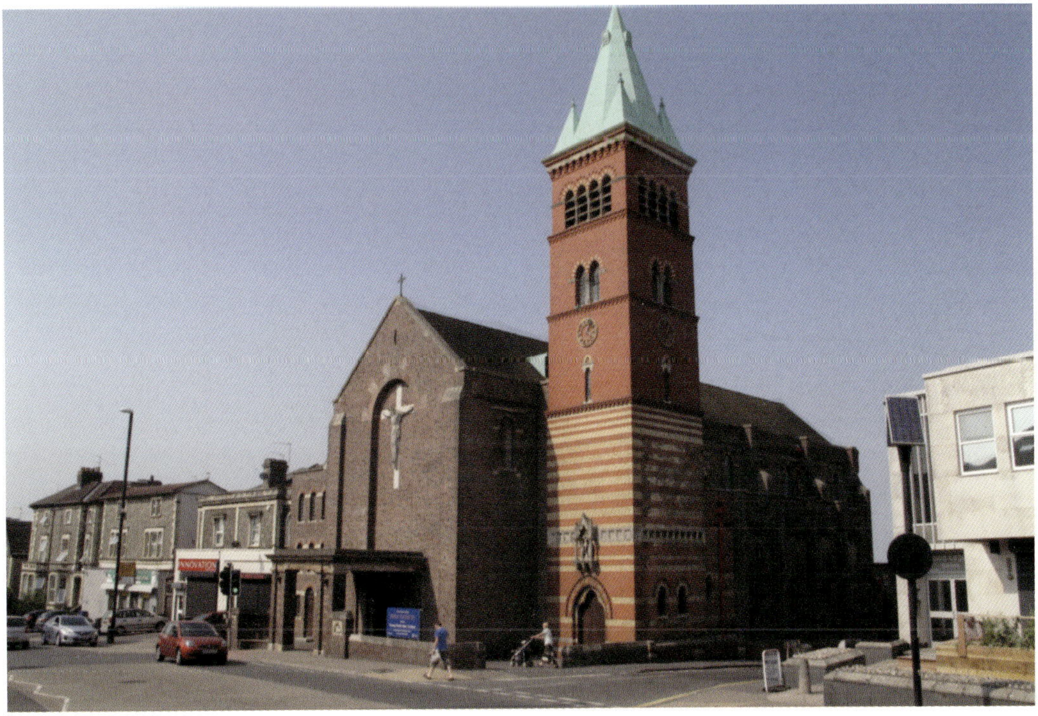

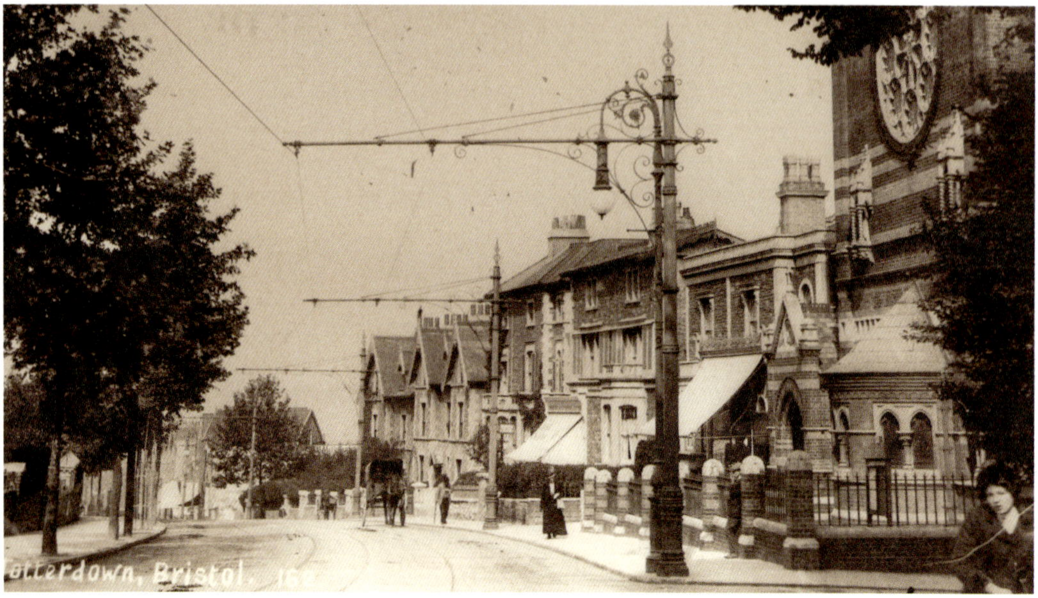

Wells Road, Totterdown, Postcard Dated 14 August 1919

Looking north along Wells Road, the altered exterior of the church of the Holy Nativity on the right is more obvious. The rebuilding of the church to the design of the architect J. M. Meredith was completed in 1955. The only bit remaining of the former church is the base and the ten ornate bands at the base of the new tower. The remains of the original church were chosen by the War Artists' Advisory Board to be recorded by the artist John Piper, who had a deep understanding of Britain's architectural history. The painting is now in Bristol Museum and Art Gallery. It is interesting to note that the buildings beyond the church remained intact after the Blitz attack.

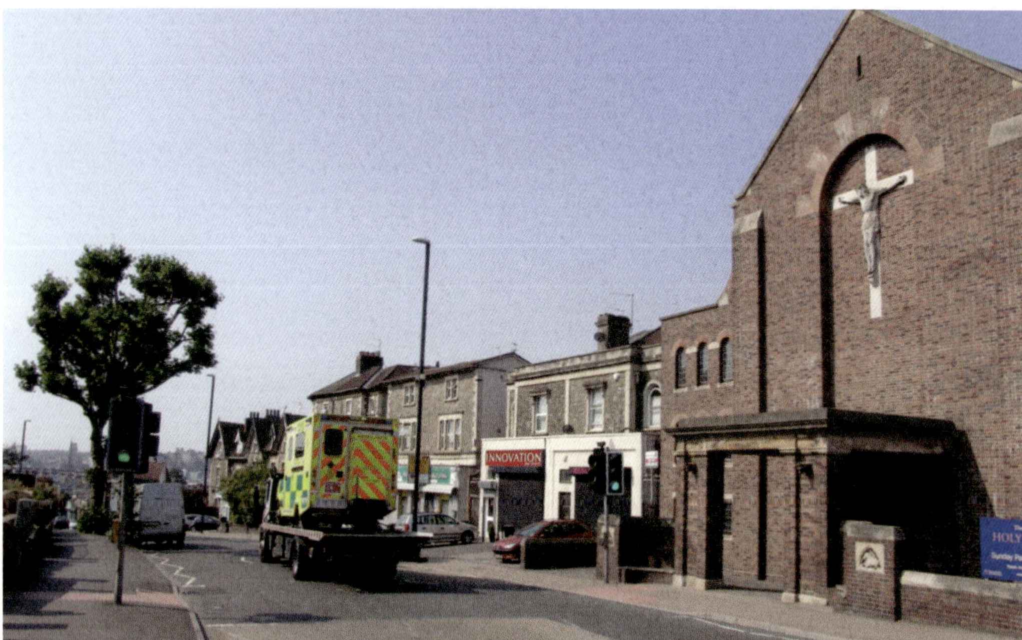

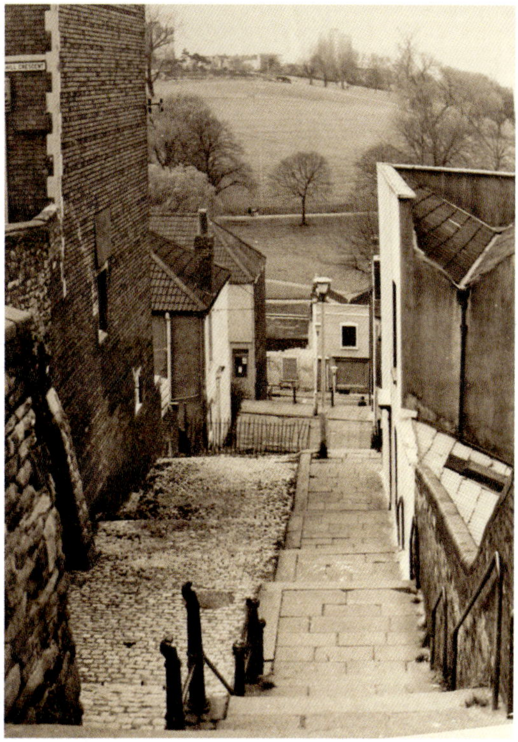

St Luke's Steps, 1972

These steps link Pylle Hill Crescent and St Luke's Road. On the 1880 map there is an indication of a path, and on the 1900 epoch 2 map they are shown as steps. In the old picture, at the bottom of the steps and across the road, the boarded up windows of the Princess Royal pub (which was subsequently demolished) are visible. The St Luke's entrance to Victoria Park is just to the right of the site of the former pub.

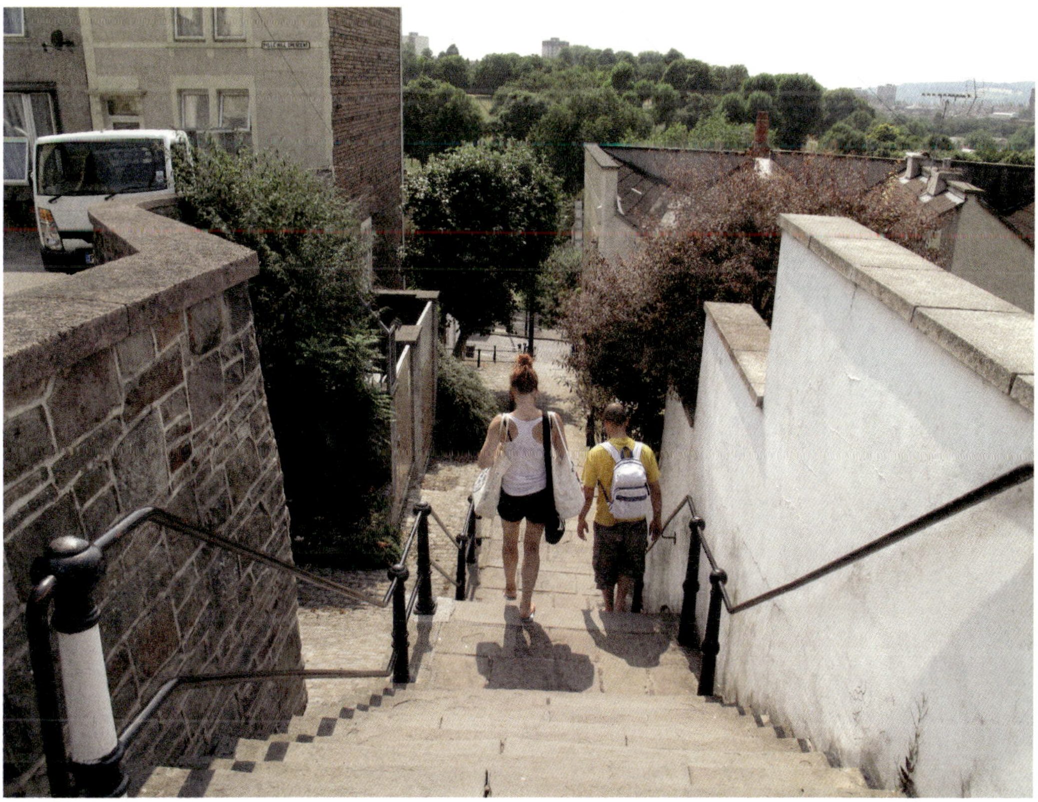

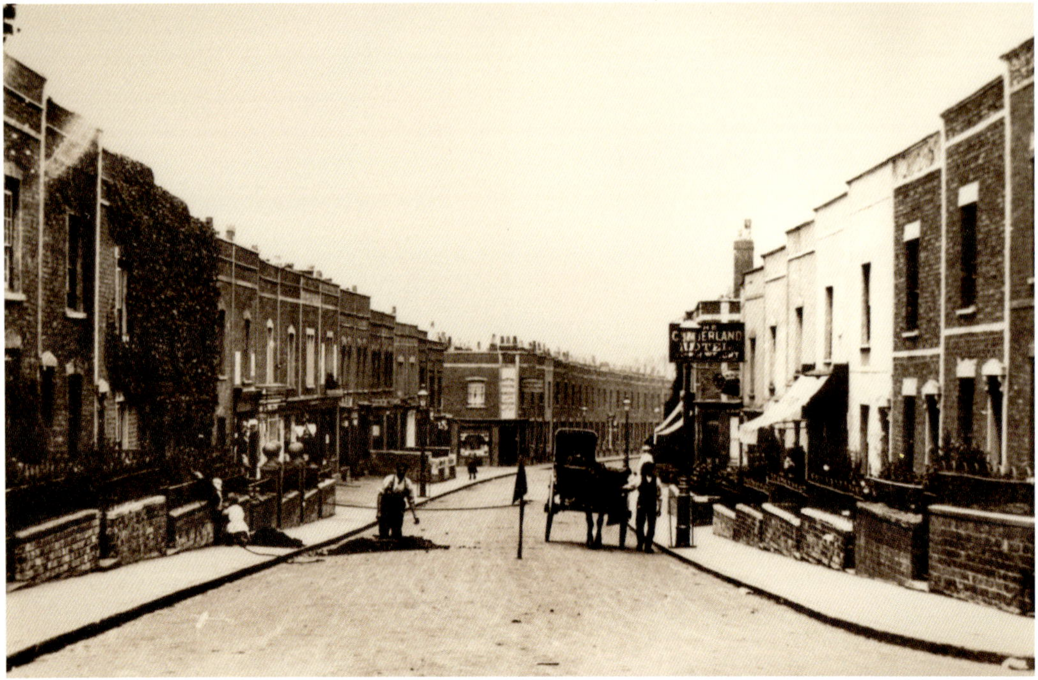

St Luke's Road, Early 1900s

These differing pictures, taken from York Road (A370), show how much clearance work has been done in what was once one of the most impoverished parts of the neighbourhood. On maps from 1880 up until 1949, the building beside the man digging a hole in the road is marked as a school. On the opposite side of the road was the Cumberland Hotel. On the crest of the hill in the modern photograph are the gaily coloured houses of Richmond Street – a trend taken up in other parts of Bristol such as Cliftonwood. 'Plots For Sale' notices indicate that the area will continue to develop and change.

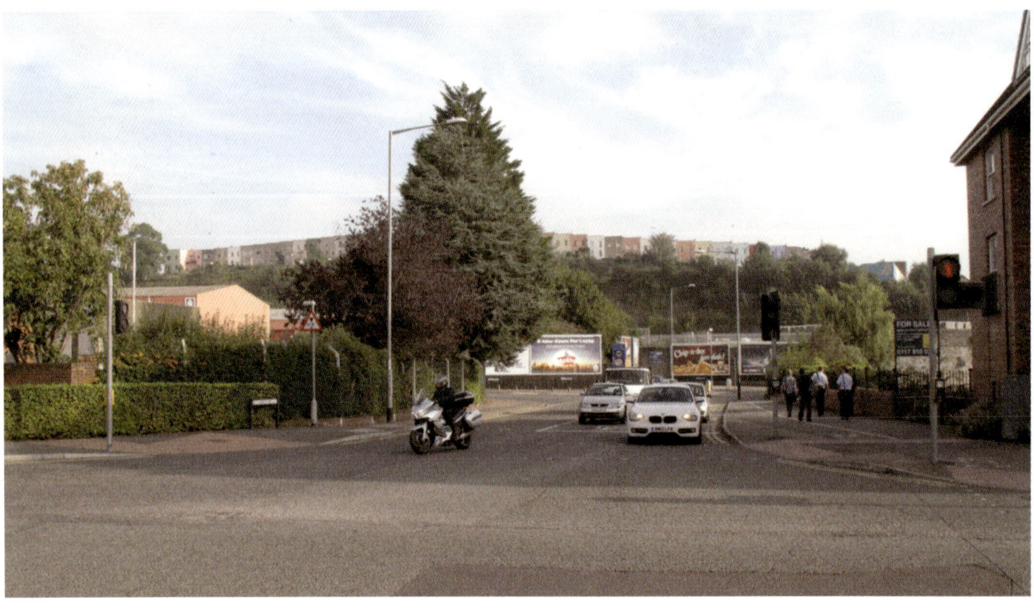

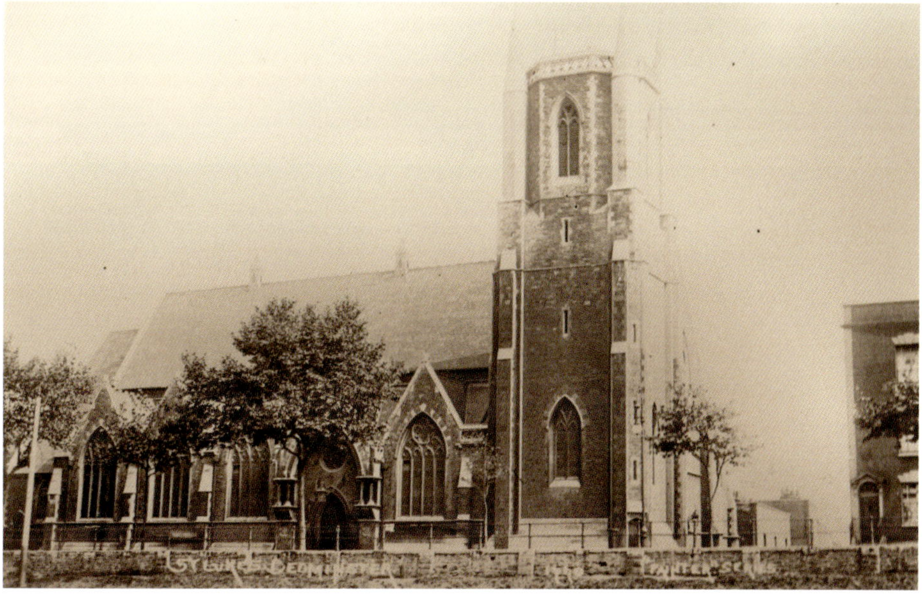

St Luke's Church, Early 1900s

Around 100 metres along the road to the right of the previous pictures stood St Luke's church, built in 1860/61 to the design of John Norton, who five years earlier had worked on the plans for the nearby St John the Baptist church. Norton, who was born and educated in Bristol, was one of the great Gothic Revivalist architects and was commissioned by William Gibbs to design the elaborate exterior of Tyntesfield in North Somerset. He also agreed in 1862 to apprentice a budding young author called Thomas Hardy, and Hardy's second wife, Florence, later wrote that 'Norton proved himself to be one of the best helps Hardy ever had'. St Luke's church was closed in 1968 and demolished in 1970. The site is now occupied by the residential blocks of St Luke's Court and Spring House.

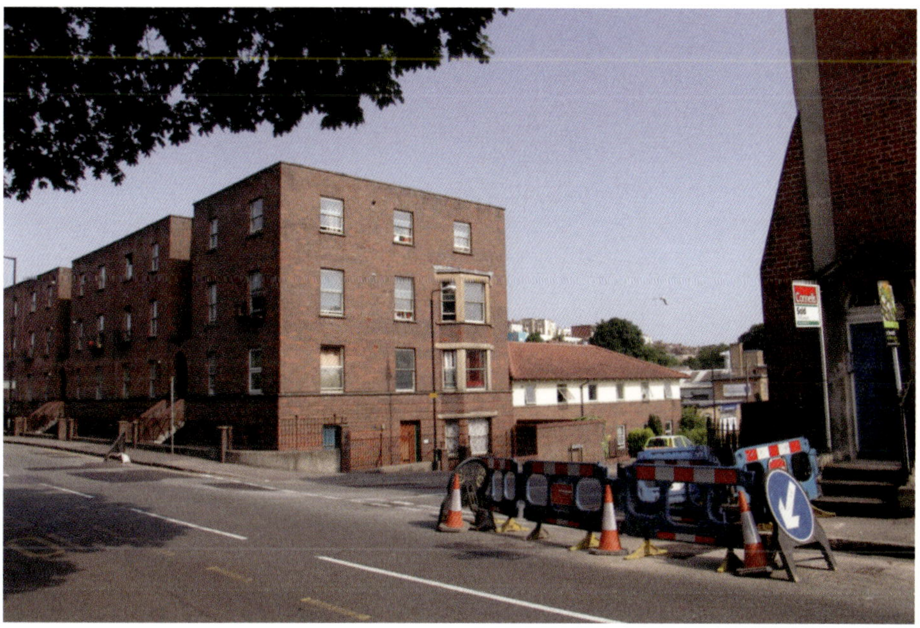

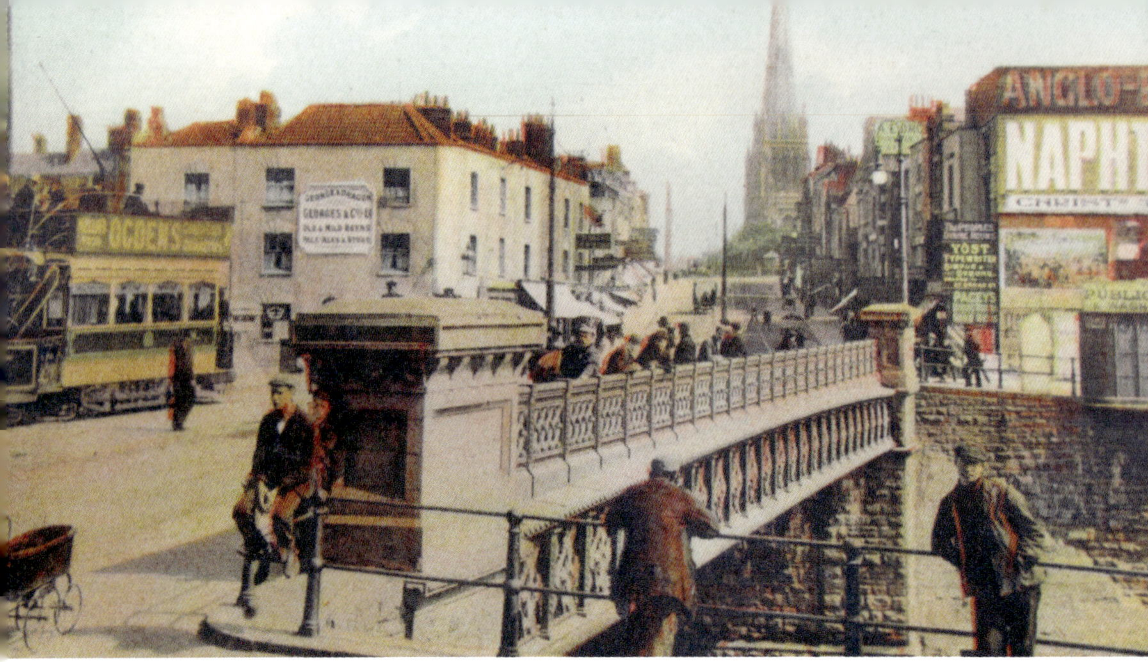

Bedminster Bridge, Early 1900s

This Grade II-listed bridge carries the A38 across the Avon New Cut. A plaque on the side says 'Cochrane/Dudley/1885'. This was the Coalbrookdale Company that produced the fine cast-iron work. It replaced the former 1809 Harford Bridge. In the mid-1960s, a concrete bridge was built to the right of this one to form a roundabout. Both pictures show the spire of St Mary Redcliffe. The George & Dragon pub has been replaced by the Waring House multistorey block of flats. In the old picture across the river, the low, grey building is a urinal, above which is the sign for public baths and washhouse.

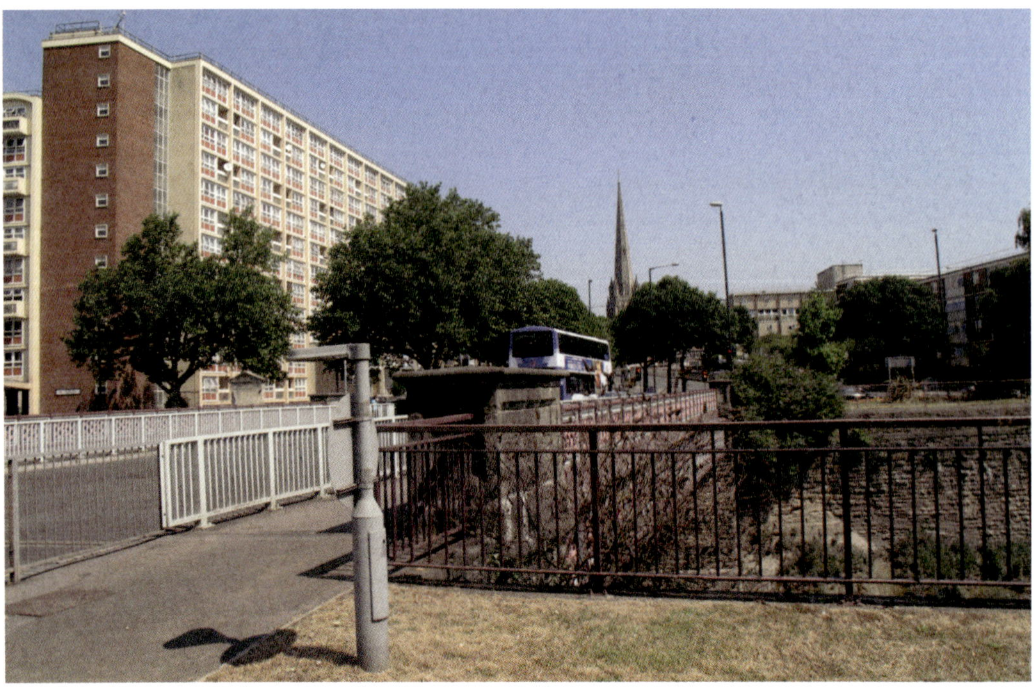

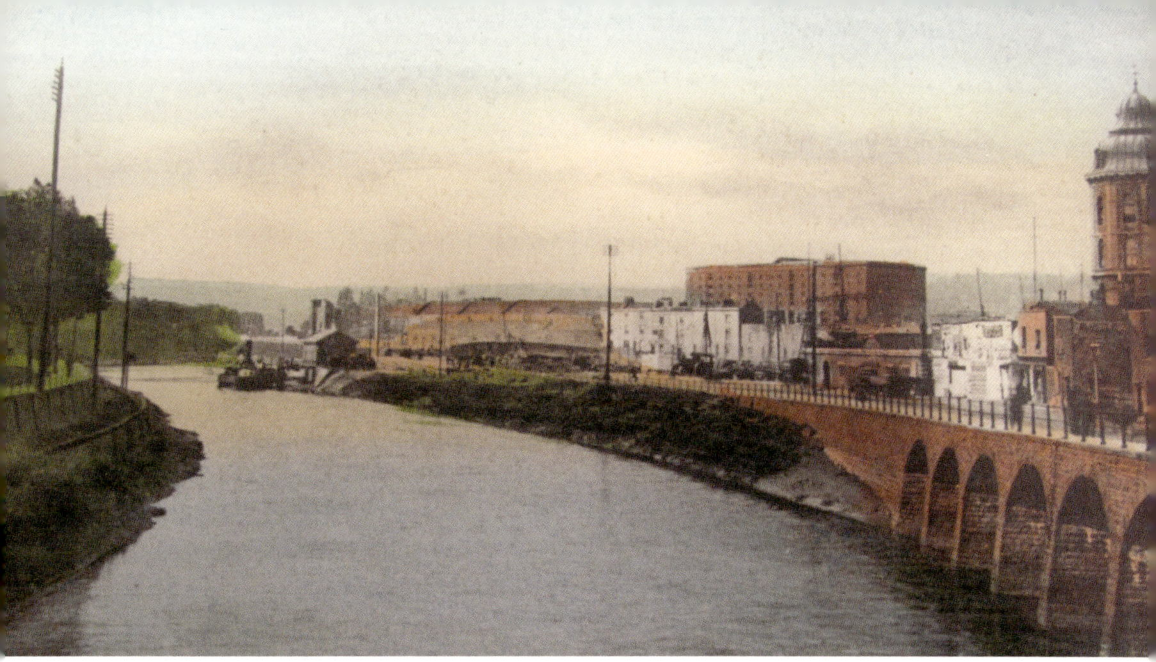

View from Bedminster Bridge, Early 1900s

This view from Bedminster Bridge looks down the Avon New Cut. The New Cut was dug in the early nineteenth century to create the Floating Harbour in Bristol's city centre so ships could berth more stably (the River Avon caused ships to become stranded on the mudbanks at low water). The original design was drawn up by William Milton in 1791. It was later adopted by William Jessop, a distinguished Georgian civil architect, in 1802. Under the supervision of Jessop's son Josias, work commenced in 1804, and five years later water was let into the New Cut for the first time. To the right in the old photograph are the bonded warehouses and the old Bristol General Hospital.

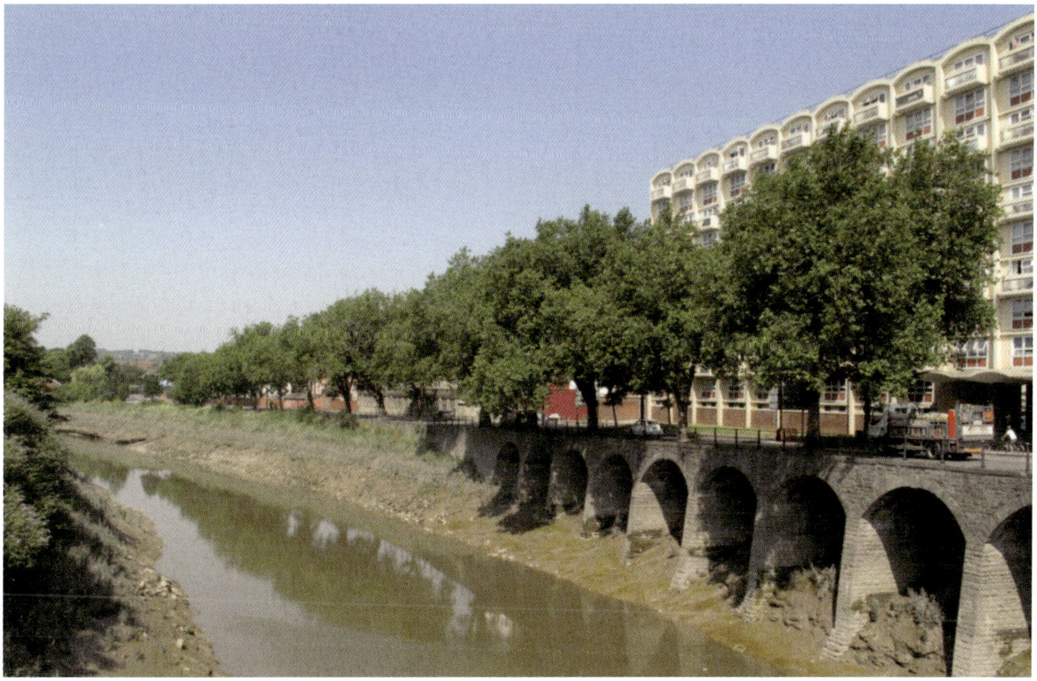

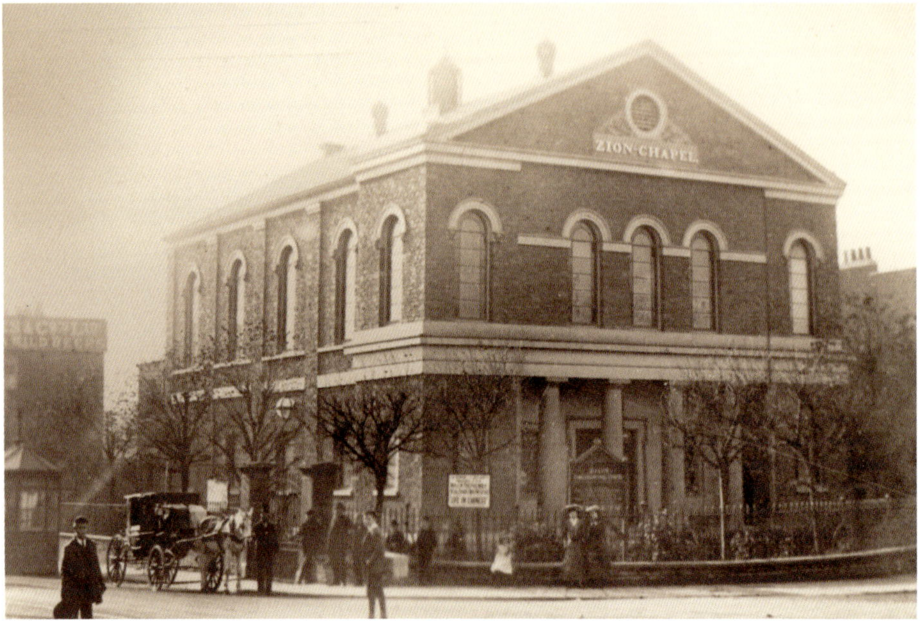

Zion Chapel, Early 1900s

This former chapel is in a prominent position at the junction of Bedminster Parade, Coronation Road and Bedminster Bridge. It was built in 1829, possibly to the design of R. S. Pope, and closed in the 1980s when it became offices over four floors. Its colloquial name is 'Church of the Vow', which refers to its foundation by John Hare, who bought the land and gave £4,000 for its construction. Hare came to Bristol from Somerset in 1773, determined to make his fortune. He spent his first night sleeping rough near this site and vowed that if he was successful he would build a church there. He was and he did. He invented a new floor covering: linoleum (the precursor to vinyl flooring).

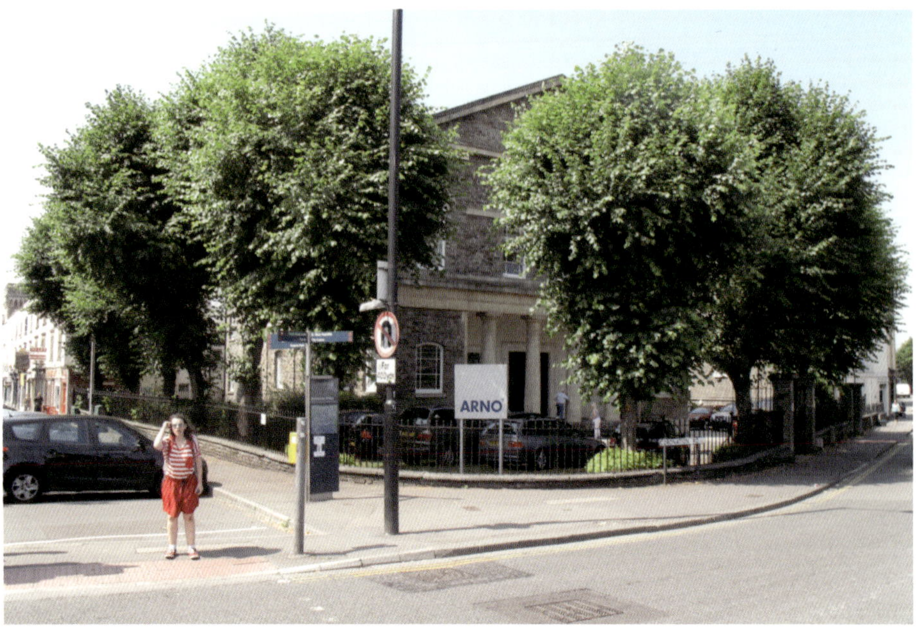

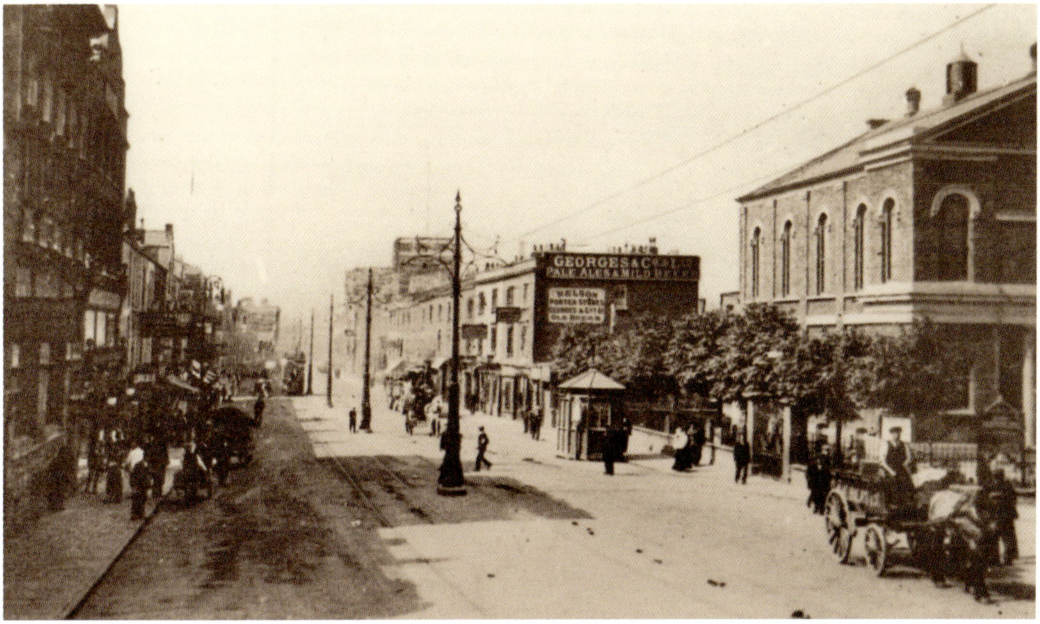

Bedminster Parade, Late Nineteenth/Early Twentieth Century

Both pictures are taken in Bedminster Parade (also known as the Causeway), looking south towards East Street. In the old picture, Zion chapel is on the right, in front of which is a cab stand. The horse manure scattered along the street is a reminder of the importance horses still played in early twentieth-century life. A steam tractor can just be made out in the centre of the picture, behind the white horse and cart. The buildings advertising George's Pale Ales in the older picture are still small commercial outlets at street level, with housing above. The coloured road marking for the bus lane has replaced the tram lines.

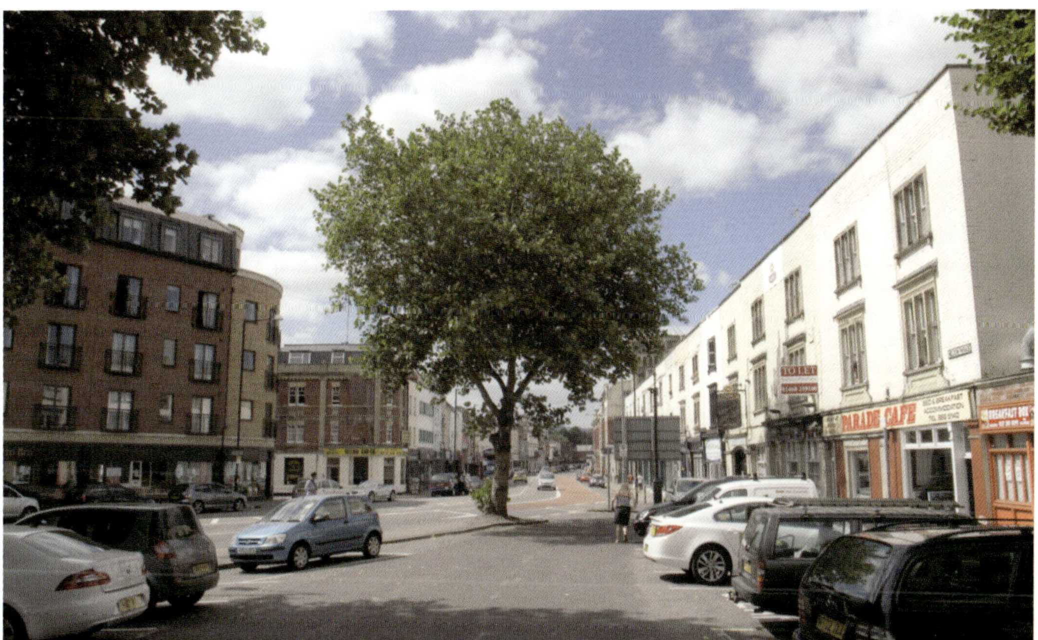

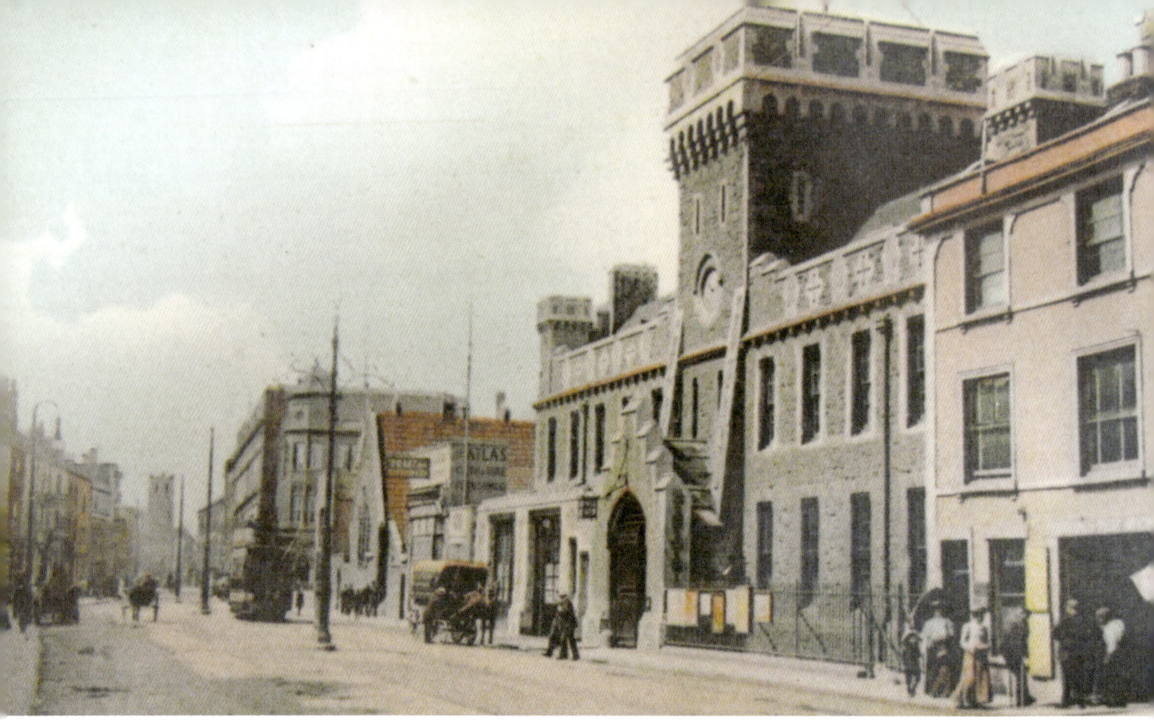

Police Station, Bedminster Parade, *c.* 1900

The former fire and police station, with its distinctive tower, is on the right. Opened in 1882 by Elisha S. Robinson, the owner of the Robinson paper factory, it was the headquarters of the B Division of the Bristol police force. The advertising outside it now is for a traditional Italian restaurant. In the distance, the tower of the church of St John the Baptist is visible, which was bombed in 1940 and finally demolished in 1967.

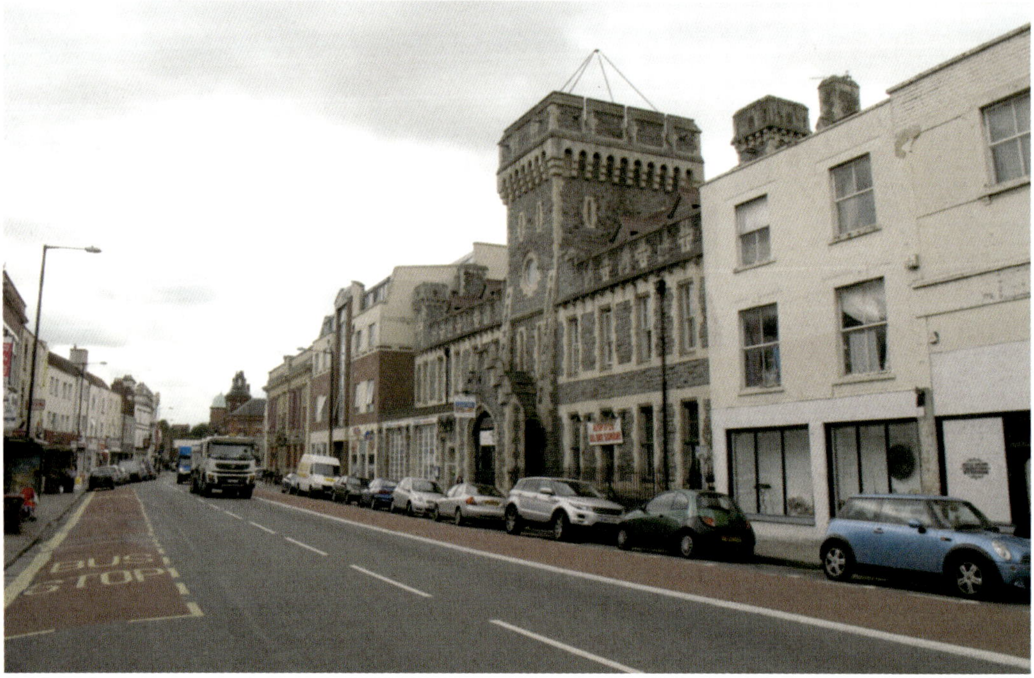

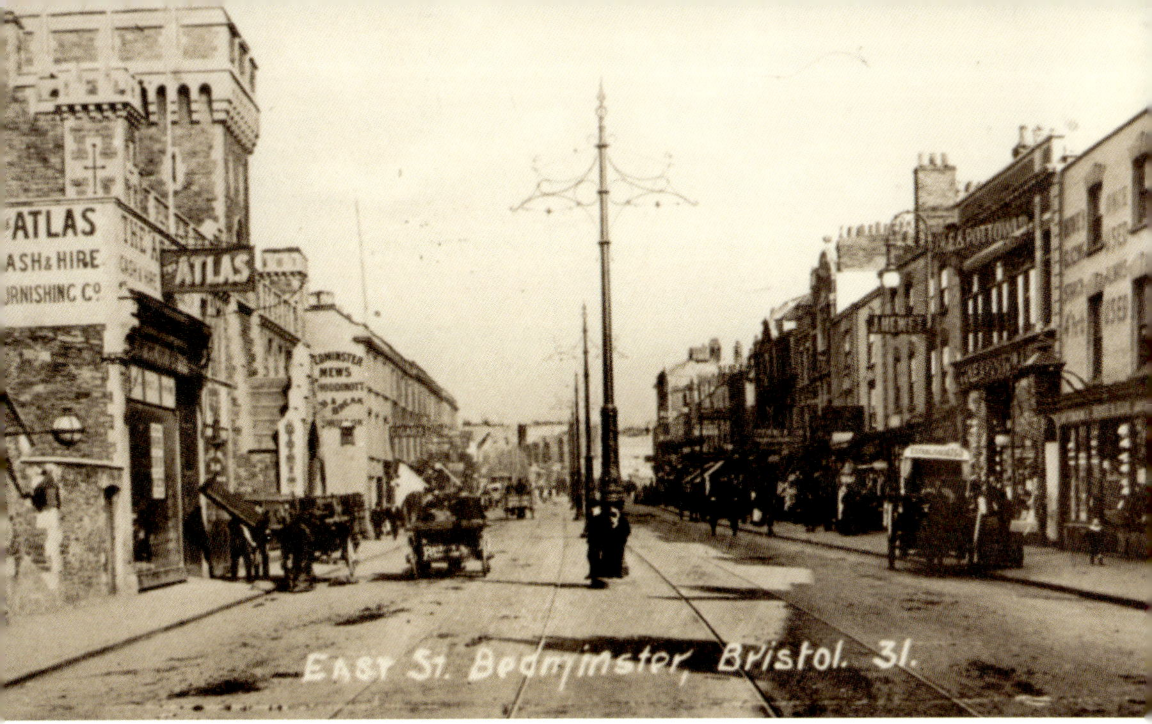

East Street, Bedminster, 1900s

These pictures are looking north towards Bedminster Bridge. The old police station is on the left. The exterior of the building remains virtually unchanged, except for the street-level fenestration. Interestingly, it was designed in the office of the architect Henry Crisp, but is in fact one of the earliest works of his pupil George Oatley, when he was only eighteen years old. Oatley went on to become the architect who was often favoured by the Wills family for some of their grand buildings, such as the Wills Memorial Tower, the Homeopathic Hospital, Wills Hall and others.

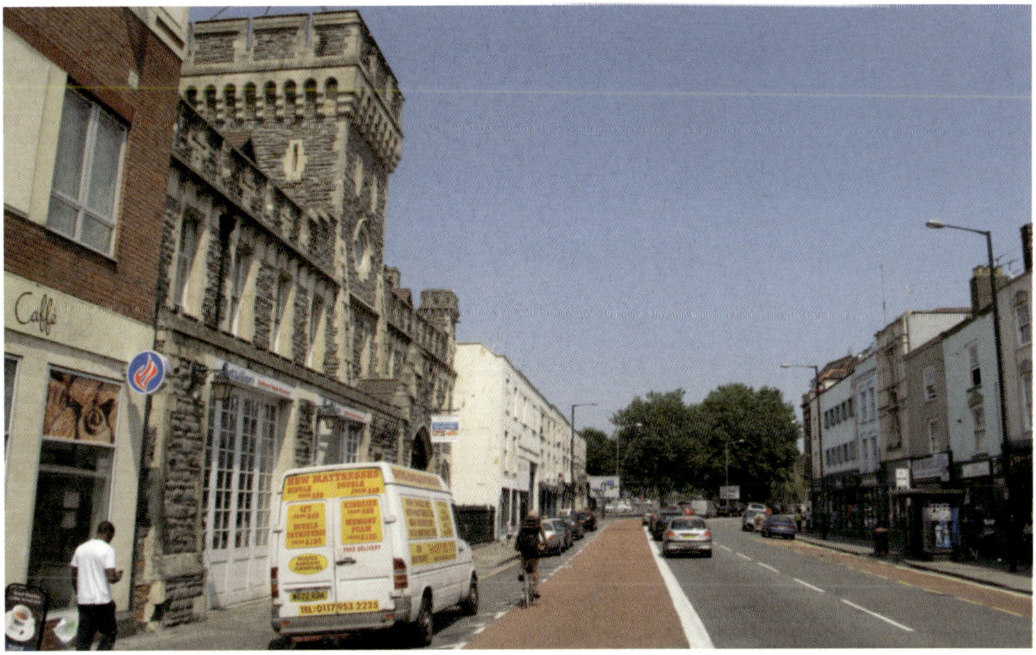

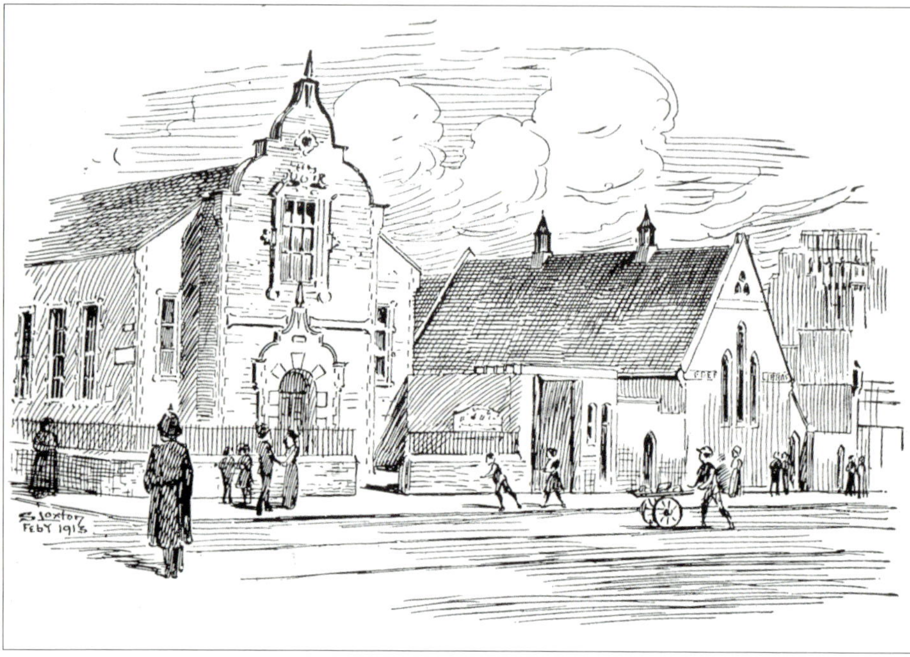

Bedminster Temperance Hall and Free Library, East Street, Pre-1913

This substantial library building below was designed by Frank Wills and opened in 1913. He used the same brick and light-coloured stone as he had for the adjacent tobacco factories designed in 1886. This building stands on the site of the Temperance Hall and of the Free Library. The drawing by Loxton, dated 1913, shows both these buildings just before their demolition. In 2005, it became the Grant Bradley Gallery. Bedminster Library has moved a little to the north, and is almost on the site of the former Free Library.

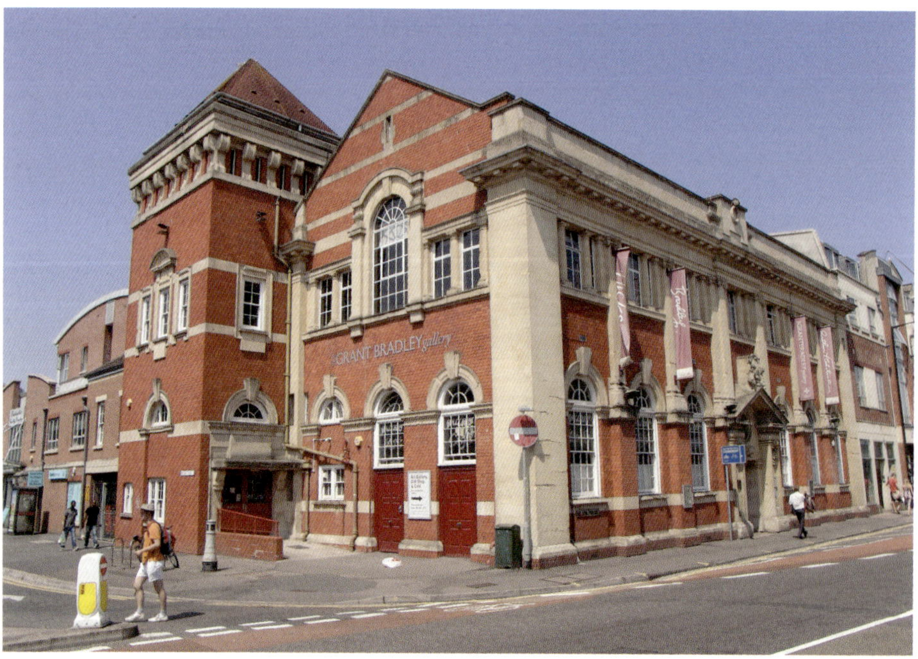

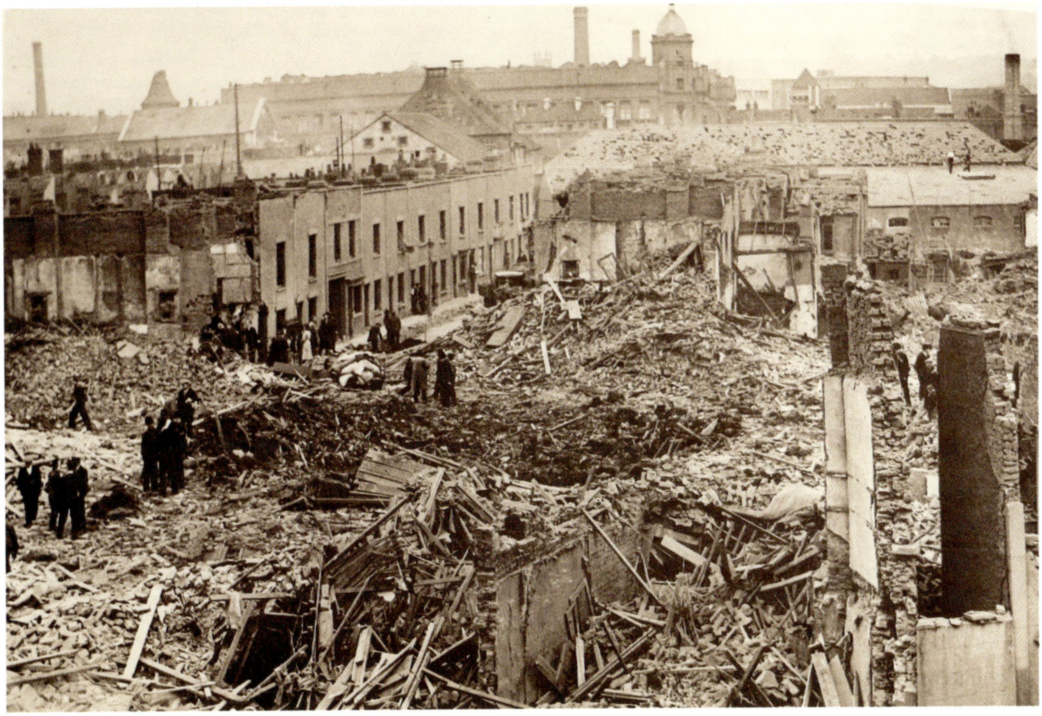

Blitz Damage, Willway Street, Bedminster

The two pictures are looking in opposite directions: the old one westwards towards the W. D. and H. O. Wills factory in East Street, and the modern photograph towards Victoria Park. This has always been primarily a non-residential street. The bombing raid on Good Friday 1941 shows the damage to the tannery, the flat area in the middle foreground. To the left of this, one can see the bell towers of the old malthouse, which remained fairly unscathed. The photograph shows that not all was lost – there is still old paving and the old wall on the site of the malthouse. Today, it is a street of mixed business use, ranging from printers to a live music club.

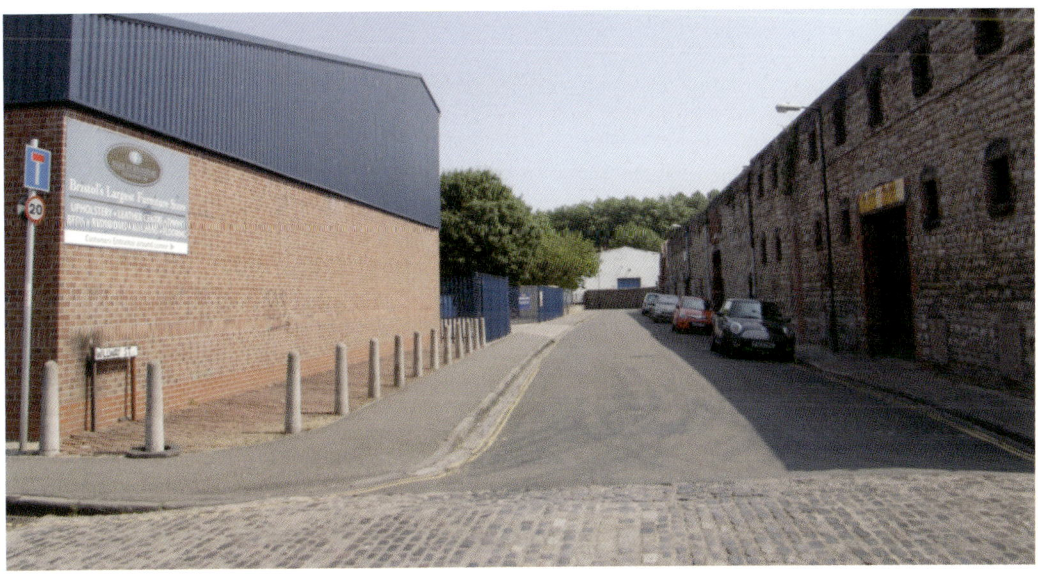

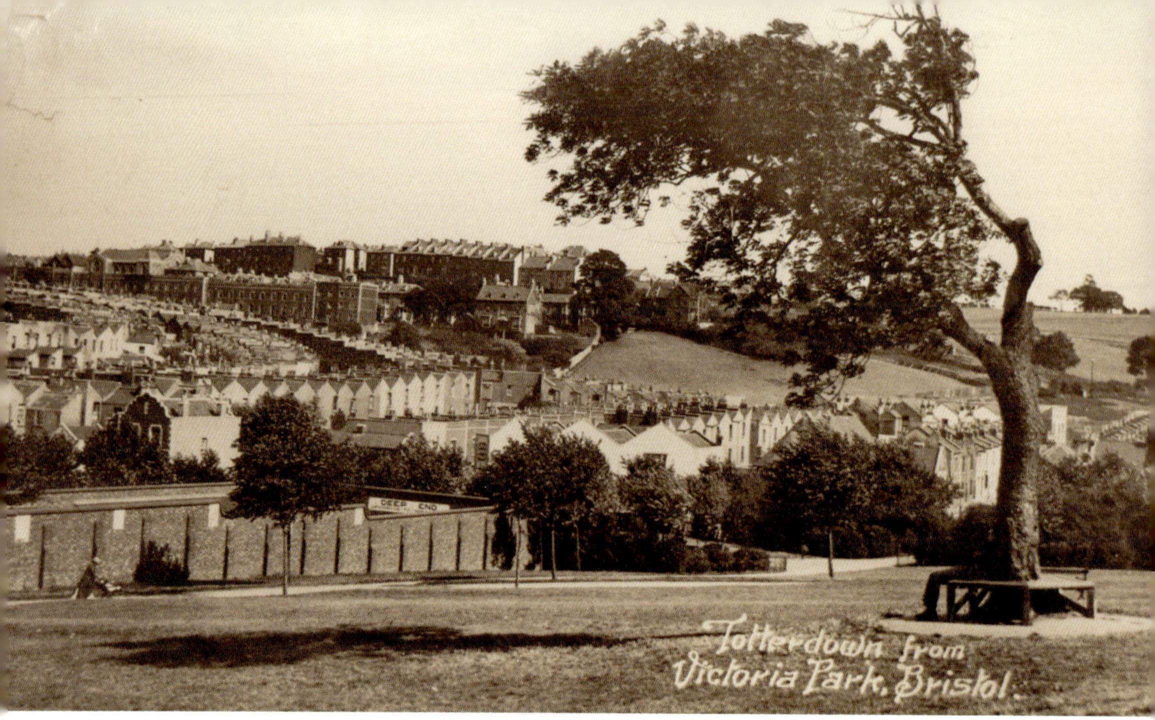

Victoria Park

By the middle of the nineteenth century, Bristol was the third unhealthiest city in England, and Bedminster was one of its most polluted parishes. When a parcel of land became available for purchase in 1887, the Bristol Sanitary Committee suggested acquiring it in order to create a 'green lung' in this part of the city. By 1889, a total of 51 acres was purchased for £20,678, and plans were swiftly drawn up for pathways, park walls, entrances and a planting scheme. Within a year, a bandstand had been added. In the rather tattered postcard above we can see how much of Totterdown was yet to be built on. At the bottom left of the postcard is an open-air swimming pool, which was installed in 1905, but sadly was irreparably damaged in the Second World War.

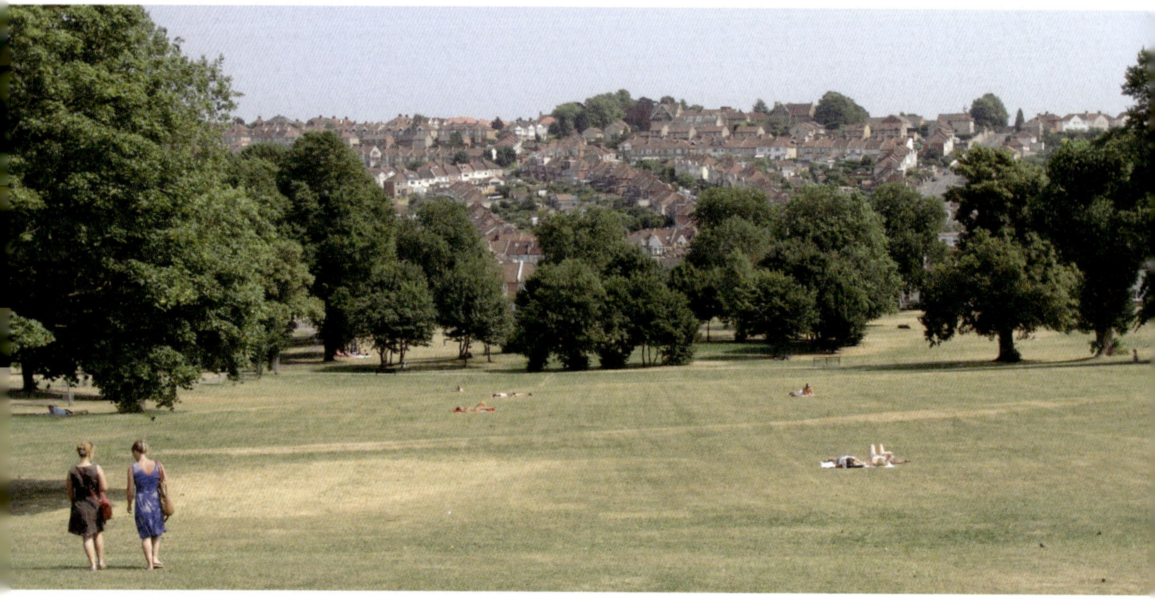

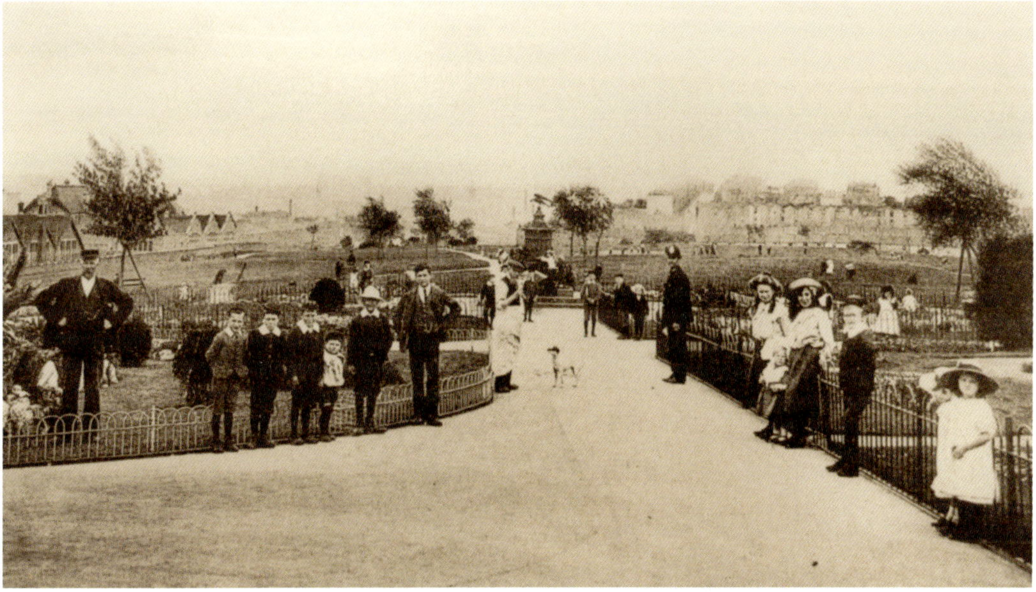

Victoria Park

Within ten years, Victoria Park had become an orderly, laid out park: there were swings, see-saws and horizontal bars, a pond at the St Luke's entrance, two drinking fountains (one can be seen in the centre of the old picture sporting a eagle sculpture), iron fencing placed around flower borders and shrubs, and four rangers employed to maintain the grounds. Grazing sheep were used as grass trimmers. One of the rangers can be seen here standing inside the protective iron railings, while on the right is a policeman standing to attention. On the far right of the modern photograph is the keeper's lodge, which now houses the public toilets.

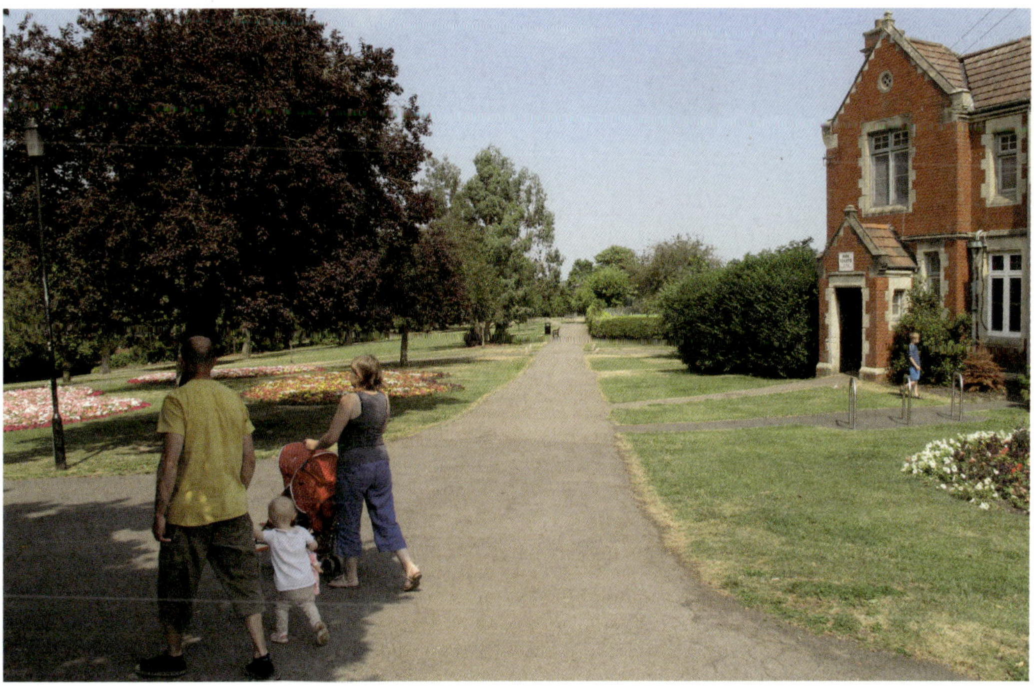

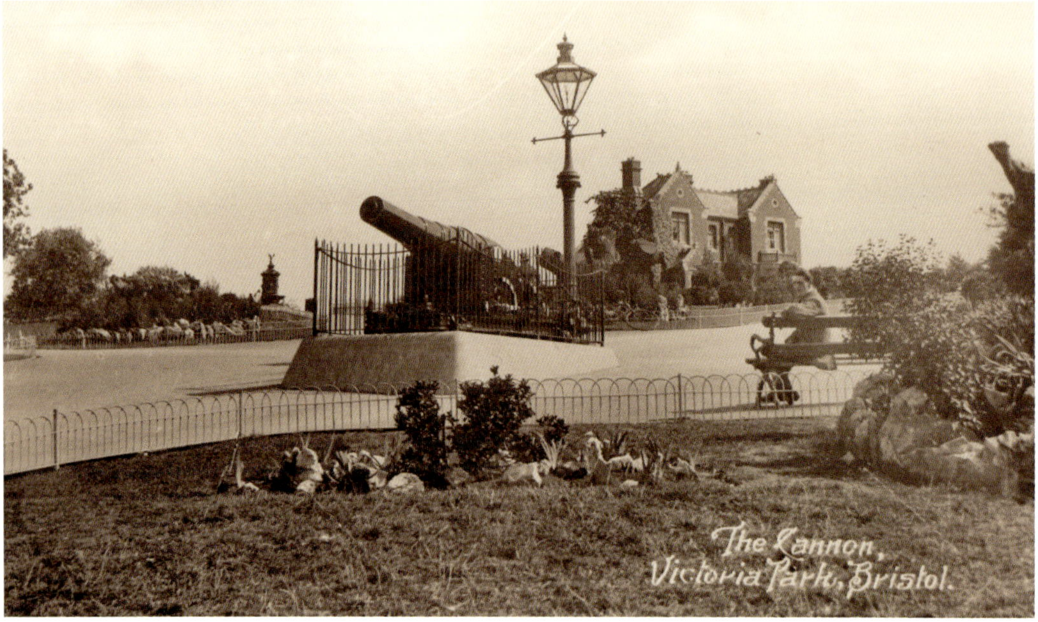

Victoria Park

A notable feature of the park was the Crimean War cannon that stood just below the Somerset Terrace entrance. It became a focal point, with paths designed to lead towards it and little rockeries placed sympathetically around it. Other attractions were added in the years up to 1918, including tennis courts and a bowling green. Sadly, the cannon and much of the iron fencing were removed during the Second World War, purportedly to help the war effort. All that remains is the lamp stand, which now has an incongruous modern top (a visible example of the amount of money invested in municipal works in the latter half of the twentieth century).

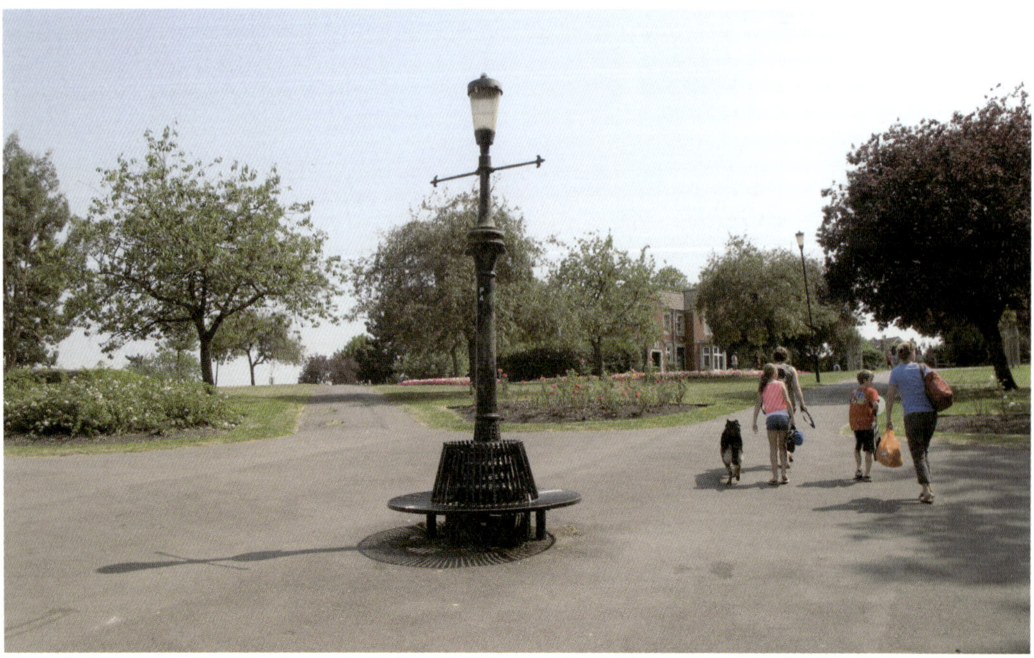

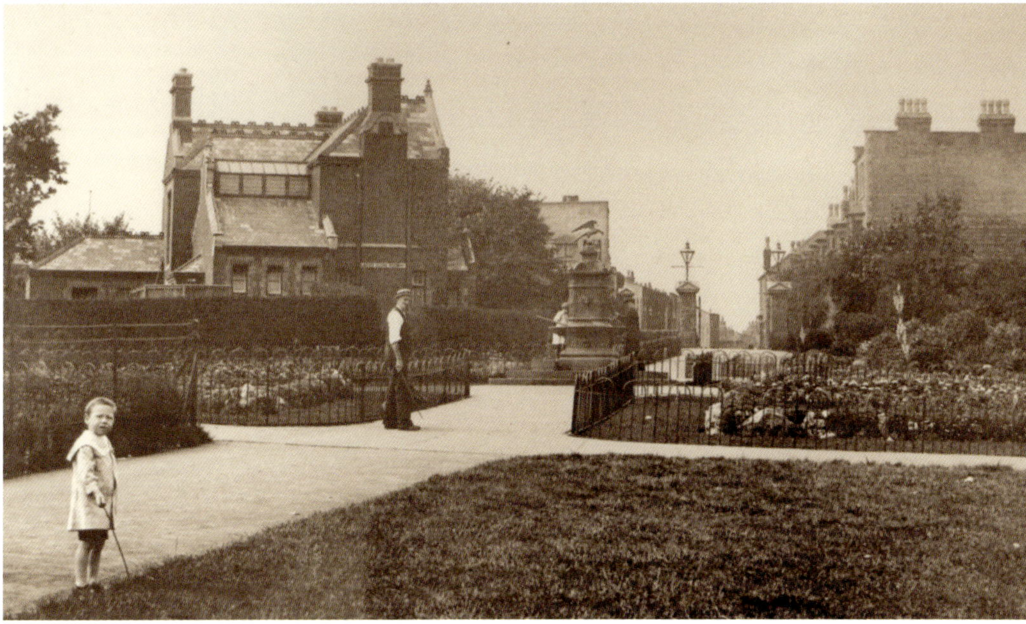

Victoria Park

The view here is along the Somerset Terrace towards one of the park's entrances. Many of the park's old features, such as the bandstand, the drinking fountains (such as the one pictured here), the urinals and the swimming pool have gone, but Victoria Park is still a much cherished haven from the bustle of the city below. Along with colourful flower beds, shrubberies and rock gardens, the park now has a pond, a wildlife area and a water maze. The latter was designed by Peter Milner and Jane Norbury, and is a modern example of the Charles maze, a special feature of which is that it has no ends. It was inspired by one of the roof bosses from St Mary Redcliffe church.

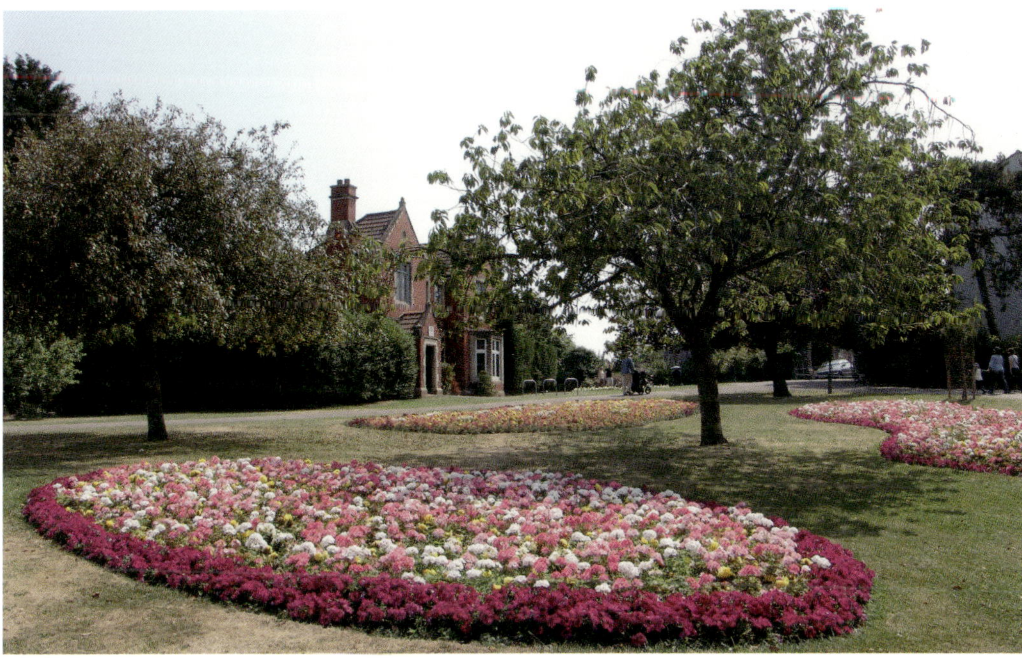

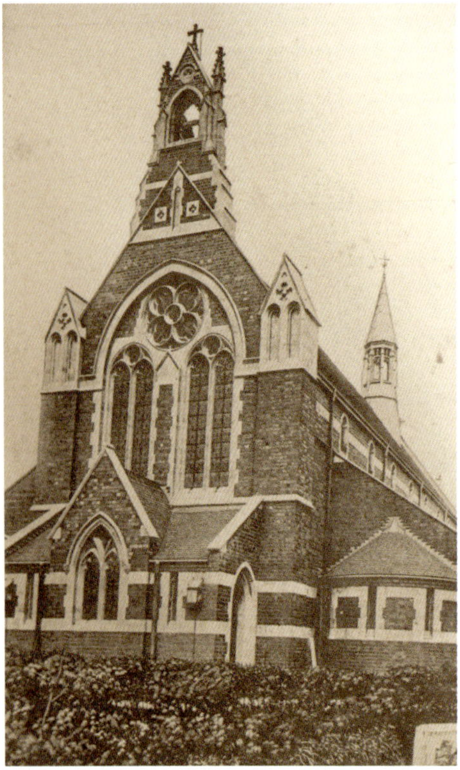

St Michael and All Angels, Bedminster, 1900s
The church is on the side of Windmill Hill between Fraser Street and Vivian Street, not far from the tunnel under the railway. The land was given by Mr A. Capper Pass, who owned the smelting works beyond the railway line. The chancel was built in 1886, to a design by E. H. Edwards, and attached to a temporary corrugated iron nave with seating for 350 people. The nave and aisles were added in 1901, to a design by J. Bevan. However, most of this was destroyed by a fire on 9 January 1926 and rebuilt to a different design by P. Hartland Thomas in 1927. St Michael and All Angels was the first church in Bristol to install solar PV cells to generate electricity.

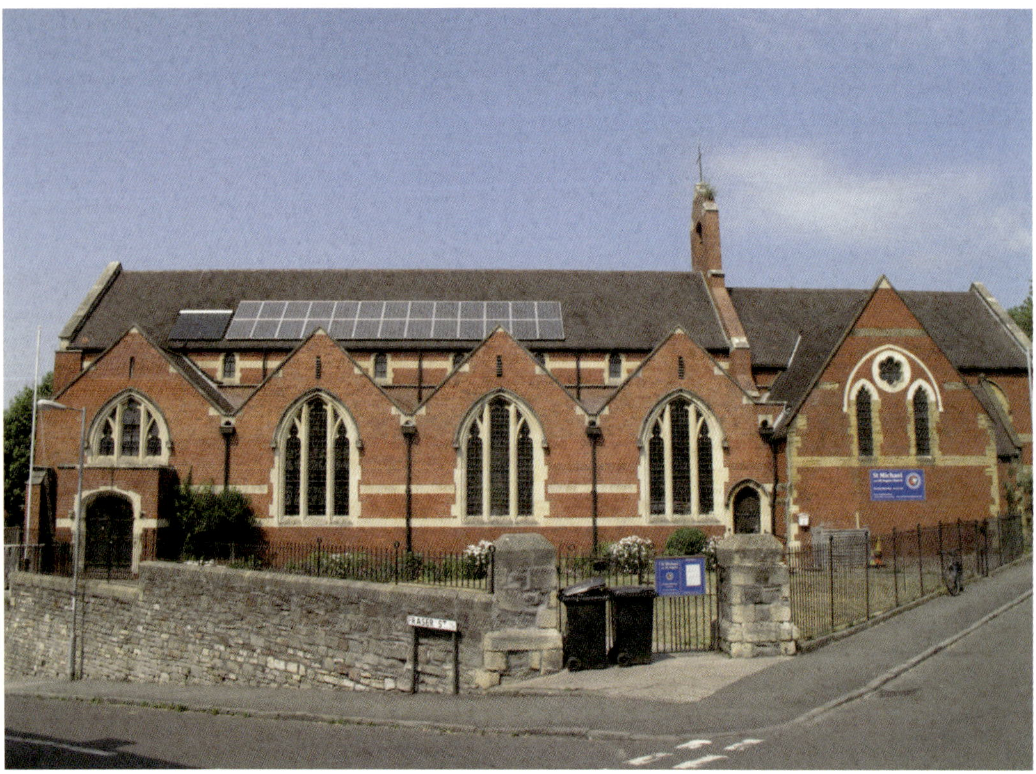

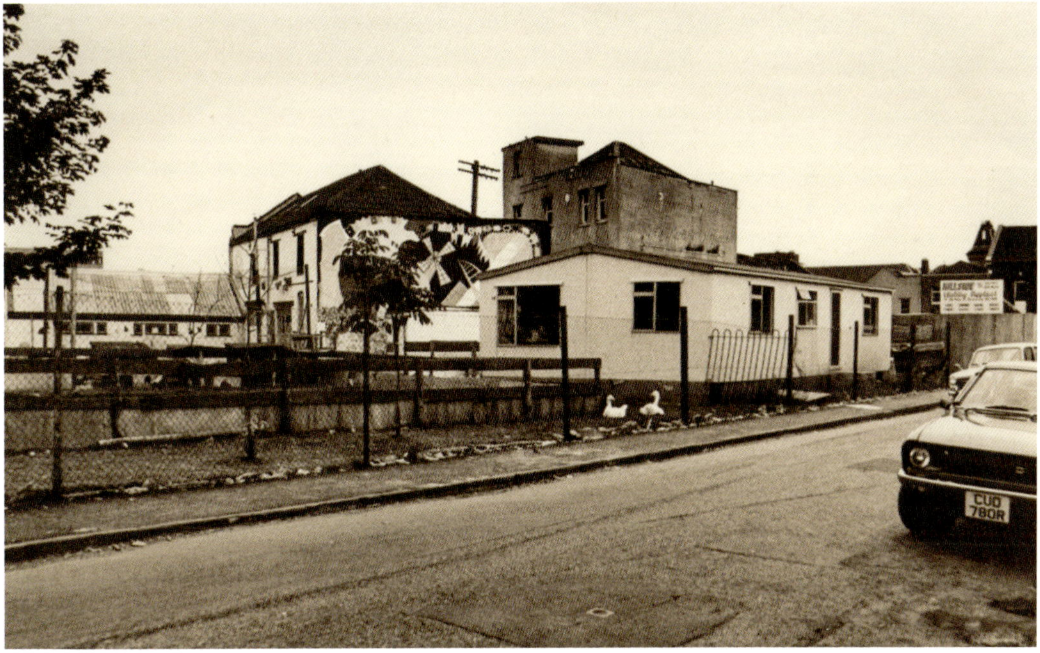

Windmill Hill City Farm, 1970s

Windmill Hill City Farm is an independent community project that aims to meet the needs of local people through a wide range of social, environmental, educational, recreational and economic activities. There is a theme of food, farming and the environment, as well as community involvement and projects. It has been, and continues to be, very successful. It started in 1976 when there was clearance of poor housing and light industry, some of which can be seen in the old picture, and where the two geese must have been some of the early farm residents. Today, there is also a commercial side with a café and shop selling produce. Local residents are justifiably proud of their community farm.

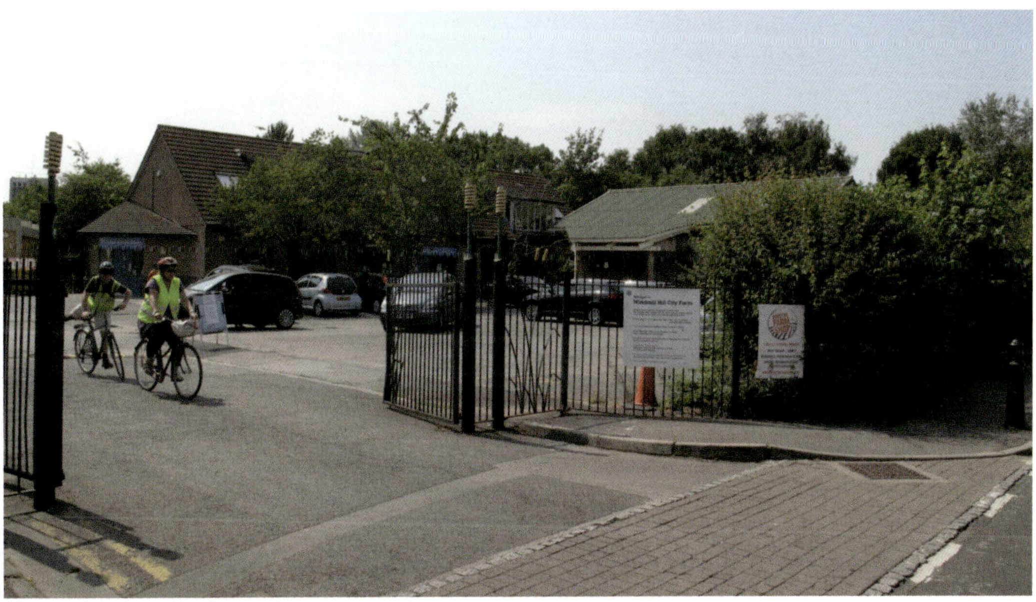

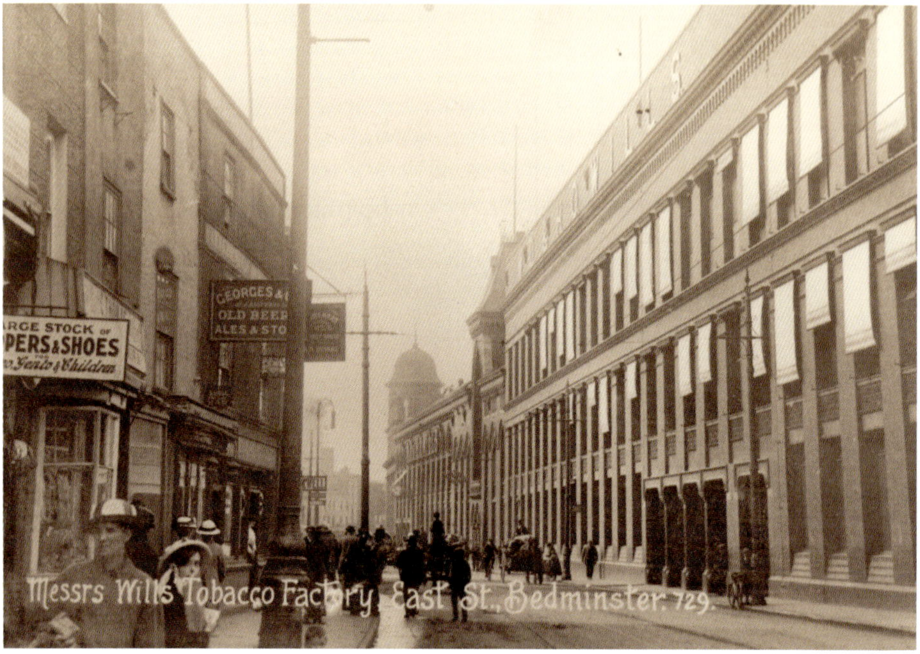

East Street, Bedminster, Early 1900s

Francis Ford's copper dome on the tower of the 1886 Wills Imperial Building can be seen in both pictures. The building on the right, where ASDA now stands, was the 1902 extension to the main building. In 1988, it was pulled down to make space for the supermarket and car park. The site has had various uses: St Catherine's Hospital, providing food and lodging for pilgrims to Glastonbury, was here from the thirteenth to the nineteenth century, and later it was the site of a sawmill. The River Malago runs through the centre of the site; it was culverted around 1900.

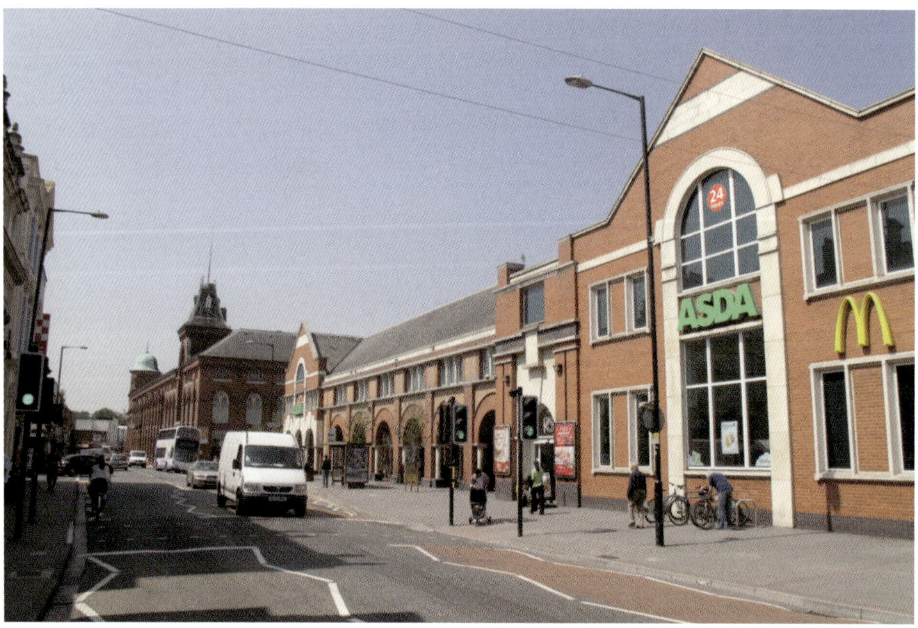

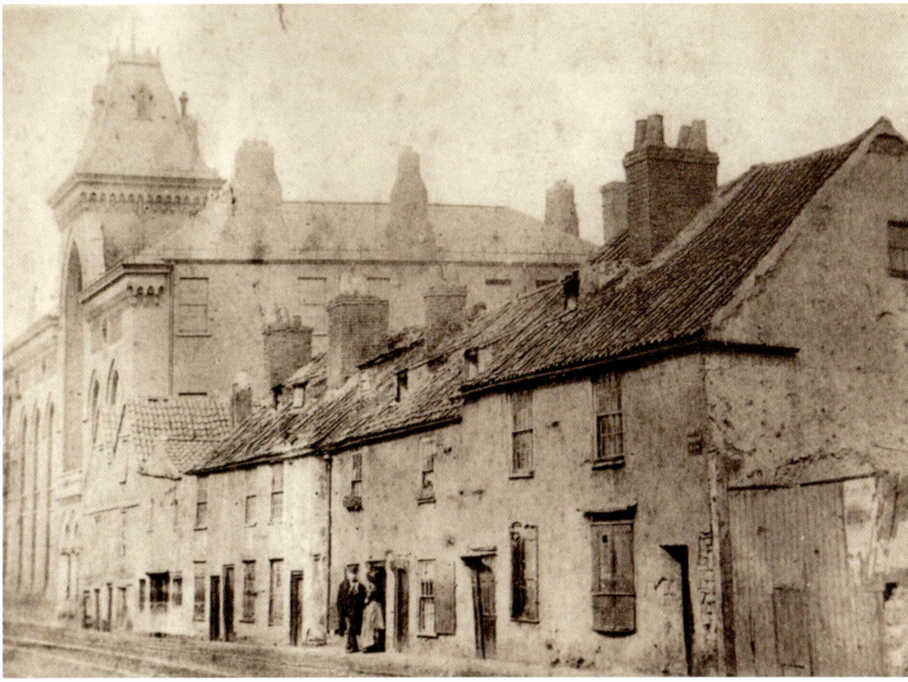

East Street, Bedminster, Late 1880s

The old picture must have been taken between 1886, when the Wills factory was built, and 1890, when this little row of cottages (called Brightbow Cottages) was pulled down (the reason given was there had been an outbreak of smallpox in them). The Malago flowed under them, and they were frequently flooded and highly insanitary.

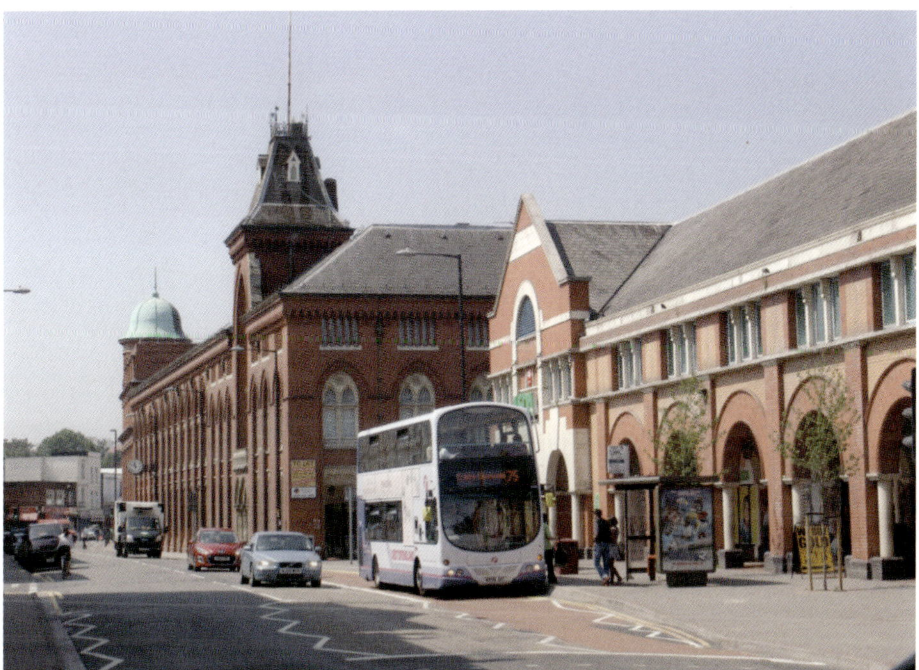

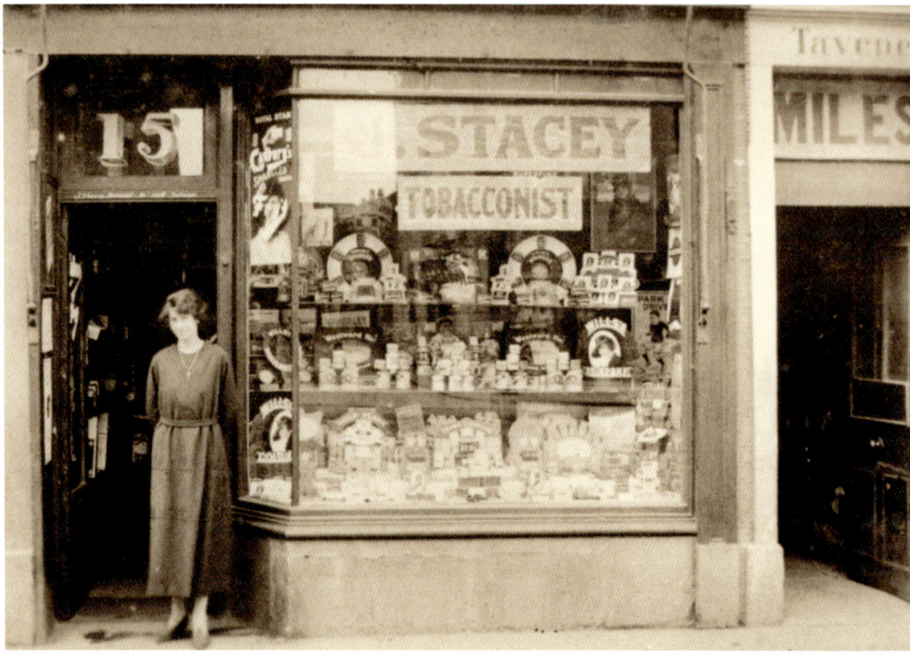

No. 15 East Street, Bedminster, 1920s

A survey of the shops in this part of East Street in the first part of the twentieth century shows the usual mixture of small businesses, such as ladies' and children's outfitters, picture frame makers, butchers, fruiterers and fishmongers. These ground-floor shops usually had more than one household living above them. Here the old tobacconist is now a house agency flanked by Inks-R-Us, selling mainly cartridges for word processors, and a pawnbroker.

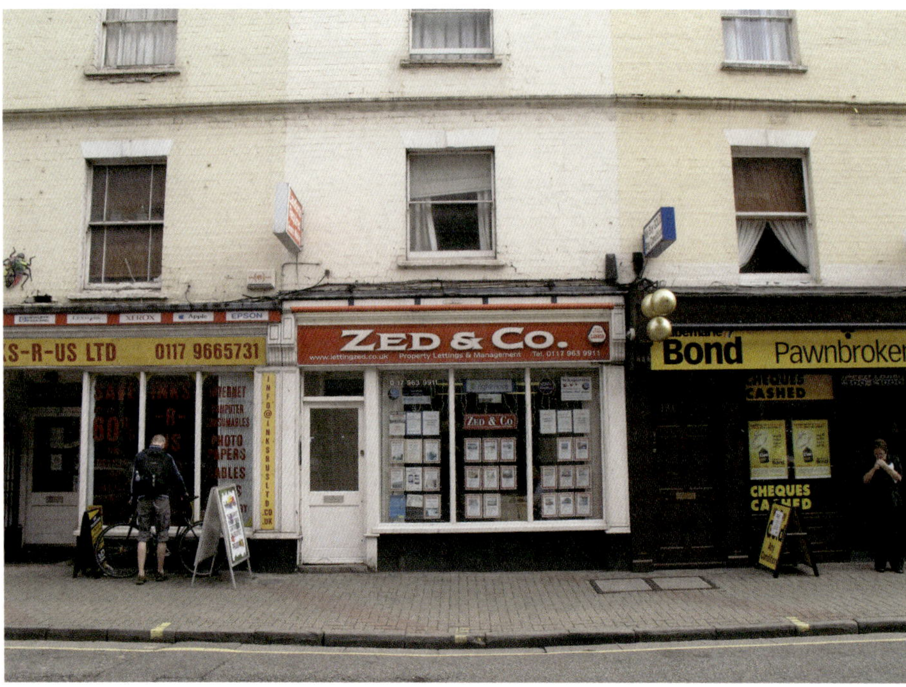

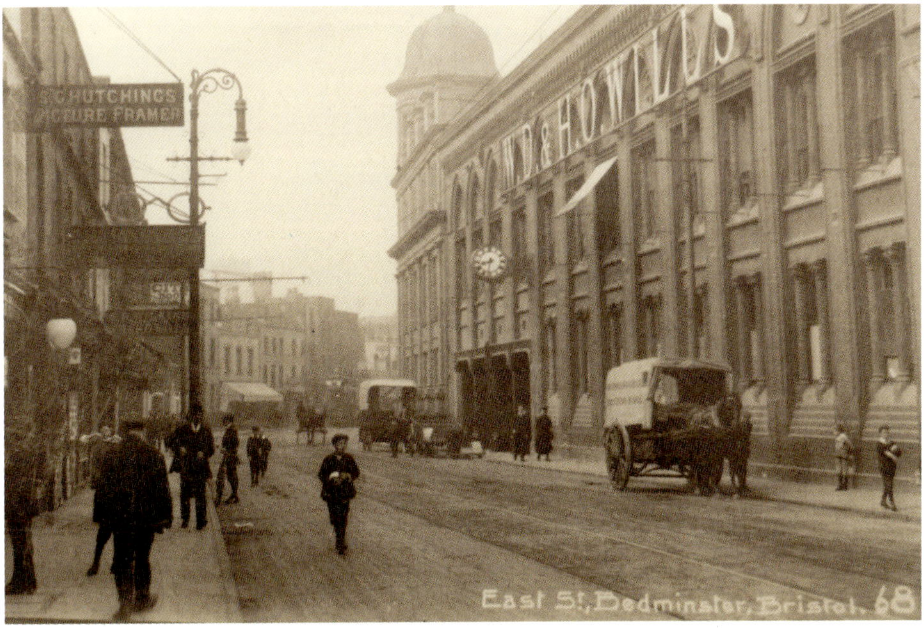

East Street, Bedminster, 1910s

These pictures are taken looking south, with the Wills No. 1 factory on the right. It was designed by Frank Wills, later Sir Frank, who was a nephew of H. O. Wills. It is in what is described as 'Edwardian Baroque' style. It opened on 27 March 1886 and continued until production was transferred to Hartcliffe in 1974. Now all that remains of the original building is the Grade II-listed façade, behind which are Regent House and Consort House that are mainly offices with some residential occupancy and retail units at street level. The Imperial Arcade is made up of nine retail outlets. On the left-hand side are signs for a pawnbroker's business, an increasingly common sight in modern-day high streets.

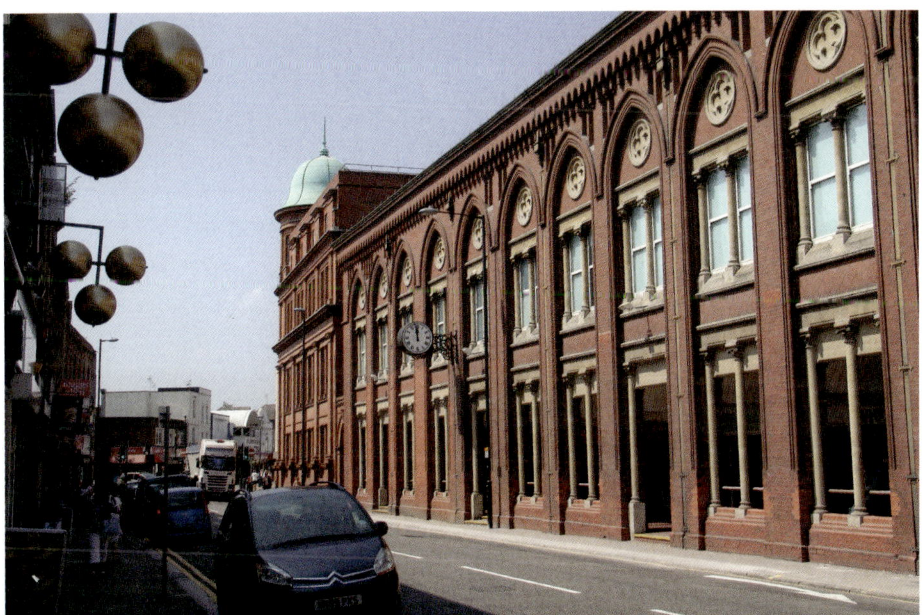

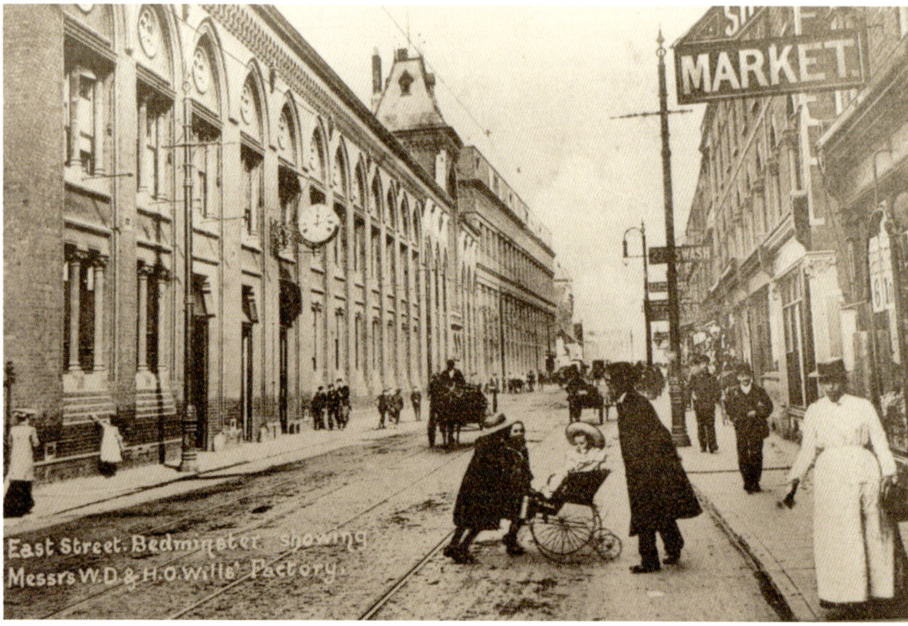

East Street, Bedminster, Postcard Dated 4 August 1906

This is looking north up East Street. The postcard shows a busy midday street scene, with women shopping and children pushing a perambulator. The building beyond the small tower on the left was pulled down to allow for Asda to be built in 1987. The large clock on its ornate metal stand has been kept and is a feature in the street. Wills was the largest employer in the area, and obtaining a job at one of its factories was considered very desirable as it meant guaranteed work, with a number of additional benefits such as a yearly bonus, a pension, a health-care programme, and various sports and social clubs.

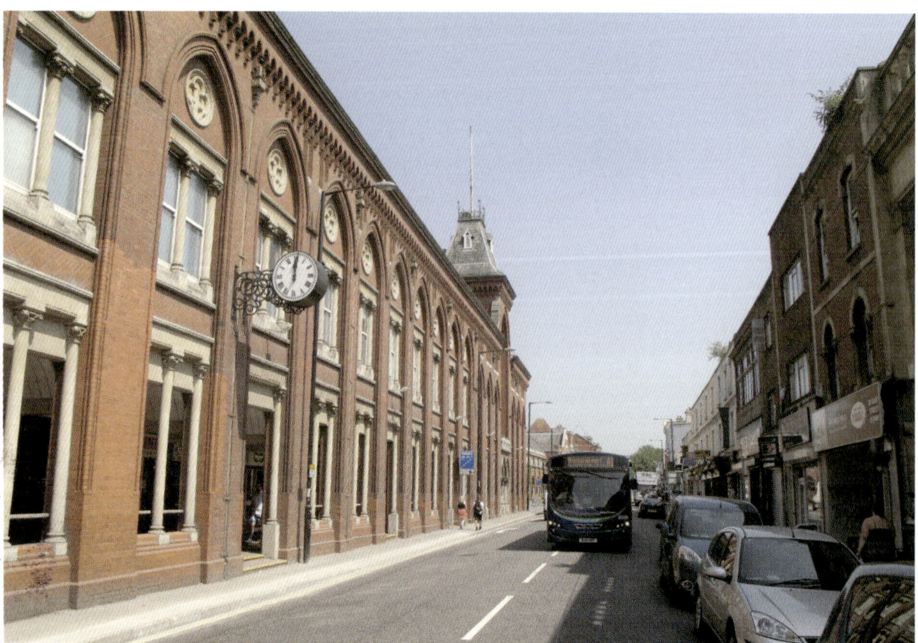

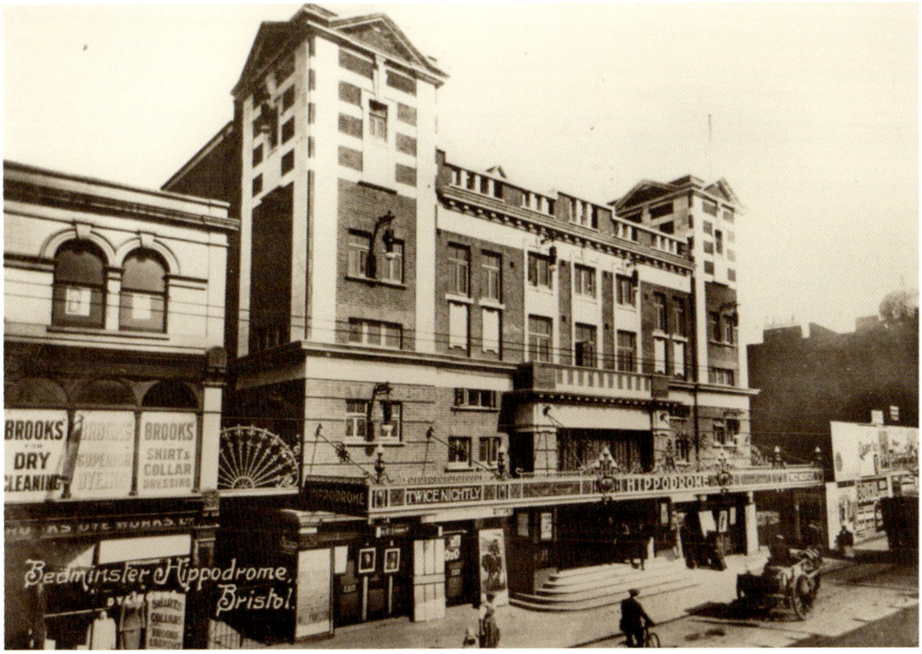

Bedminster Hippodrome, 1920s

The Bedminster Hippodrome stood in East Street in the block of properties between Essex Street and Lombard Street. It was built by Bertie Crewe. He was an architect who specialised in theatres and is credited with forty one establishments, including Sadler's Wells. The Hippodrome opened on 7 August 1911 as a variety theatre. It quickly ran into financial difficulties, partly because the proprietor, Walter de Frece, was unable to obtain a licence for dramatic performances. It was bought by Oswald Stall in 1914, and was opened as Stoll's Picture Theatre in April 1915 (although it retained its Hippodrome name). The film being shown when the picture above was taken was a 1922 British silent film called *Dick Turpin's Ride to York*. The Hippodrome was bombed on 5 January 1941; the remains were demolished in 1954.

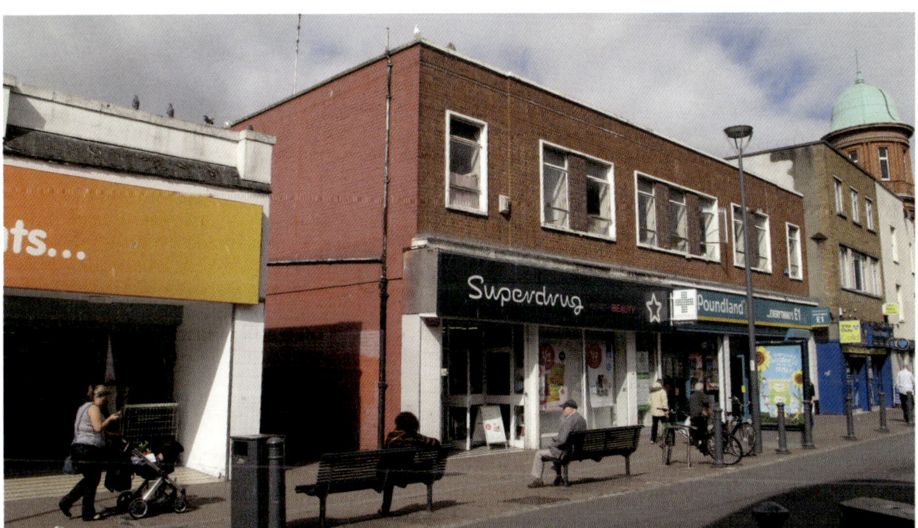

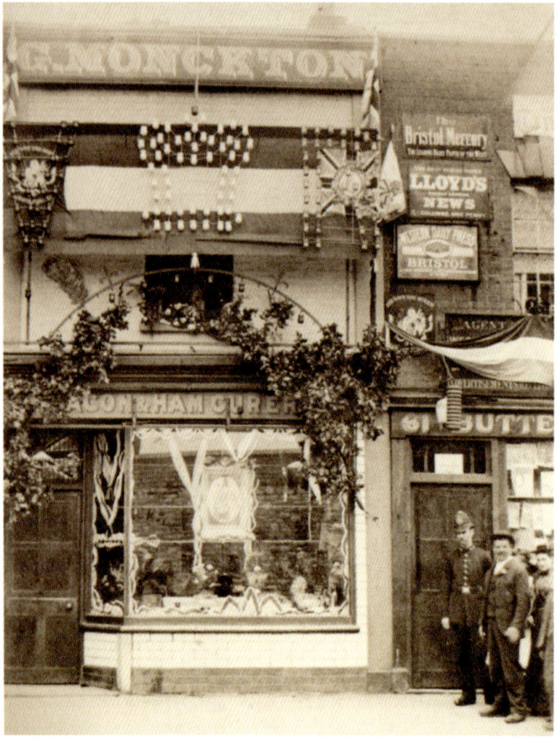

No. 59 East Street, Bedminster, 1890s
A fine example of the continuation of shop use, No. 59 was run by the Monckton family for many years at the turn of the twentieth century, before changing to Robinson's (which is still remembered by locals today) and then Kelvins. The decorations outside the shop (*left*) were put up in celebration of Queen Victoria's Diamond Jubilee in 1897.

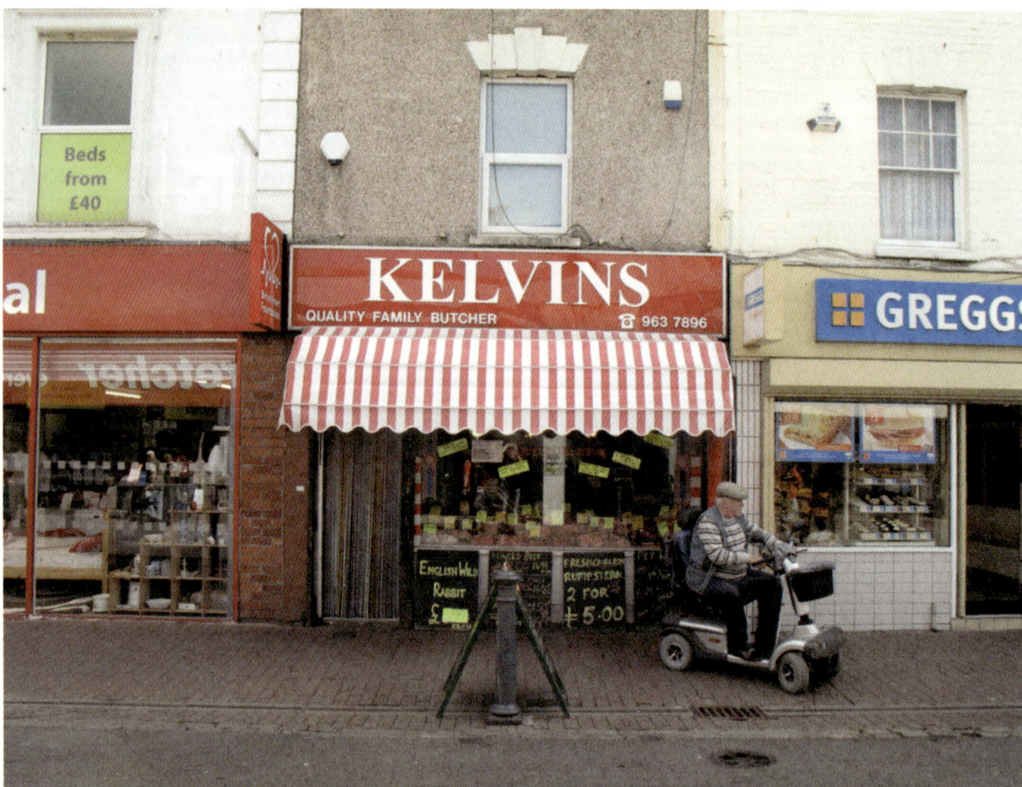

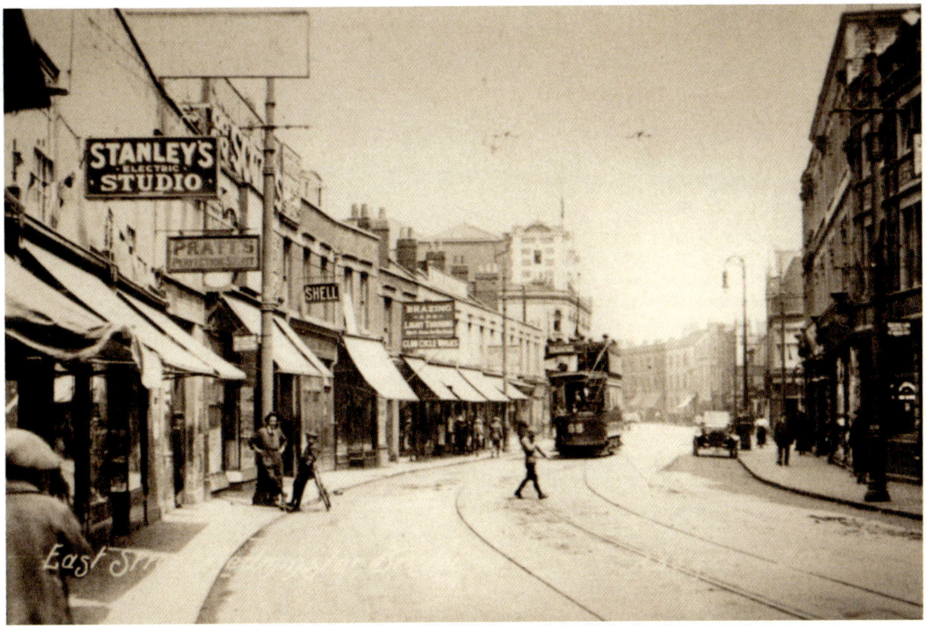

East Street, Bedminster, Early 1900s

In the postcard, the Hippodrome looms in the distance. The photograph is taken at the point where East Street becomes a pedestrian zone, with only buses, taxis and delivery vehicles permitted. There are likely to be more changes soon: in 2012/13, Bedminster was one of the twelve pilot areas in the government-funded scheme for rejuvenating high streets headed by Mary Portas, and was given £100,000 of Business Improvement District (BID) funding.

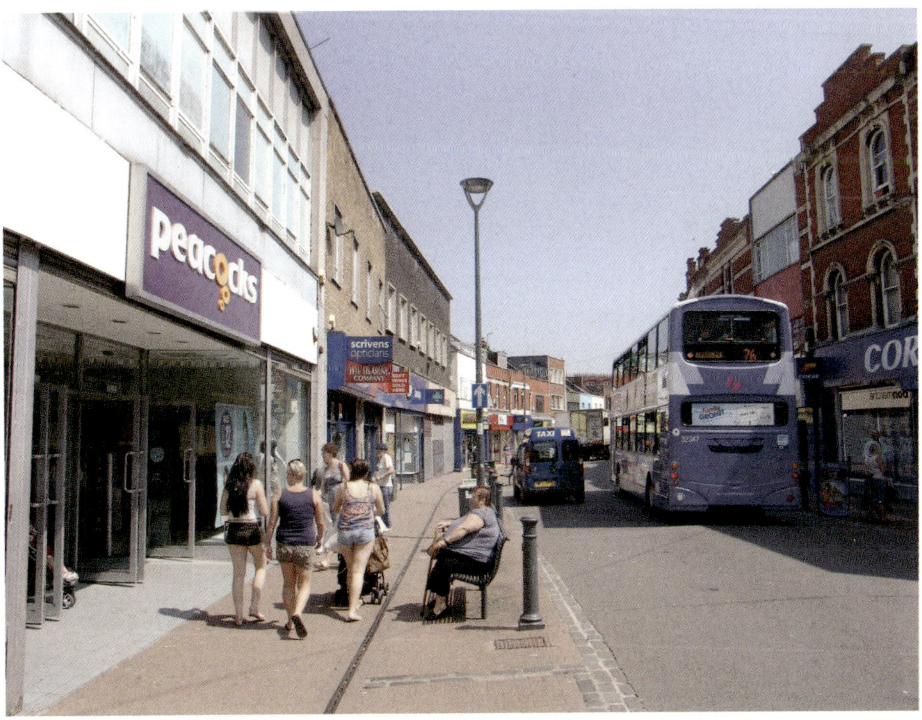

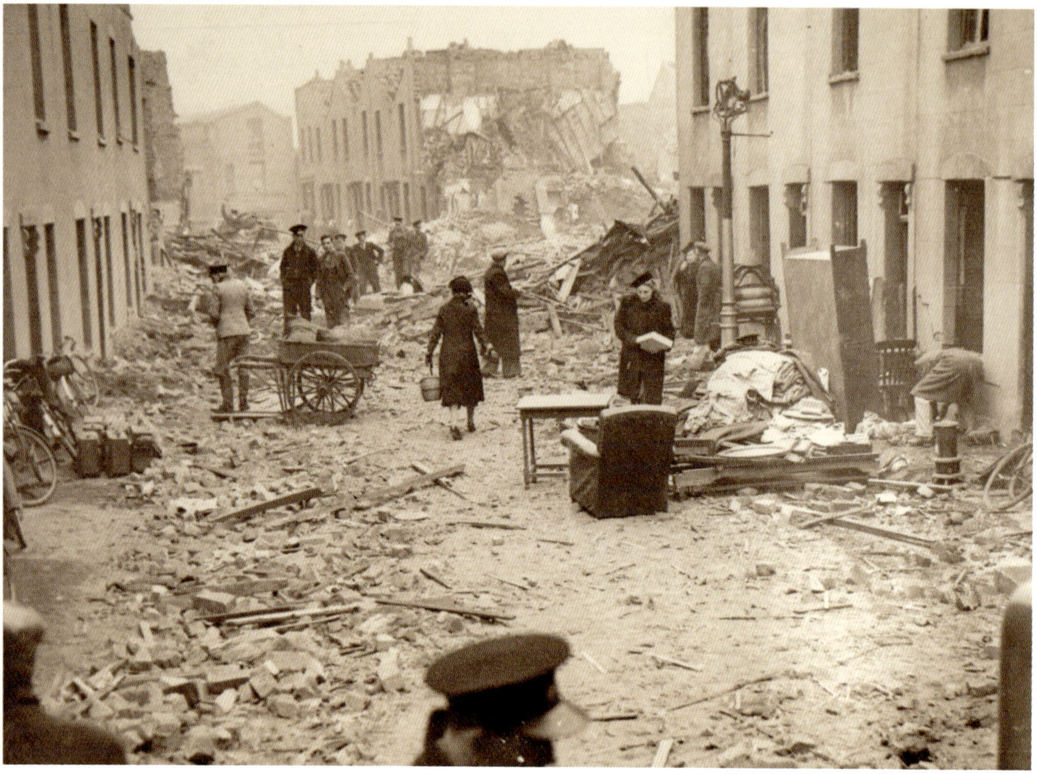

Blitz Damage, Stafford Street

Stafford Street is reached by turning east off East Street down Mill Lane. As can be seen, it was severely damaged in April 1941 it is said by a single bomb. It was not rebuilt as a residential road. The 1880s map shows twenty-one terraced houses on the west side and fourteen on the east, with the open River Malago flowing past the southern end.

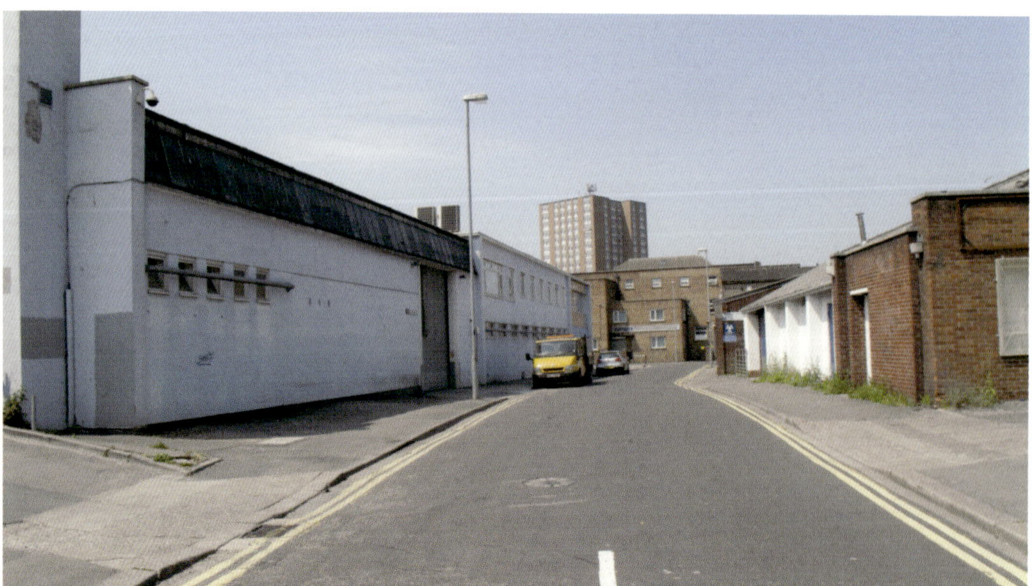

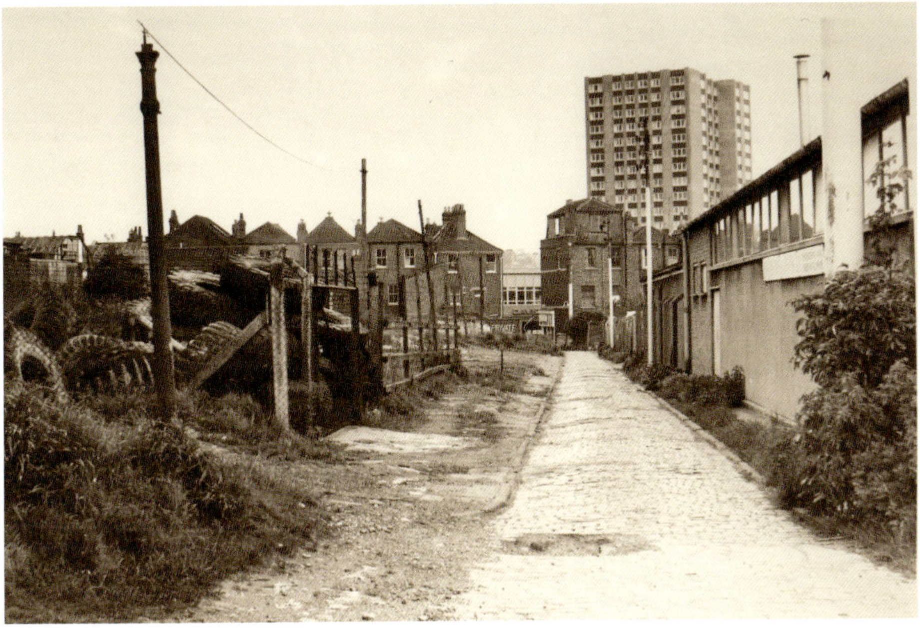

Little Paradise, Bedminster, 1970s

Little Paradise – named after an orchard previously on the site – is parallel and to the south of Stafford Street. It was built in around 1840, primarily to accommodate mining families. Despite its name, it was no paradise; the terraced houses were small and when first built had no water supply or drainage, and it quickly became a slum. The houses were pulled down in 1961, and the only indication of its previous existence is the patch of cobbled street in the 1970s photograph. Today, the building on the left is St Catherine's Court, which is sheltered accommodation for older people, and further down, a car park. On the right are warehouses. In the distance is the tower block of Northfield House.

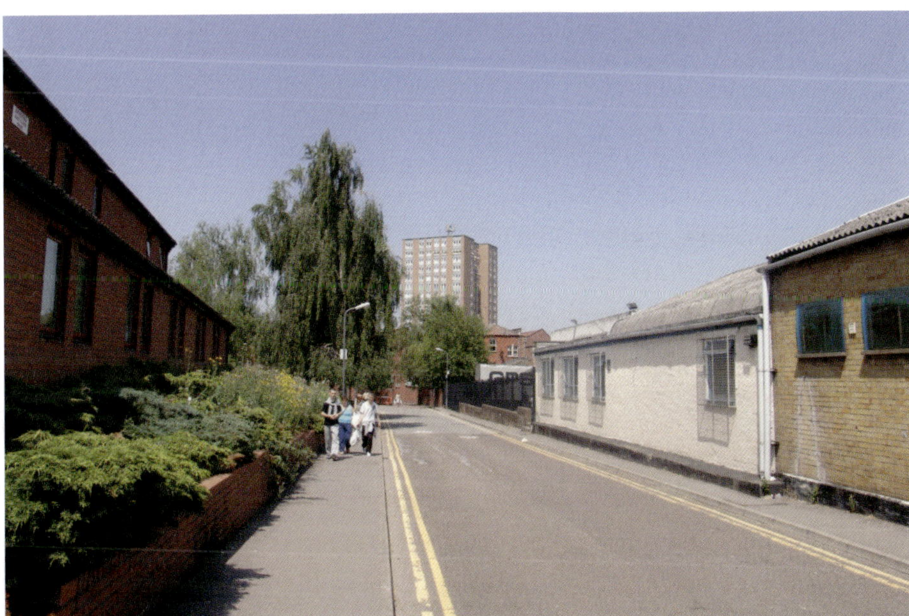

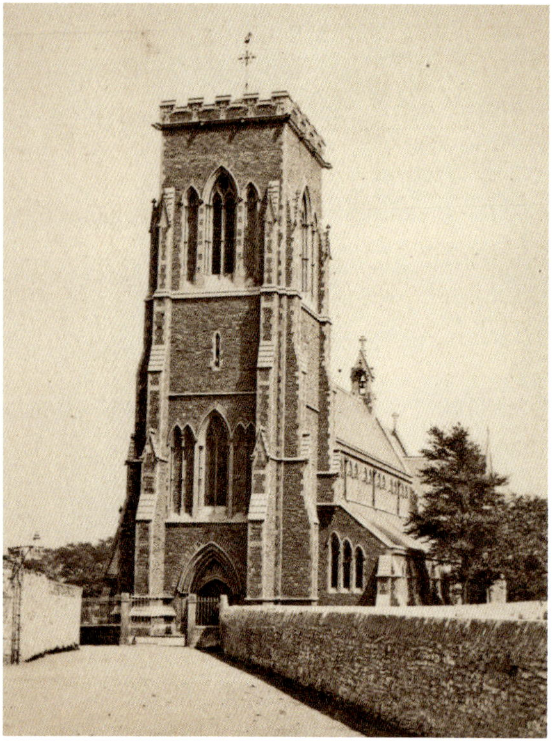

Church Road, Bedminster, Early 1900s
On the east of East Street, Church Road leads up to where the church of St John the Baptist stood. The foundations of this church may be older than any other in Bristol. The earliest records date to 1003, and it is the presumed site of the original Anglo-Saxon minster of Bedminster. In the twelfth century, it became the mother church of St Mary Redcliffe and Abbots Leigh. The church received a direct hit on 24 November 1940 during the Blitz. Much of the building survived as a ruin until it was finally demolished and levelled in 1967.

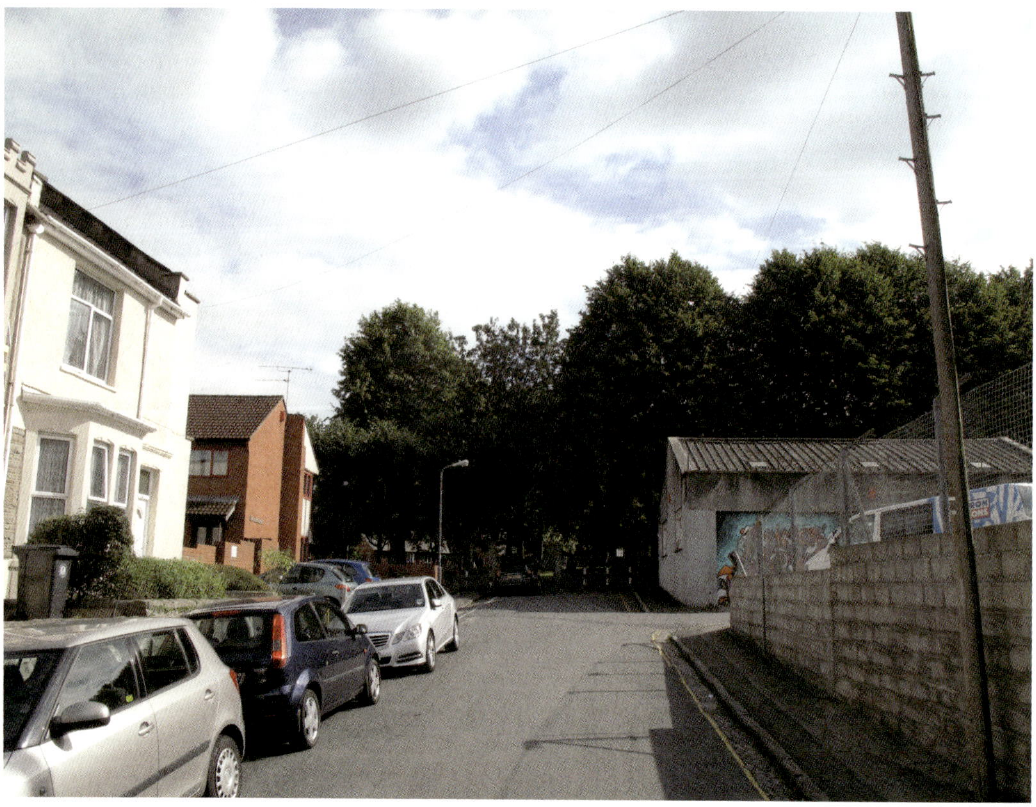

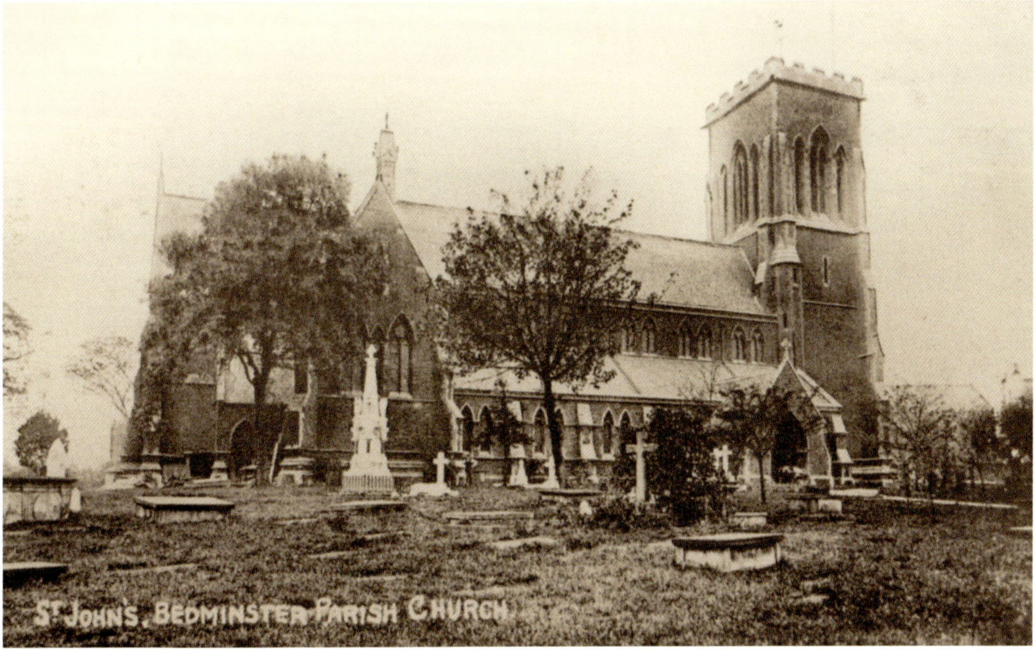

St John's Church, Bedminster, Early 1900s

The original church was burnt down in September 1645, by the order of Prince Rupert during the second siege of Bristol in the Civil War, and not rebuilt until 1663. In 1854, it was decided to build a new and larger church to the design of John Norton (see St Luke's church). After the destruction wrought by the Blitz, the tombs and headstones were removed and it became a small public park fringed with imaginative housing, which replaced damaged terraces. The inset shows a sculpture of the Green Man by local artist Steve Joyce.

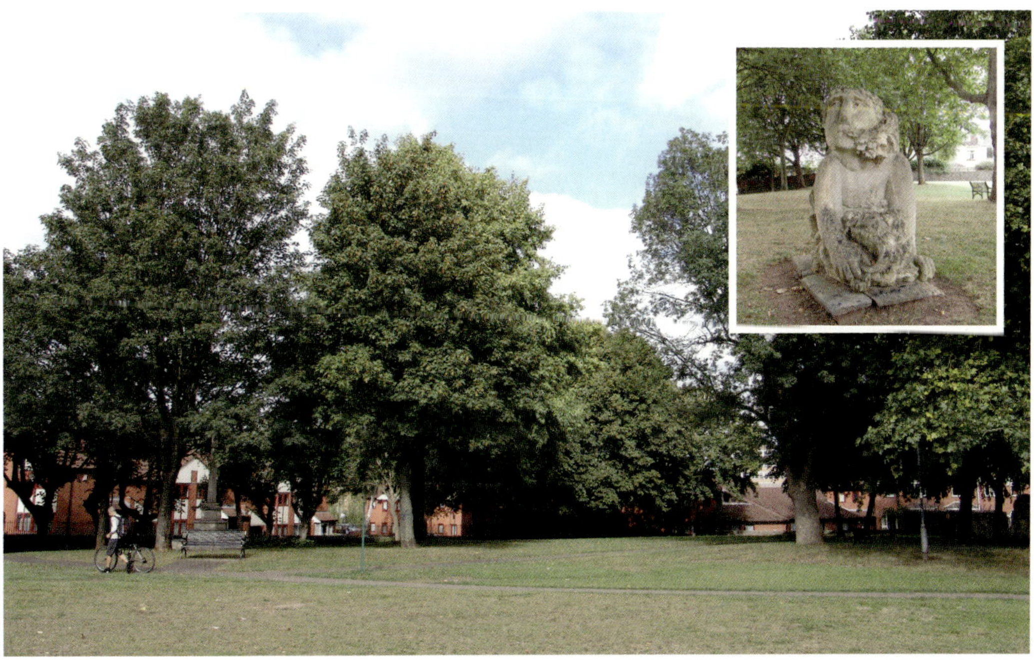

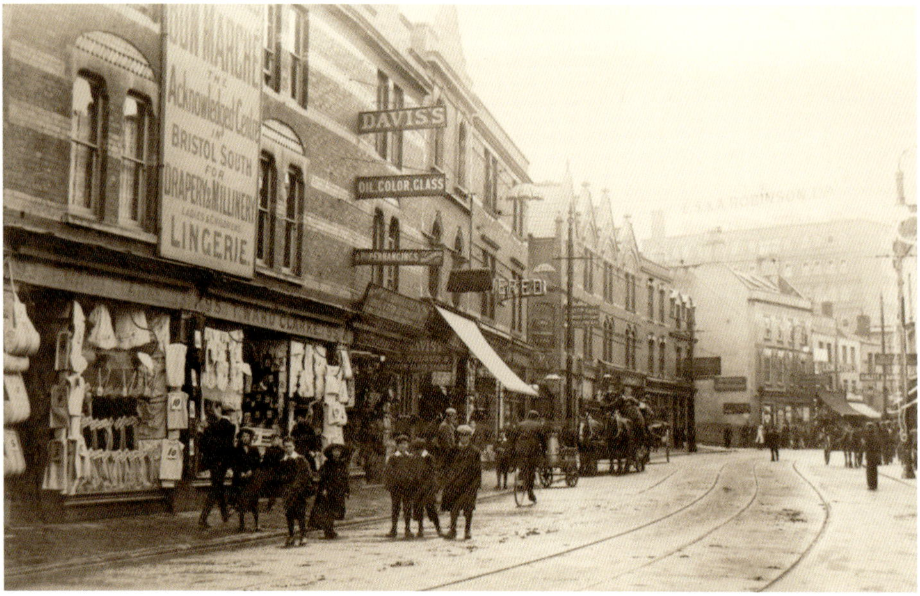

East Street, Bedminster, Early 1900s

The postcard in the early 1900s shows the intriguingly named Bon Marché store, which claims to be the 'Acknowledged Centre in Bristol South for Drapery, Millinery and Ladies Lingerie'. One of the things that would strike a modern shopper walking down this stretch of Edwardian East Street is the grandeur of the buildings – they are three stories with interspersed layers of different coloured bricks and impressive façades. Some of them have roofs with elegant pointed gables. It is interesting to compare these with the simpler buildings in Bedminster Parade at the other end of the street. In the distance is what is now called the Robinson Building and, although no longer a Robinson factory, it still has 'E. S. & A. Robinson Ltd Colour Printers' displayed high on the building.

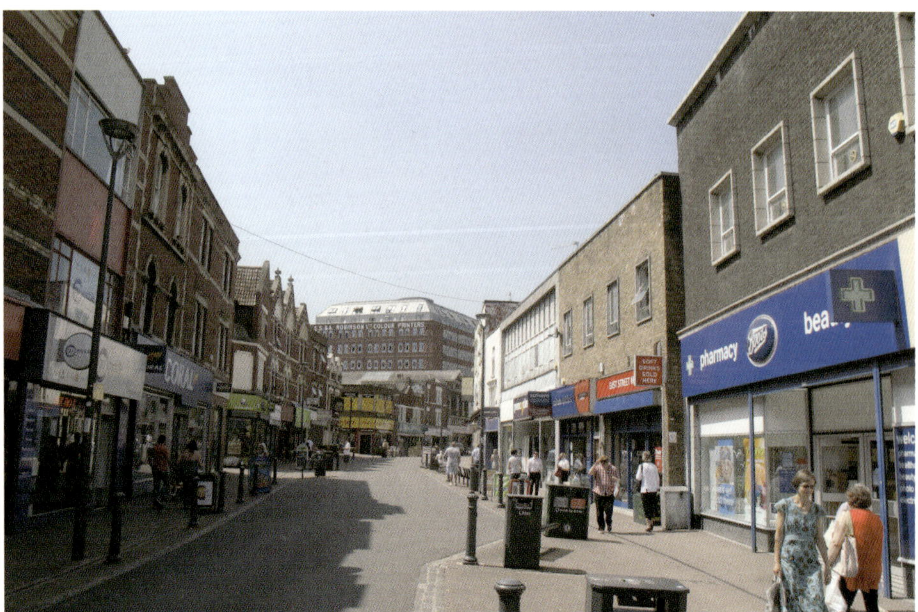

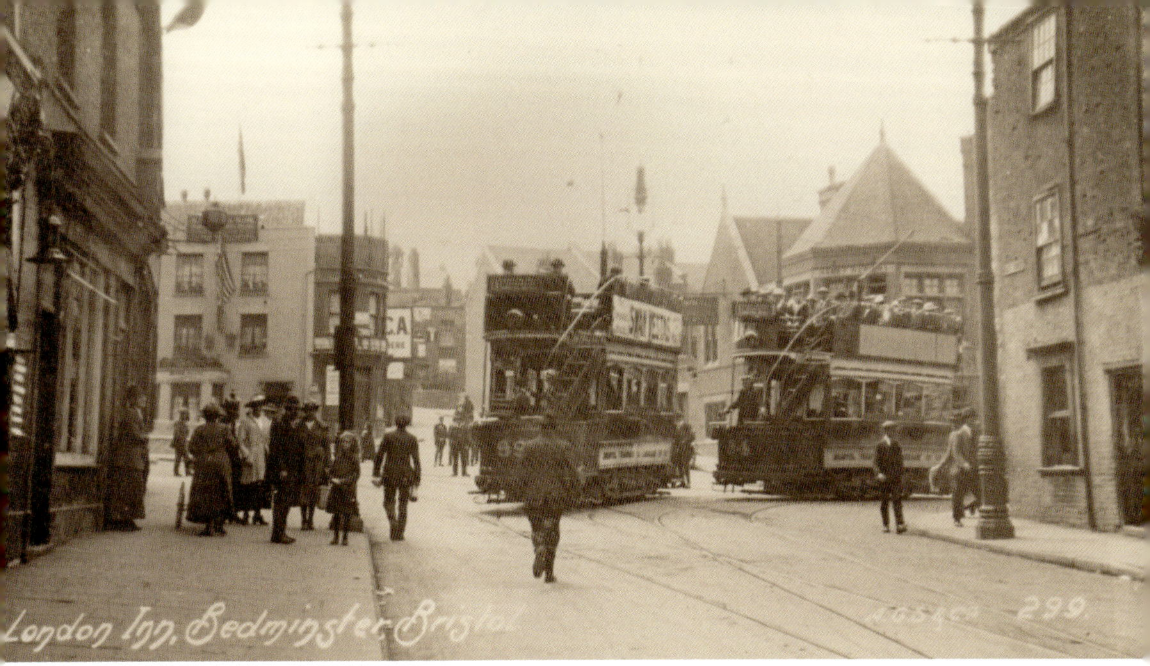

London Inn and East Street, Bedminster, 1910s

The inn has stood on this prominent location for around 400 years. The original building was replaced by the present one with its distinctive pointed roof and tall chimney in 1895. Today, it is seen as straddling the junction of East Street, Cannon Street and British Road. The inn is not exactly in the same spot as it used to be, as it was necessary to make a wider entrance to British Road, but it is within metres of being so.

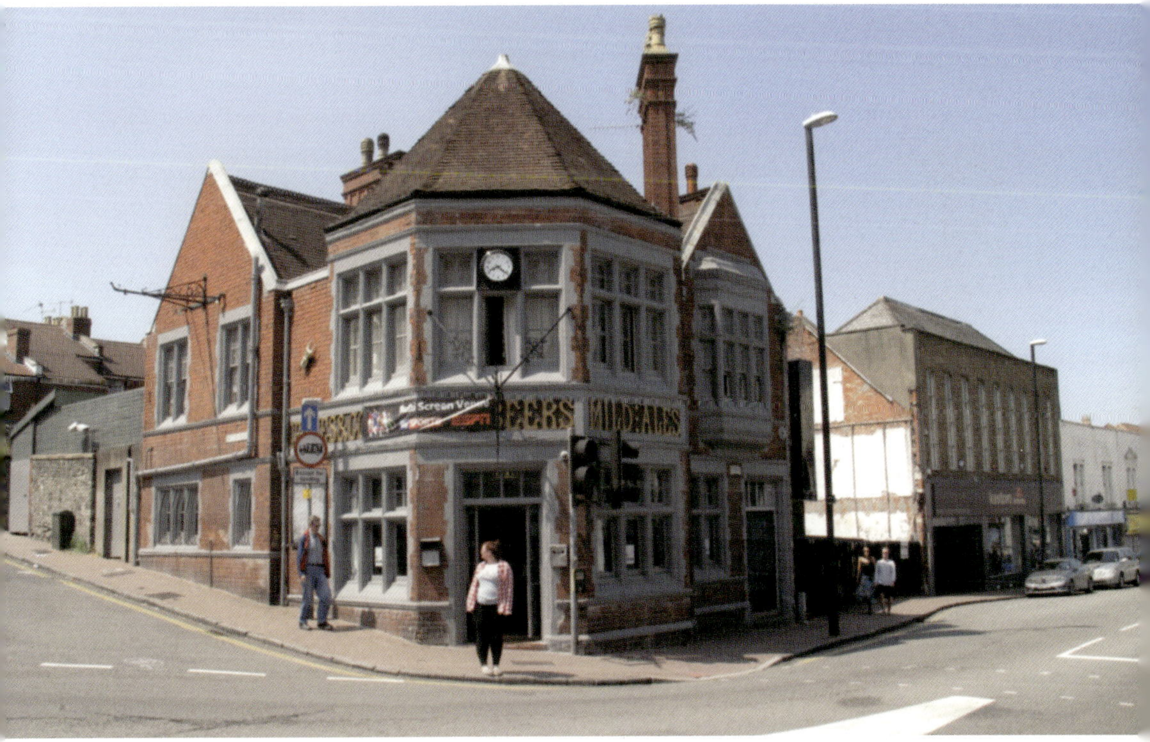

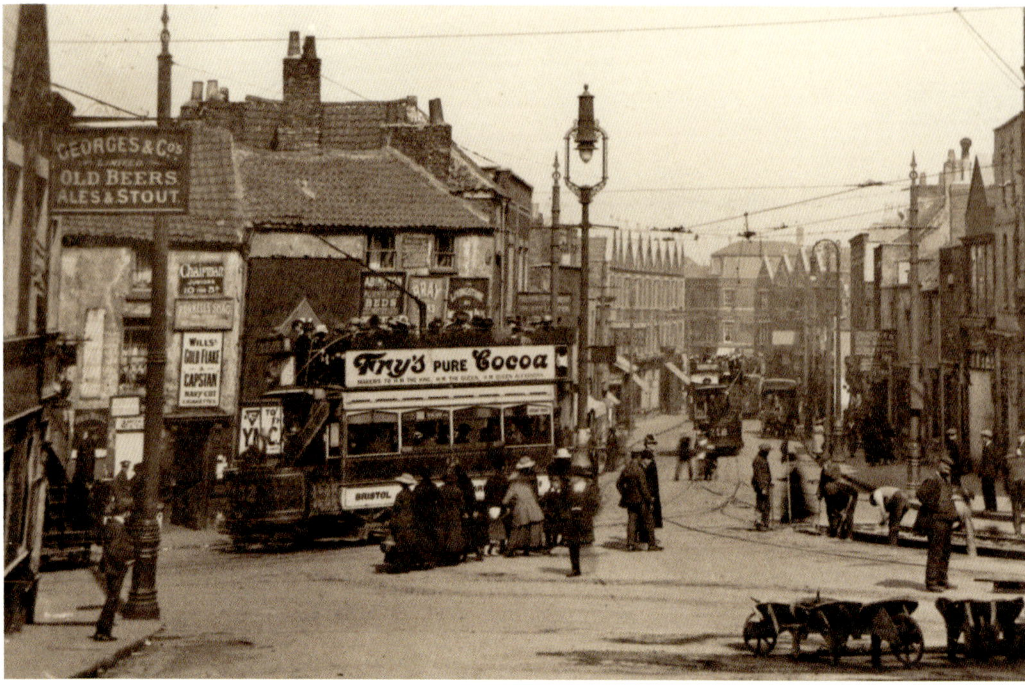

East Street Junction, Bedminster, Early 1900s

This street junction has certainly changed. The building in the foreground on the left is the London Inn. The new building across the road on the left is now a bank, but the buildings on the right remain as small businesses. The advertising in the postcard is interesting. Fry's was another major Bristol employer. On the left of the tram is a sign for the YMCA – possibly drawing attention to the one in Totterdown. The other advertisement on the wall for Wills' Gold Flake is rather superfluous, as it was only processed a few hundred metres down East Street. Judging by the activity in the foreground of the postcard above, road works are not just a modern irritant.

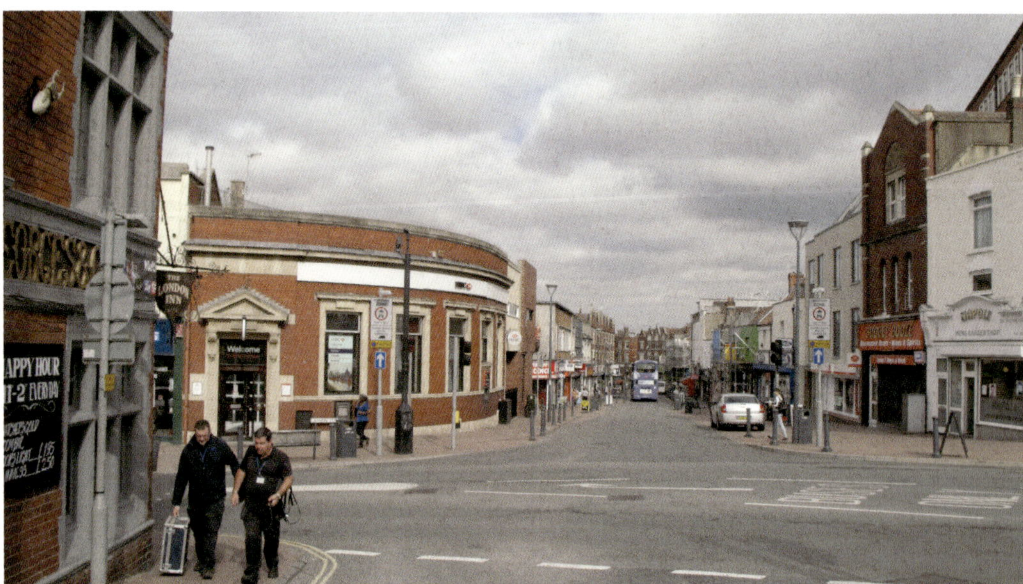

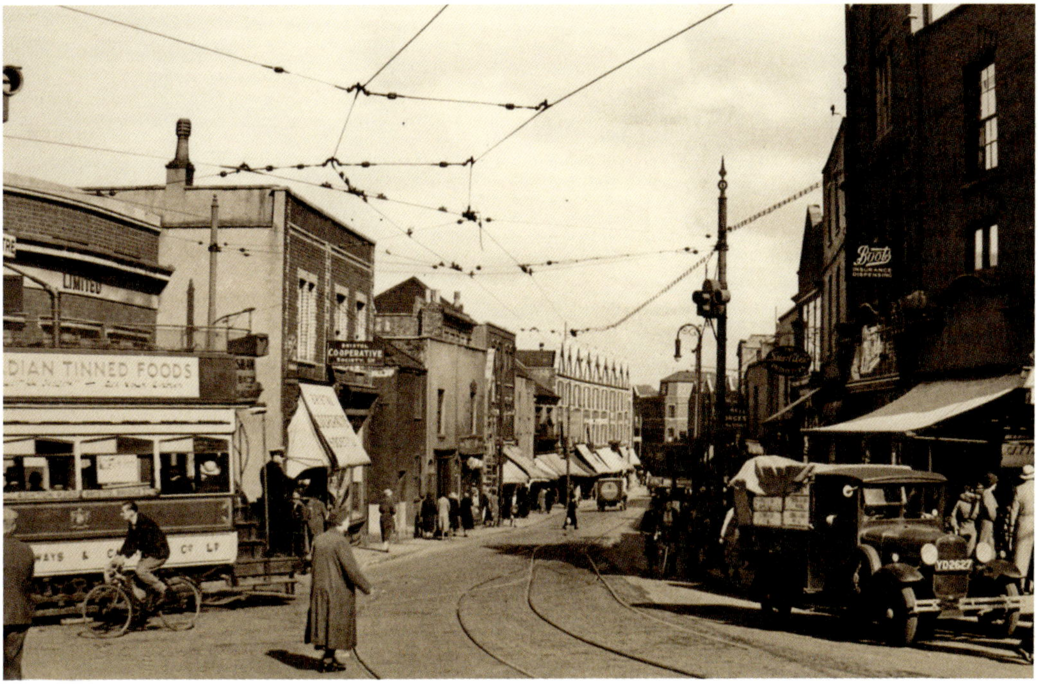

East Street Junction, Bedminster, 1935

The old photograph of the end of East Street was taken approximately thirty years after the one on the previous page. Deliveries were now being made by vehicles rather than horse and cart. The overhead web of electric cables are a reminder of the importance trams still played in 1930s life. Pedestrianisation has now transformed the south end of East Street.

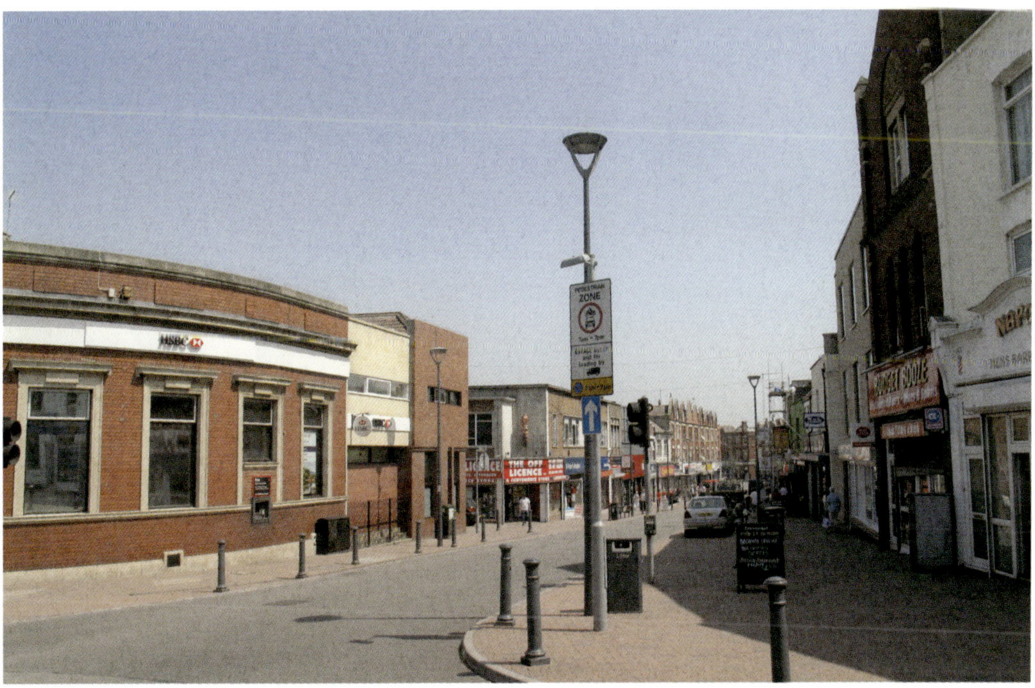

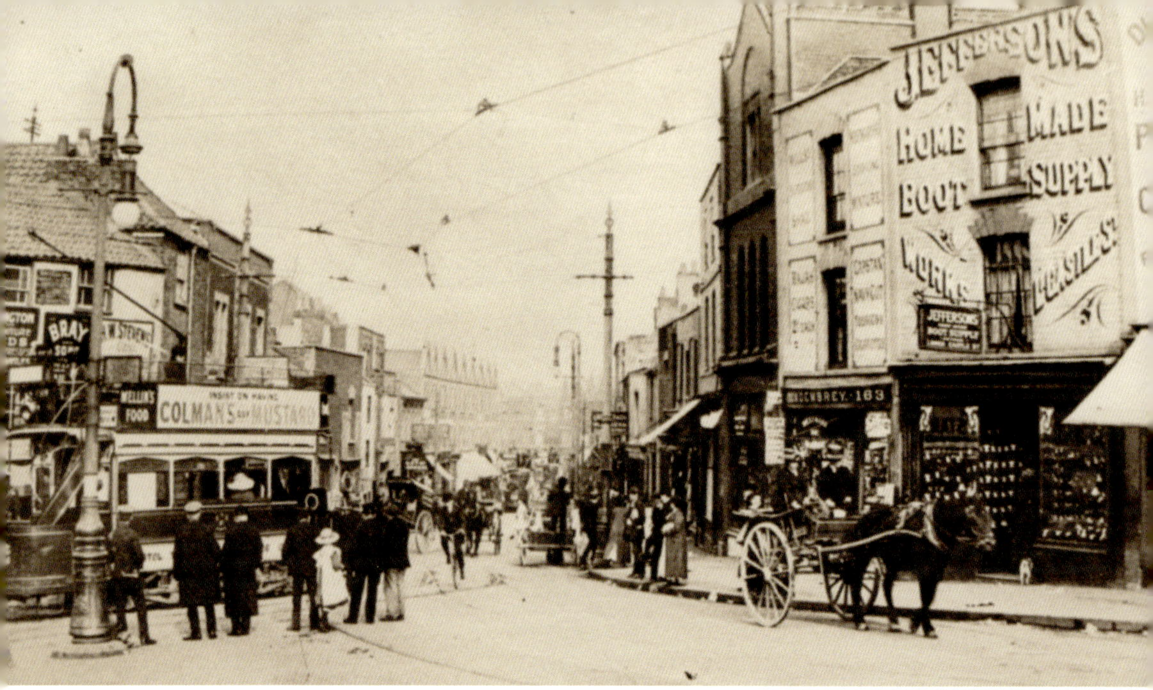

East Street Junction, Bedminster, 1909

The postcard shows a rather congested East Street with horse-drawn vehicles, carts and a tram jostling for position. It is a reminder of what a vibrant place Bedminster had become. Looking down the street, the pointed gables of one block can be seen in both pictures. On the left side of the photograph there is a new skyscape, with the top of Northfield House peeping over the HSBC bank. The buildings on the right-hand side have not changed, except for their use, with a house agent replacing the bootmaker.

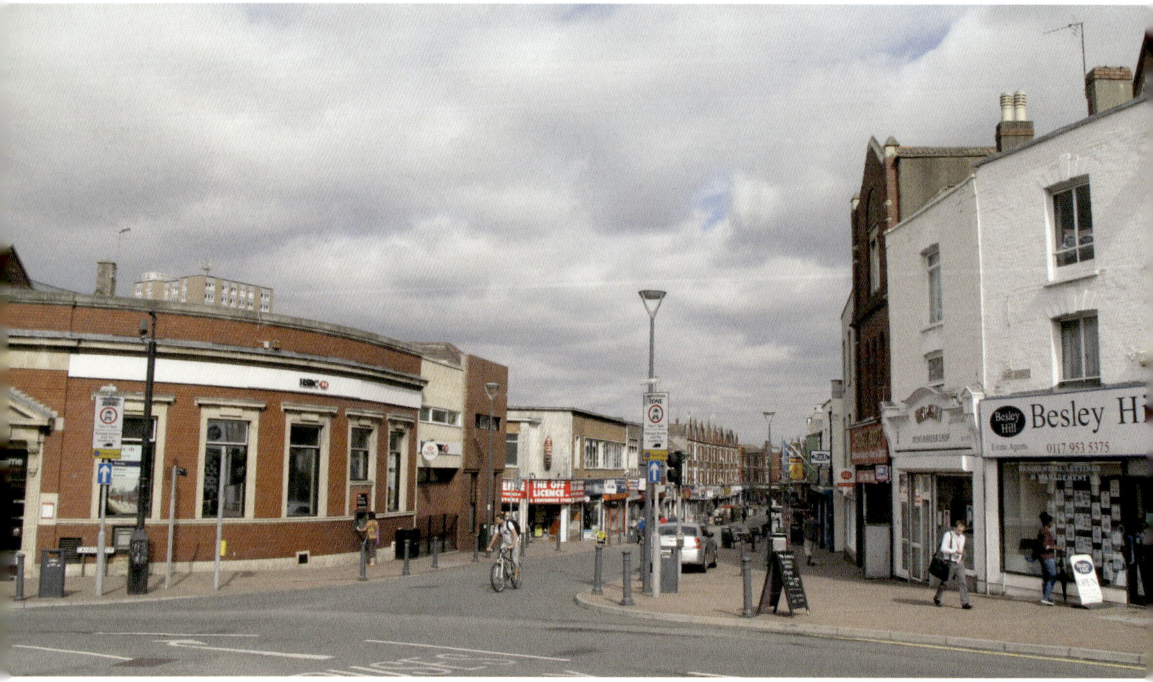

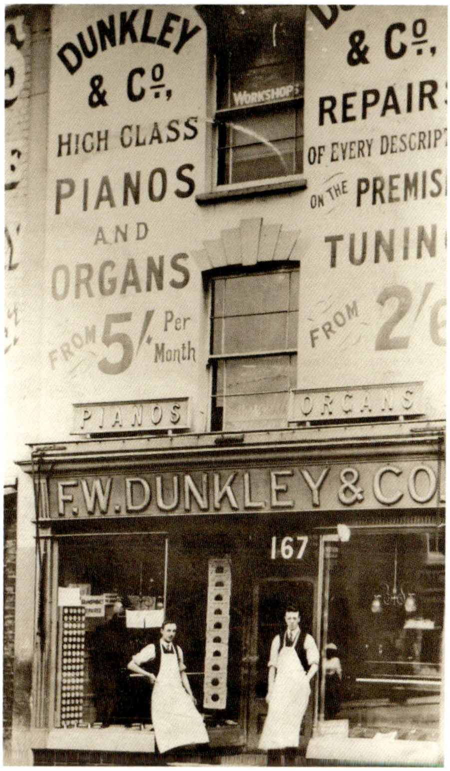

No. 167 East Street, Bedminster, Early 1900s
F. W. Dunkley & Co.'s shop is next door to Jefferson the bootmaker in the previous pictures, and is sited where East Street bends round towards the junction with West Street. It is an interesting comparison between the two ages when a piano was rented for home entertainment, just as televisions and video players were also hired until fairly recently. In the background of the photograph, the upper floors of the Robinson Building are visible.

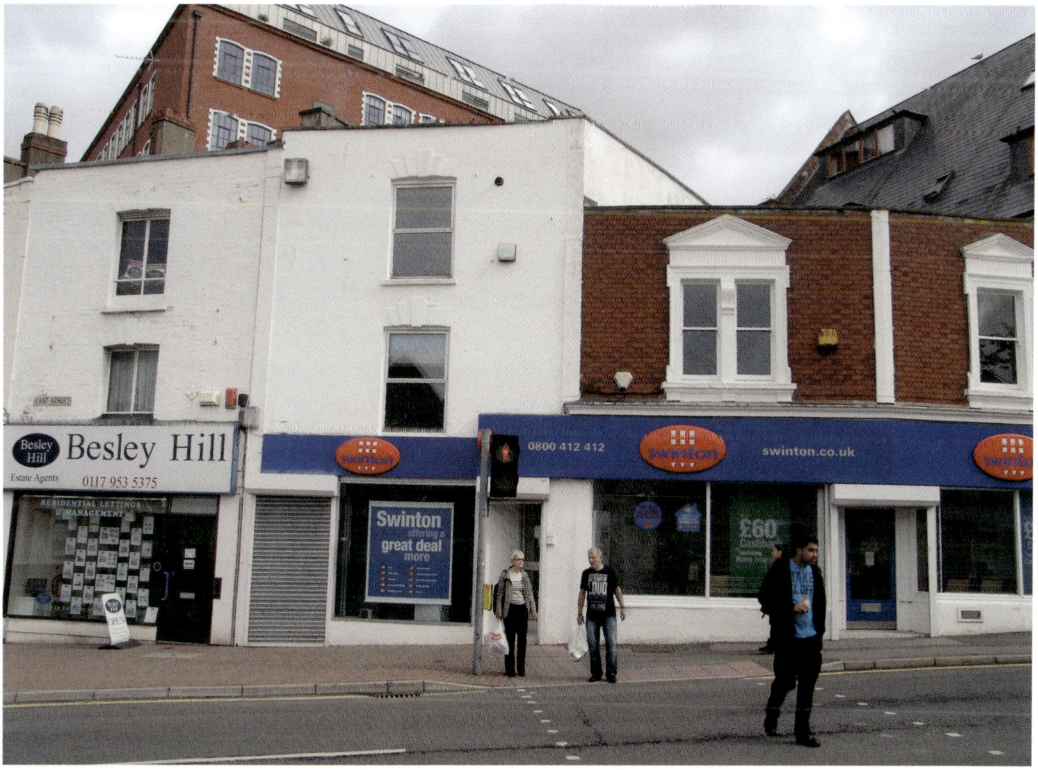

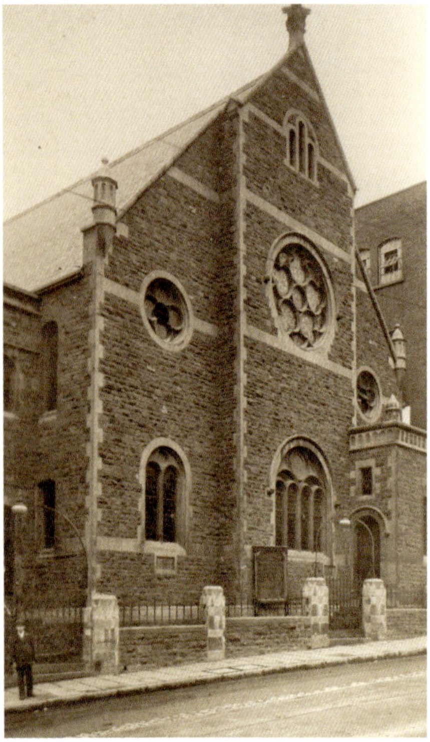

East Street Chapel, Bedminster, Postcard Dated 14 August 1913

The Baptist congregation was formed in 1884, and they built their chapel in 1893. It was deconsecrated in 2003, and is now twelve apartments. It was built beside the 1887 Robinson's Printing & Stationery Works, which at that time was a one-storey building. In 1902, due to lack of space, they expanded upwards. They jacked up the roof and inserted two more floors. The brickwork is different below and above the notice 'Cameron Balloons'. This Robinson's factory produced envelopes and cardboard boxes. Now the factory produces between 150 and 200 hot-air balloons each year, with 70 people working for Donald Cameron's family firm.

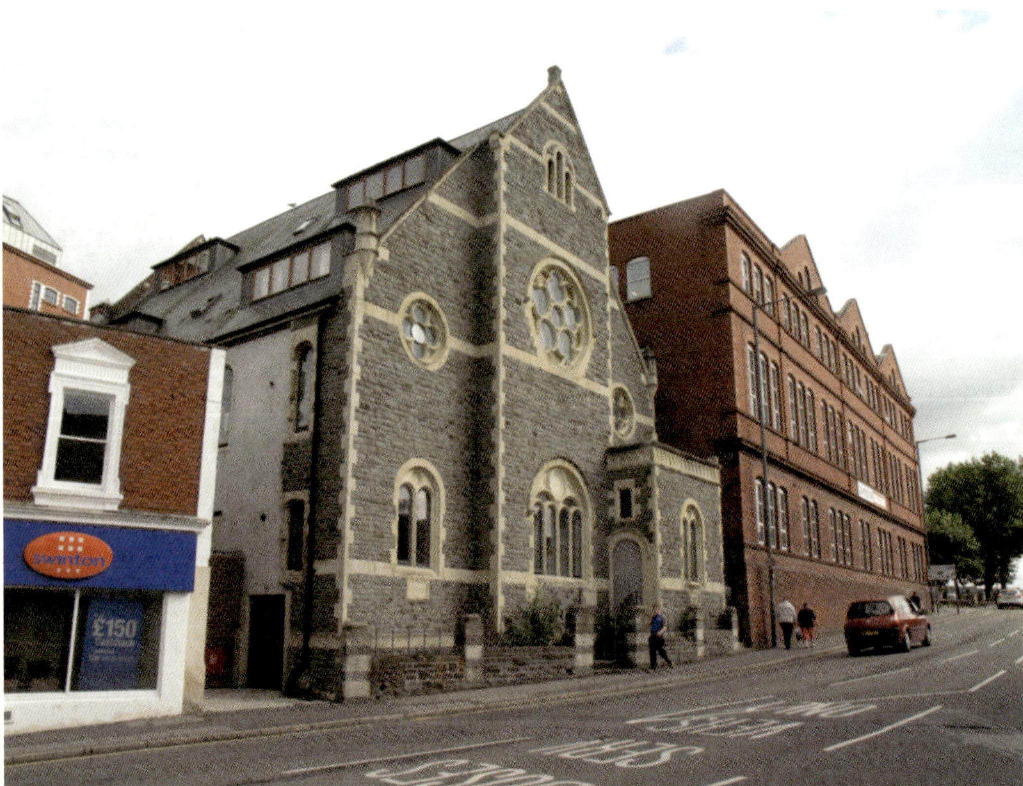

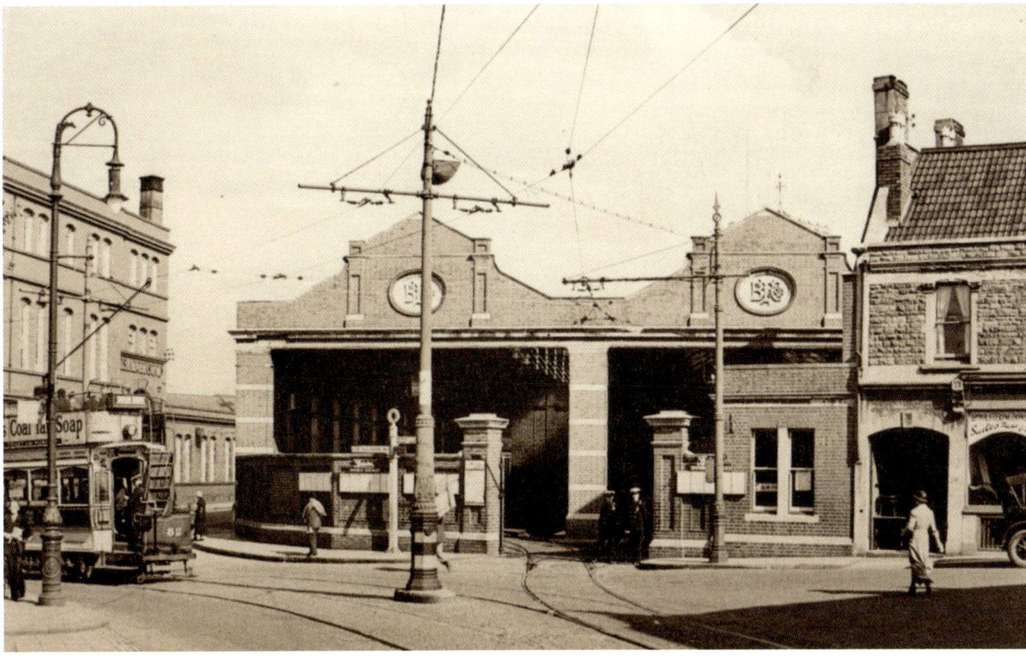

Bedminster Tram Depot, 1935

The photograph shows the tram depot six years before it was destroyed in a bombing raid in 1941. The site is now a McDonald's drive-through and car park. Standing outside the old depot are two tram drivers in their uniforms and caps. The tram passing by to the left is advertising Wright's Coal Tar Soap (a change from the more familiar brands such as Coleman's Mustard and Fry's). The Robinson Building stands on the left.

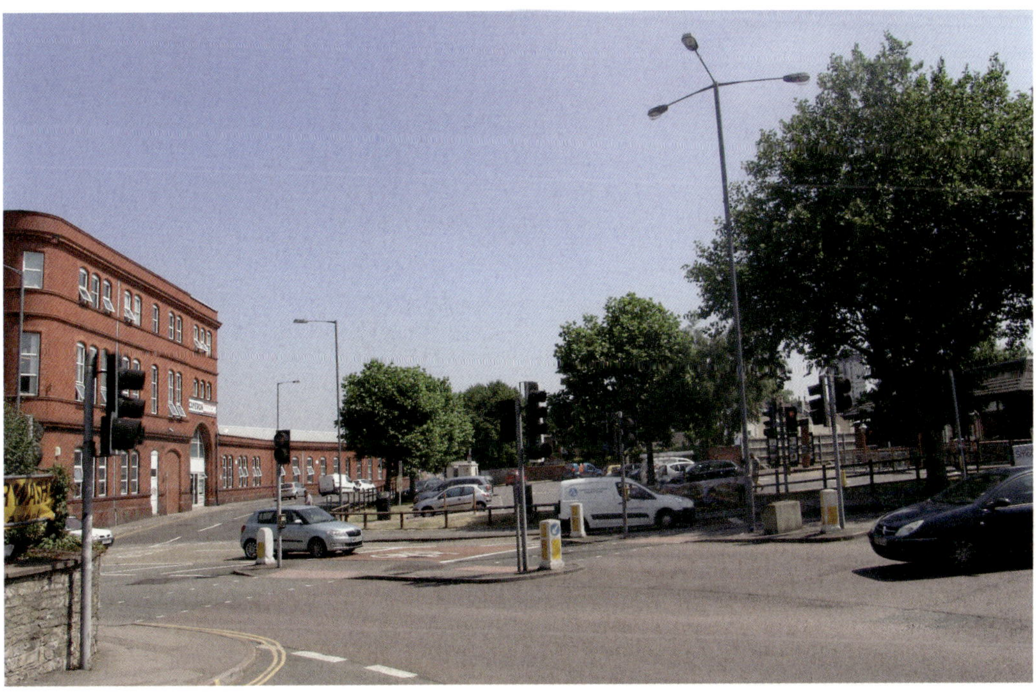

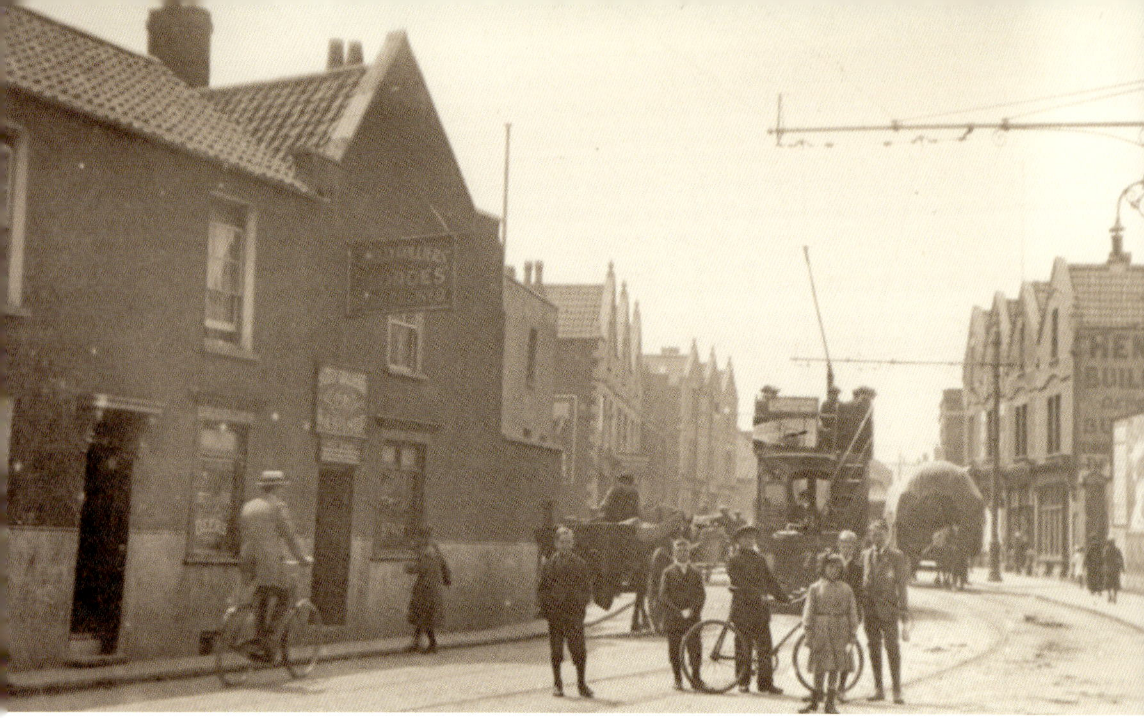

West Street, Bedminster, *c.* 1920

These pictures are taken looking south in West Street. At first sight they look dissimilar, but the buildings on the right-hand side are the same. On the left of the postcard, beside the upright man wearing a hat on his bicycle, is the Jolly Collier pub, whose doors are still open. The houses beyond, with the steep-pitched roofs, are now the Tesco Express seen on the left of the photograph. The postcard also has a horse pulling a cart piled with hay (probably fodder for working horses kept in nearby stables).

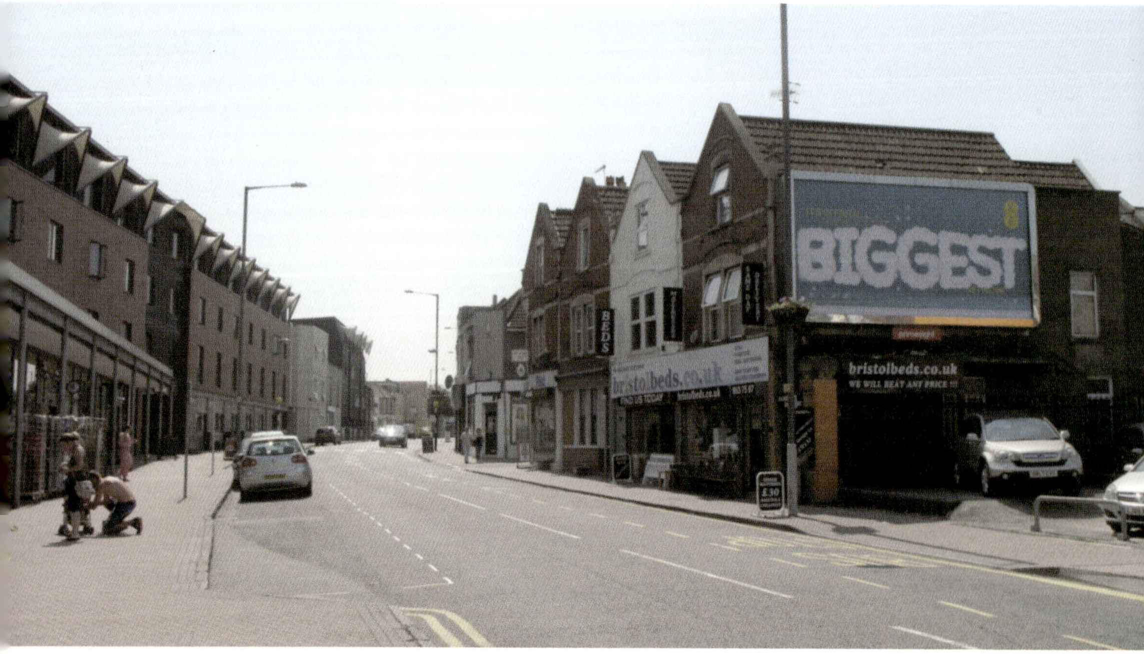

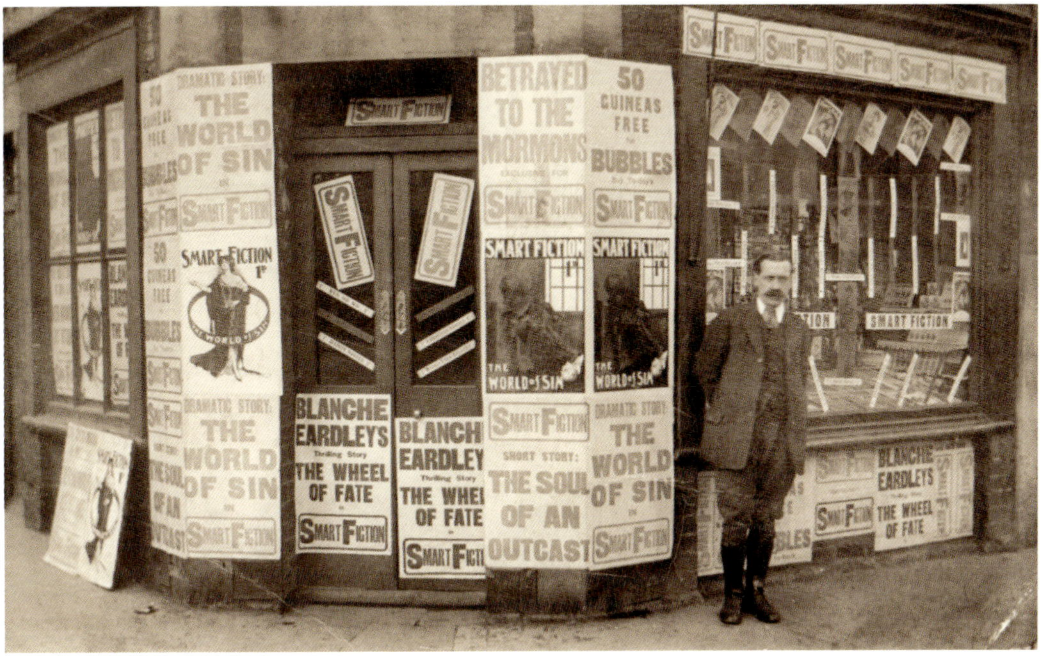

No. 120 West Street, Bedminster, 1900s

Halfway down West Street on the corner of Rowey Street stood this exuberantly festooned corner shop. The 'thrilling story' *The Wheel of Fate* advertised abundantly on the shopfront was by Blanche Eardley, who is now only remembered for a court case in which she accused a London theatre manager of infringing her civil rights for demanding she remove her yard-wide hat during a matinee performance of a play.

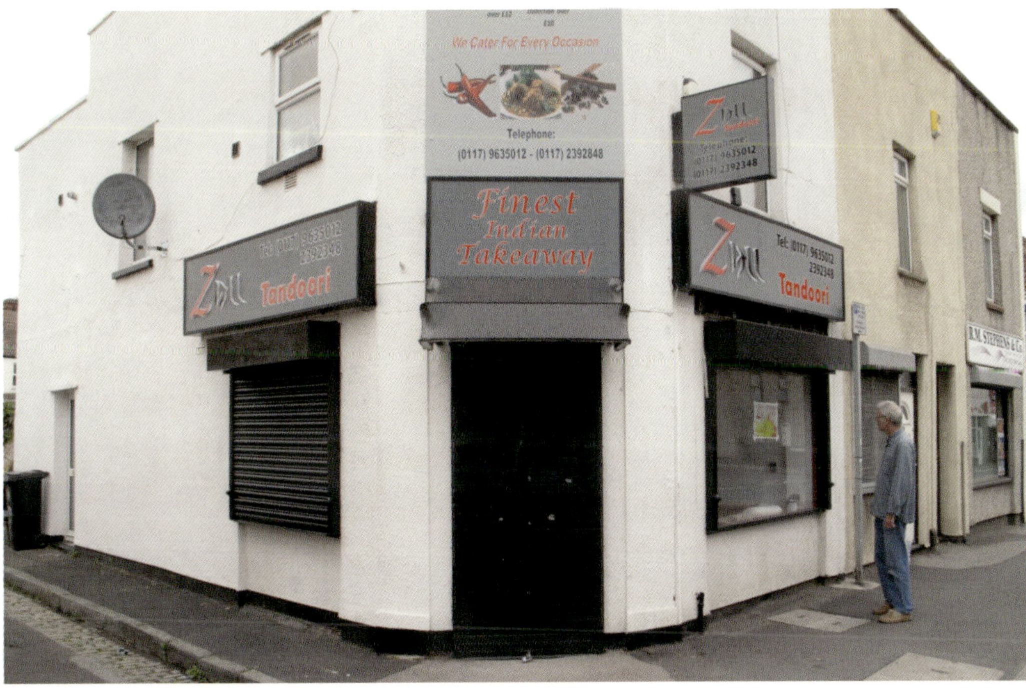

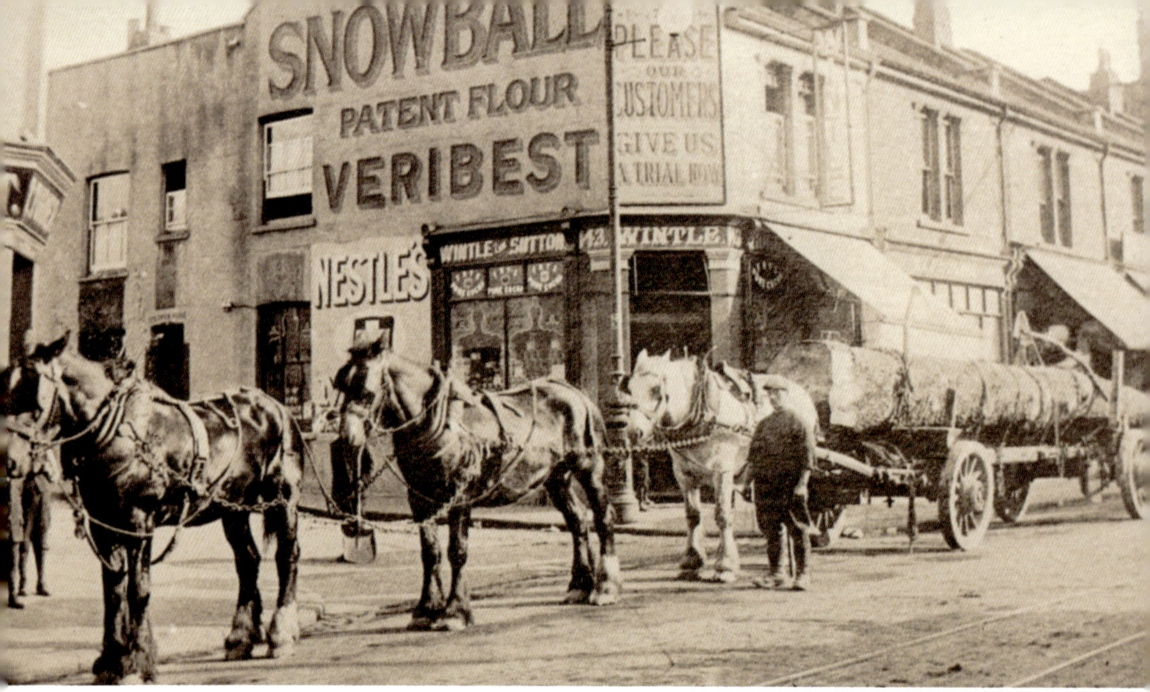

No. 143 West Street, Bedminster, Early 1900s

These pictures are around midway along West Street, with Bartletts Road on the left. Wintles shop, a small family grocer, has turned into a small supermarket. The team of shire horses pulling a tree trunk (probably from Ashton) has stopped in the road in order to turn left into a timber yard in Ireton Road, which is opposite Bartletts Road. The chains, which are attached to the wagon, are fixed onto heavy collars round the horses' necks. Their reins are not used for guidance; shire horses are noted for responding to spoken orders.

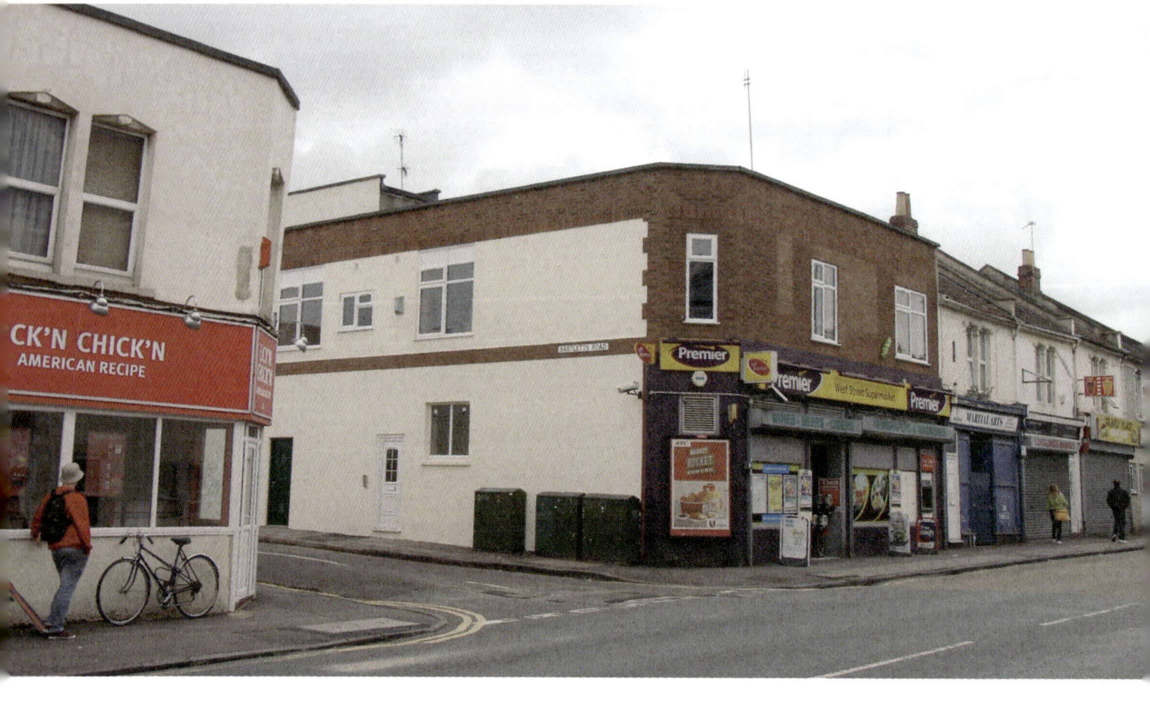

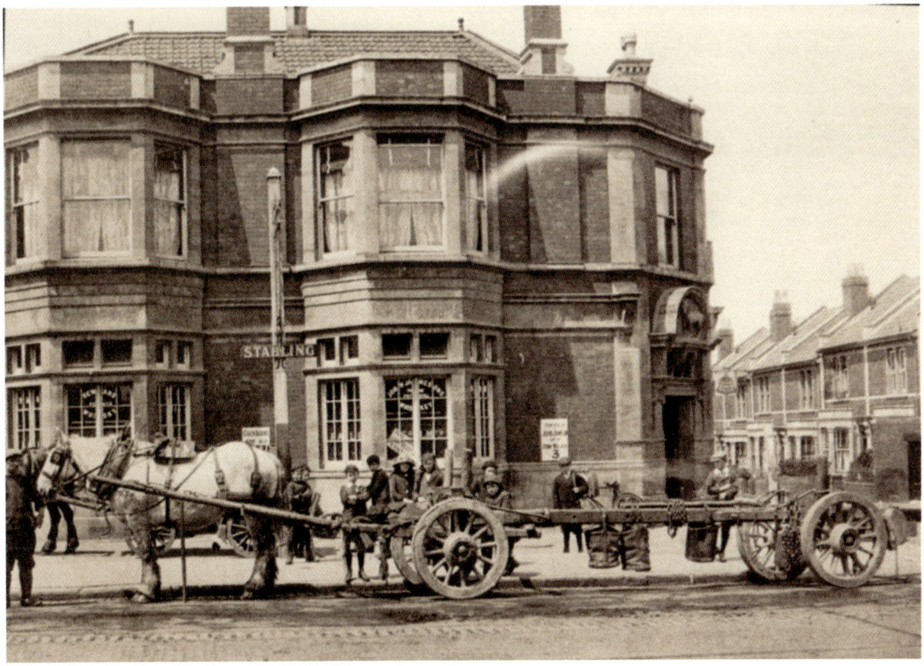

The White Horse, West Street, Bedminster, Early 1900s

The horse and wagon is drawn up in West Street with Chessel Street in the background. The 1845 Ashmead map shows a White Horse public house on this site. The pub in the picture was rebuilt in 1901. This looks like the same horse that was in the former picture and there are three nosebags tied on to the wagon, which suggests that there were snacks of oats for its companions. In 2011, planning permission was granted for change of use from a pub to six residential flats and a café/bar. Conversion work is being undertaken behind the barrier. The white horse emblem above the entrance has survived so far, and it is hoped it will be retained.

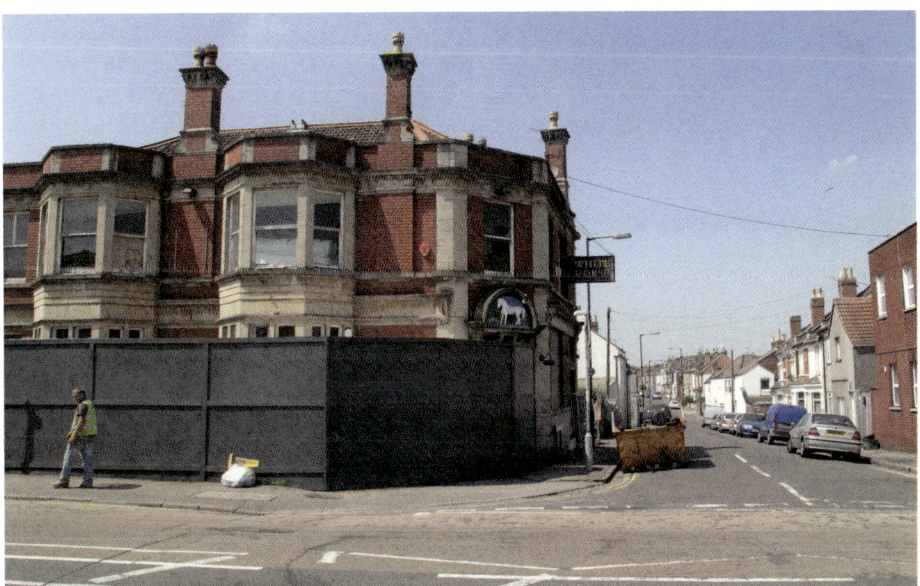

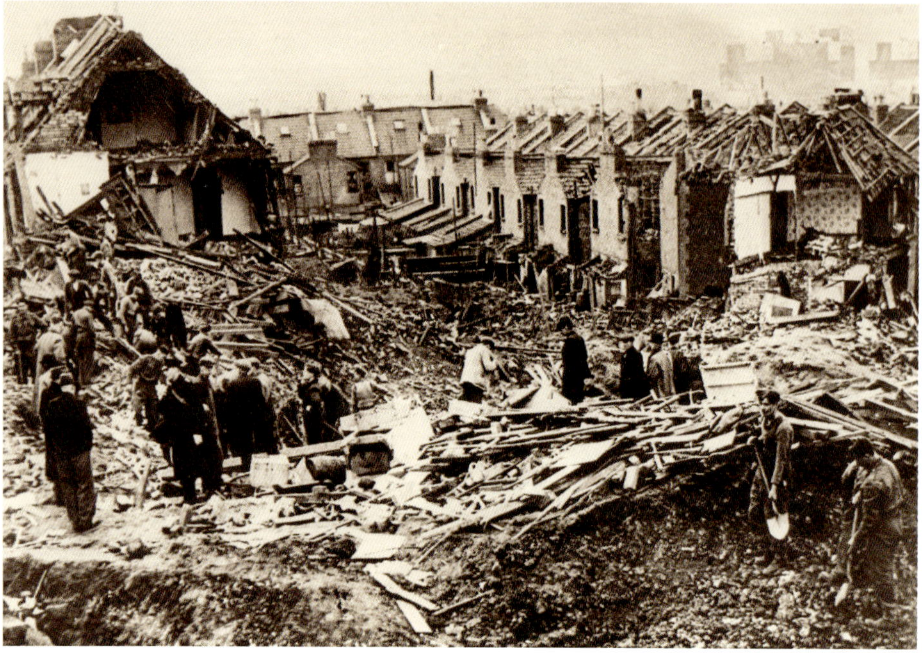

Blitz Damage, Palmyra Road, Bedminster

Palmyra Road links West Street with where Luckwell Road becomes Duckmoor Road. Unlike neighbouring roads, it never was a street of standard terraced houses. Here we see once again the devastation wrought by incendiary bombs. The modern photograph shows some post-war infill of housing. In the distance, Ashton Gate football ground is visible, behind which rise the slopes of Ashton Court. In 1901, the census reports show that there were twelve houses. All those registered as householder were in work locally, only two were over thirty-five, 50 per cent came from Bristol and 50 per cent from towns and villages in Somerset. No wives had outside employment. By 1911, there were thirty-seven houses. All the householders and children of working age were employed, along with one wife.

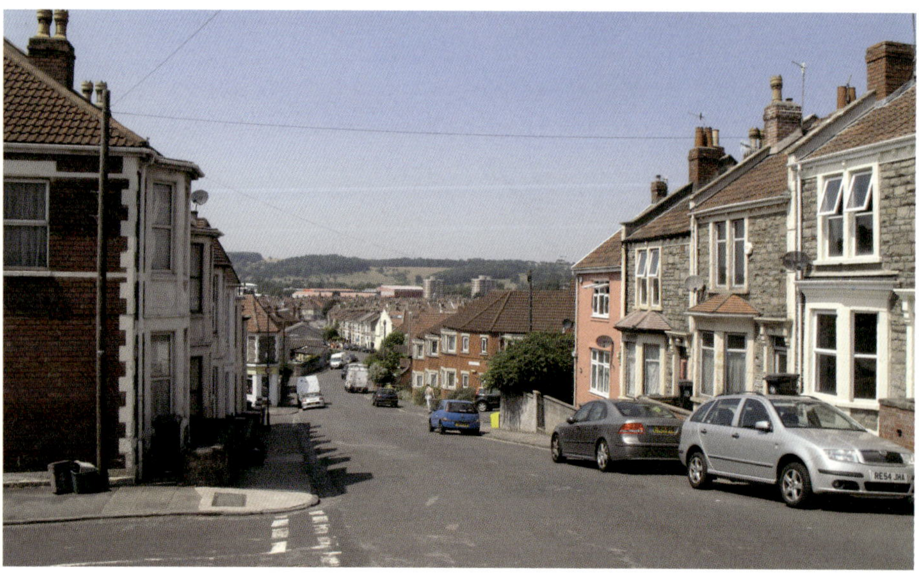

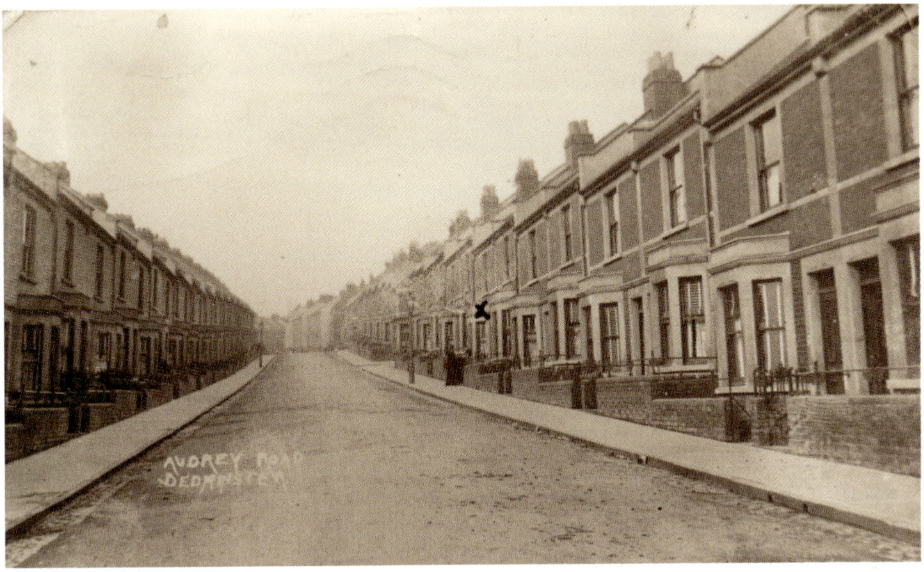

Aubrey Road, Bedminster, Postcard Dated 28 August 1918

Aubrey Road runs from Luckwell Road to Chessel Street, with St Aldhelm's church at its northern end. The 1880s map shows this land as covered by orchards. The 1901 census records sixteen houses, all with a married couple, and all except one in the age range twenty-two to thirty-six. There were no working wives, and the men were either in local industry or self-employed. Ten years later, out of the 116 houses, only one of the original families remained. Again, the male householders were employed locally. Only two wives worked (both dressmakers), and all the offspring past school age were also working. The 'X' on the old postcard probably marks the house of the sender of the card.

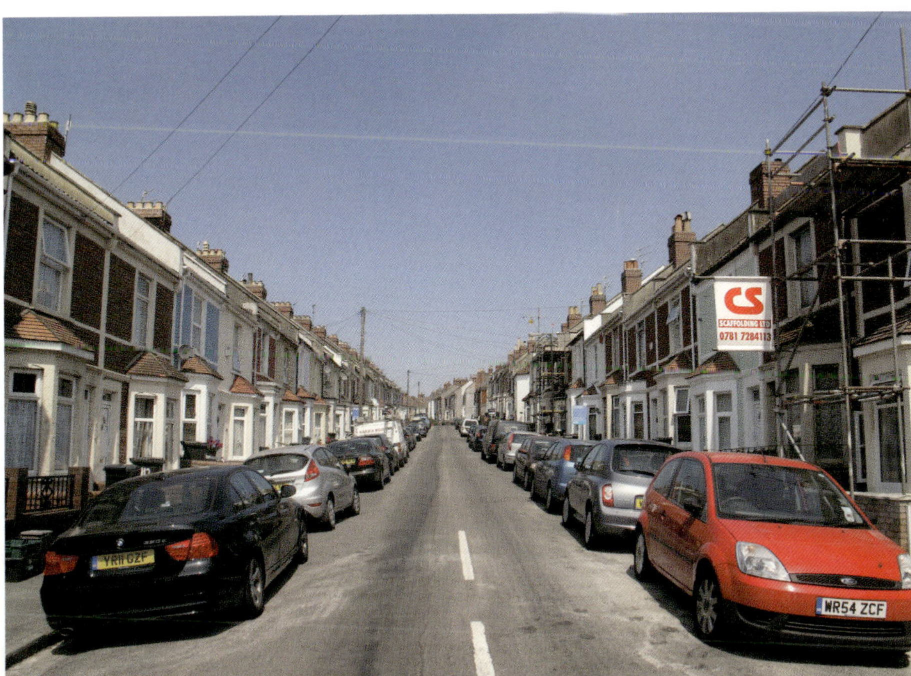

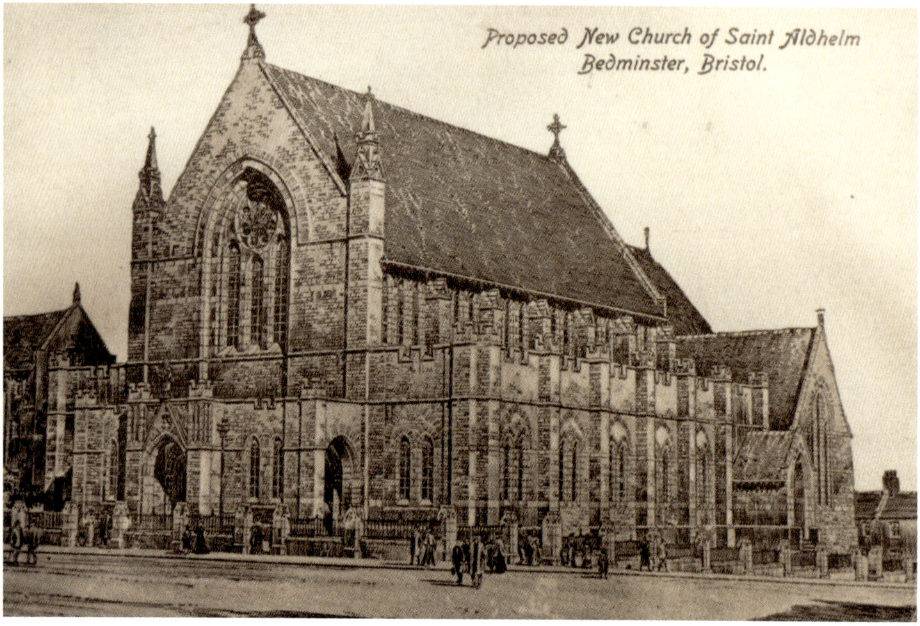

St Aldhelm Church, Bedminster, Early 1900s

The church is in the Chessels area, and stands at the junction of Chessel Street and Aubrey Road. The picture shows the proposed design by William Venn Gough, which was built in 1900. Venn Gough also designed the main building of the nearby South Street School, and the church of the Holy Nativity on Wells Road. This church, like most of the other churches and chapels in the area, was built in response to the population boom in the nineteenth century. It remains a very active church.

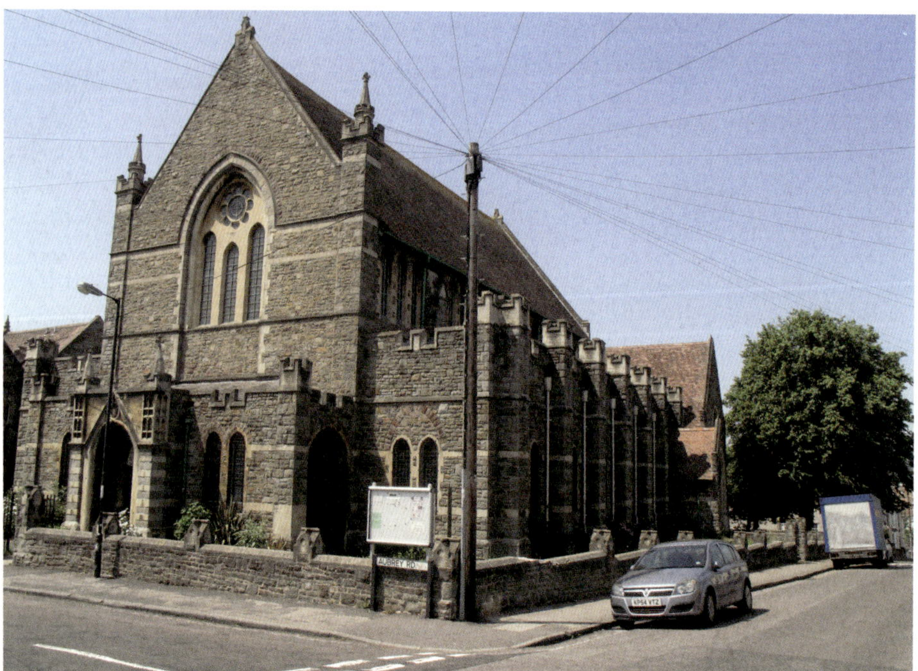

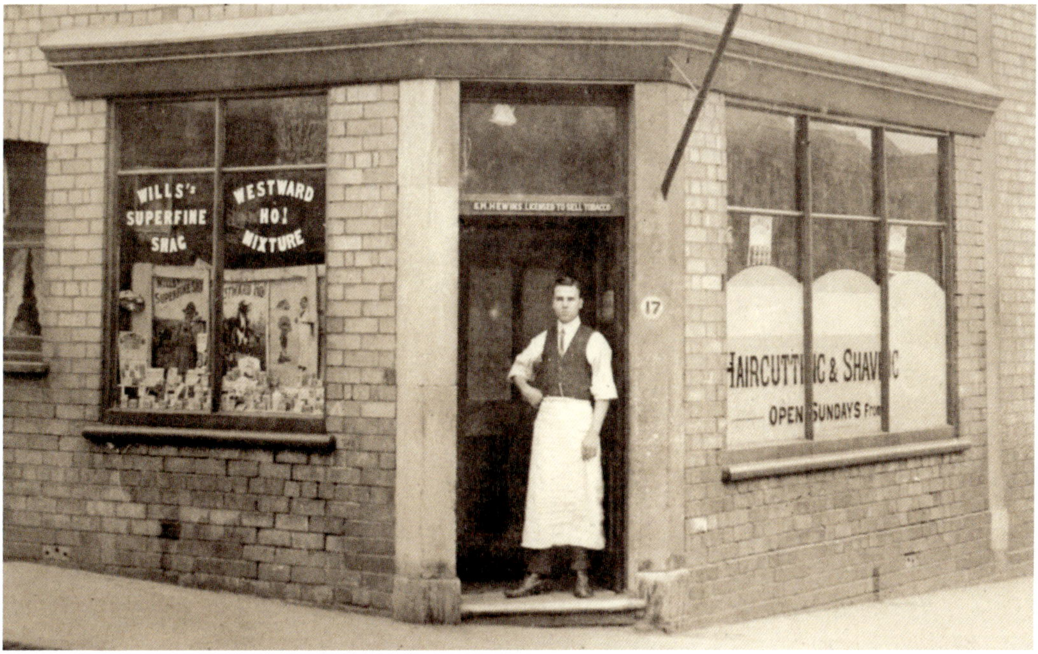

No. 17 North Street, Bedminster, 1910s

The street artist is livening up the hoarding, behind which stood No. 17 North Street, a barber's shop (also licensed to sell tobacco) owned by S. M. Hewins. Unusually, it states that it opens on Sundays. The area has quite a lot of graffiti artwork on its walls; in former years the writing on the walls was done by shops advertising their goods and services.

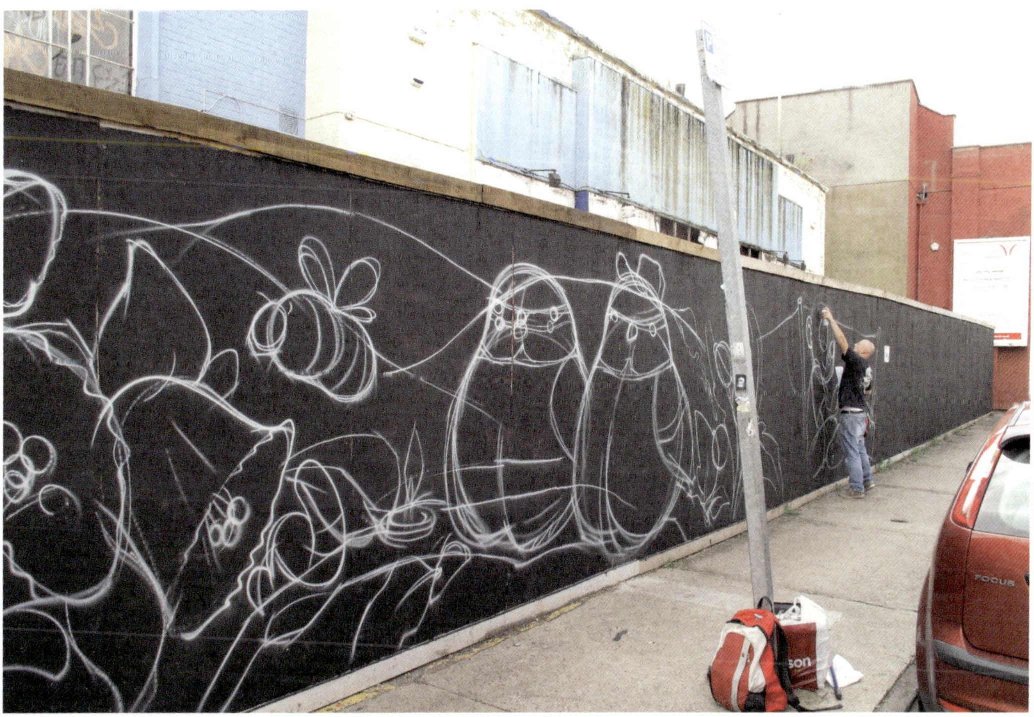

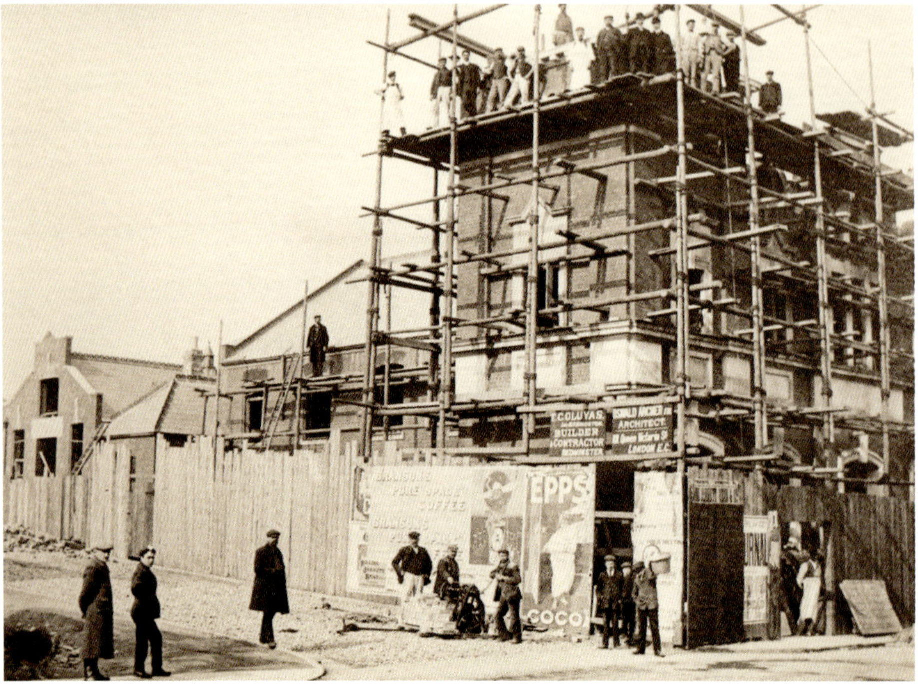

Salvation Army, Bedminster, Early 1900s

This building is on the corner of Dean Street and the very short Booth Street. Lady Emily Smyth (from Ashton Court) laid one of the foundation stones in 1907. It is on the edge of the Dean Lane colliery, which finally closed in 1909. The land was given by Lady Smyth to the city and it subsequently became Dame Emily Playpark. The Salvation Army was well known for its dedicated charitable work, and for living in the community they were helping to support. The chimney in the modern photograph is a reminder of the industrial past on this site. In the background is Northfield House.

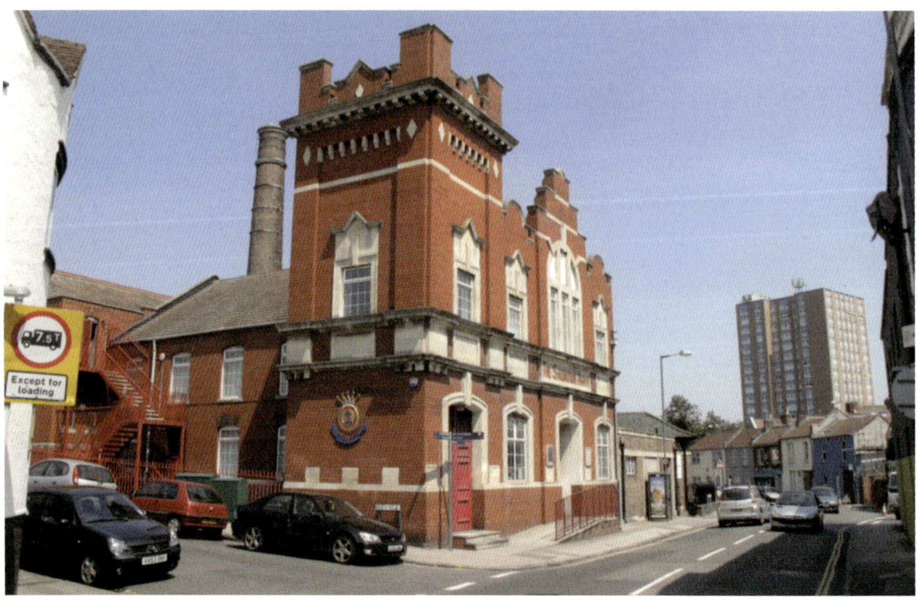

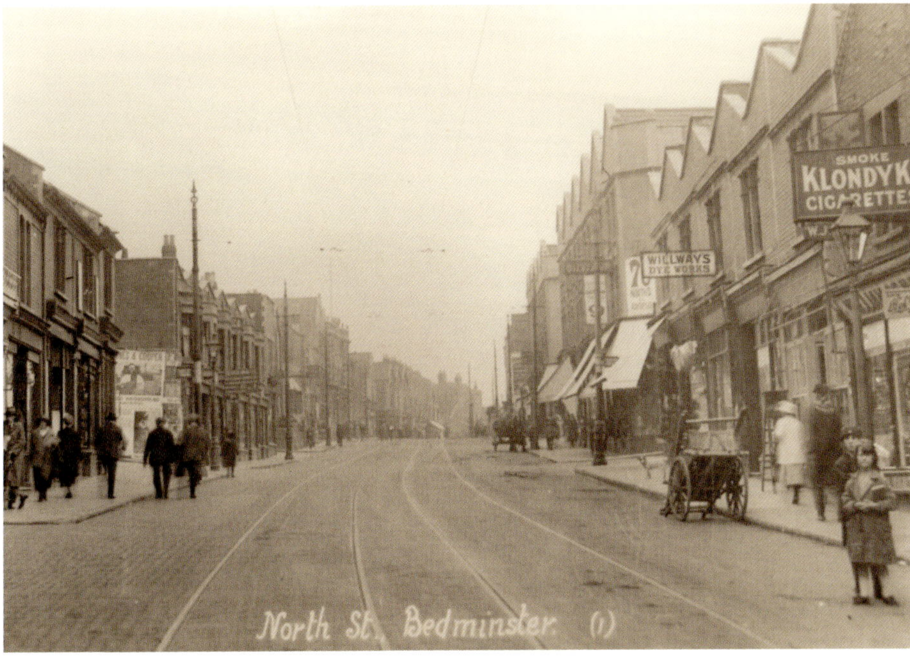

North Street, Bedminster, Early 1900s

North Street is still made up of primarily small, independent shops, but gone are the handcarts and the shop awnings. Klondyke Cigarettes were made in a factory just south of Redcliffe Bridge, which could trace its origin back to 1813. In 1901, the Imperial Tobacco Company was formed with thirteen tobacco and Cigarette-making companies (including Edwards, Ringer and Biggs, the makers of Klondyke cigarettes) joining together. Imperial was dominated by Wills. The block of flats on the left is Gaywood House.

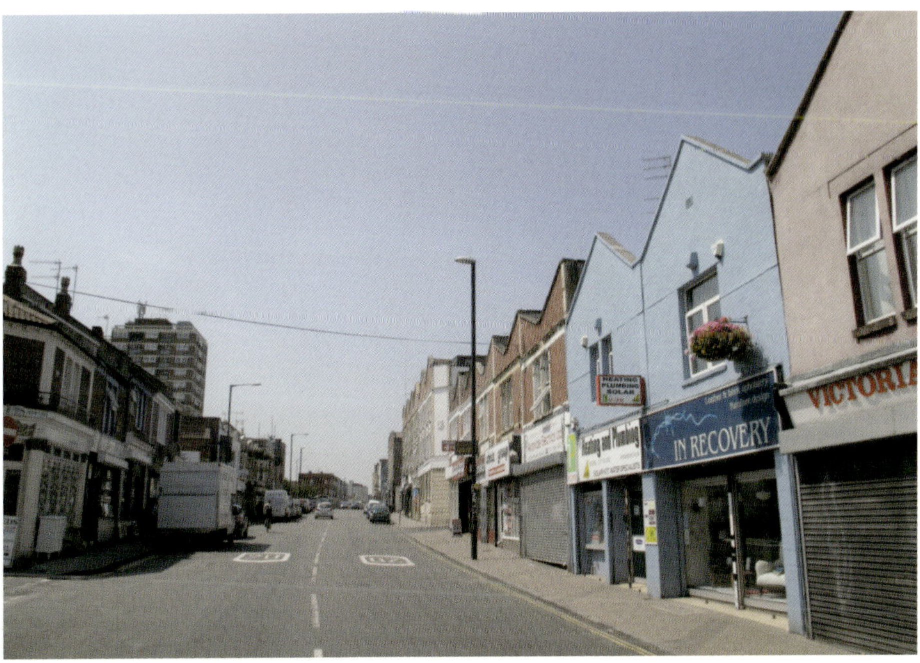

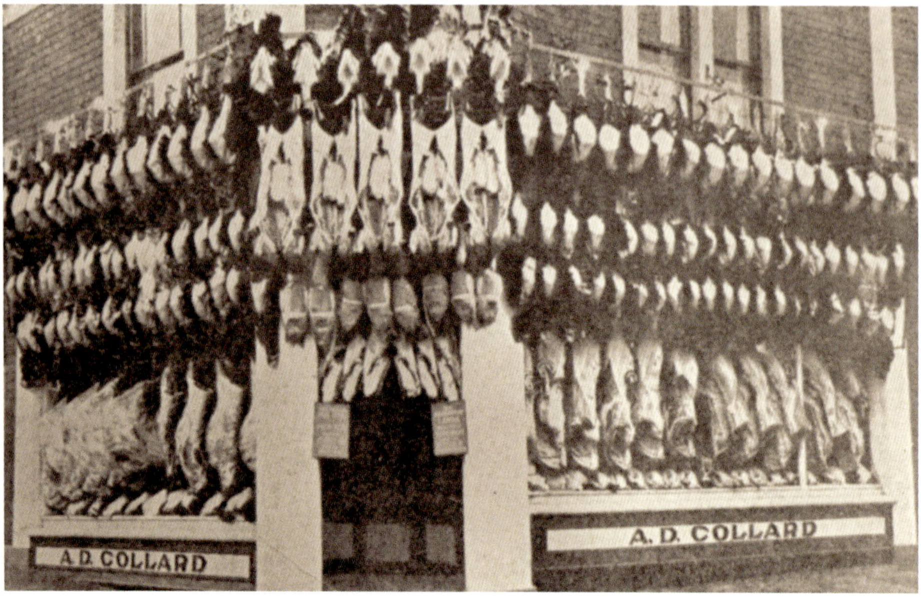

No. 57 North Street, Bedminster, Early 1900s
Collard's was a well-known family butchers in North Street. Alfred Daw Collard and his strong-willed wife, Louise, ran the shop in the early twentieth century, and their son Alfred Henry continued the family business. The personal service with customers often found in local stores such as Collard's engendered a sense of community spirit. The orderly displays of carcasses that once hung from metal hooks outside the shop have now been replaced by second-hand clothes. The A. D. Collard sign can still be seen at ground level, an evocative reminder of its past life.

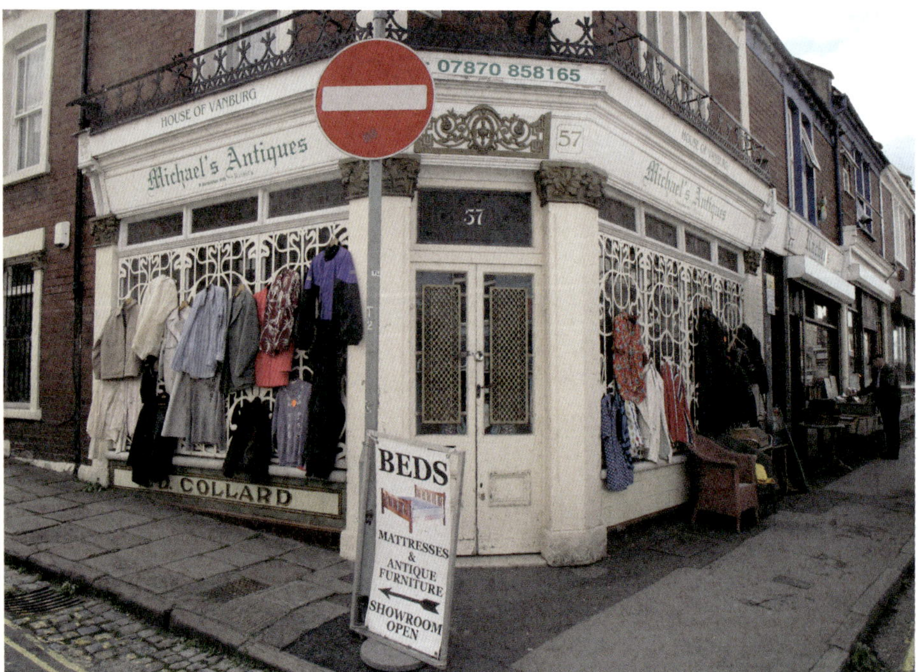

Hebron Chapel, Bedminster, Early 1900s

The chapel was built to the design of Henry Crisp in 1853 as the result of an ecclesiastical schism, which resulted in the formation of United Free Methodists. It was built before the surrounding streets of terraced housing, as seen in the 1855 Ashmead map. It was a substantial church with seating for 470. Capper Pass, who owned nearby smelting works, contributed to the funds. In the 1970s, the building was sold to the Spiritualists, but was redundant by 2000 and converted into apartments. In the burial ground, which was saved from being built on by local protest in 2003, lies Mary Baker (1791–1864), a noted impostor who went by the name Princess Caraboo. She pretended to be from a far-off island kingdom and fooled Bristolians for some months.

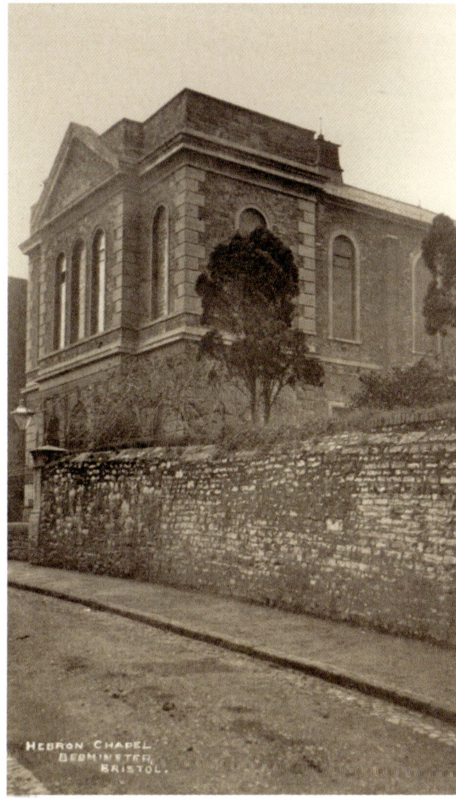

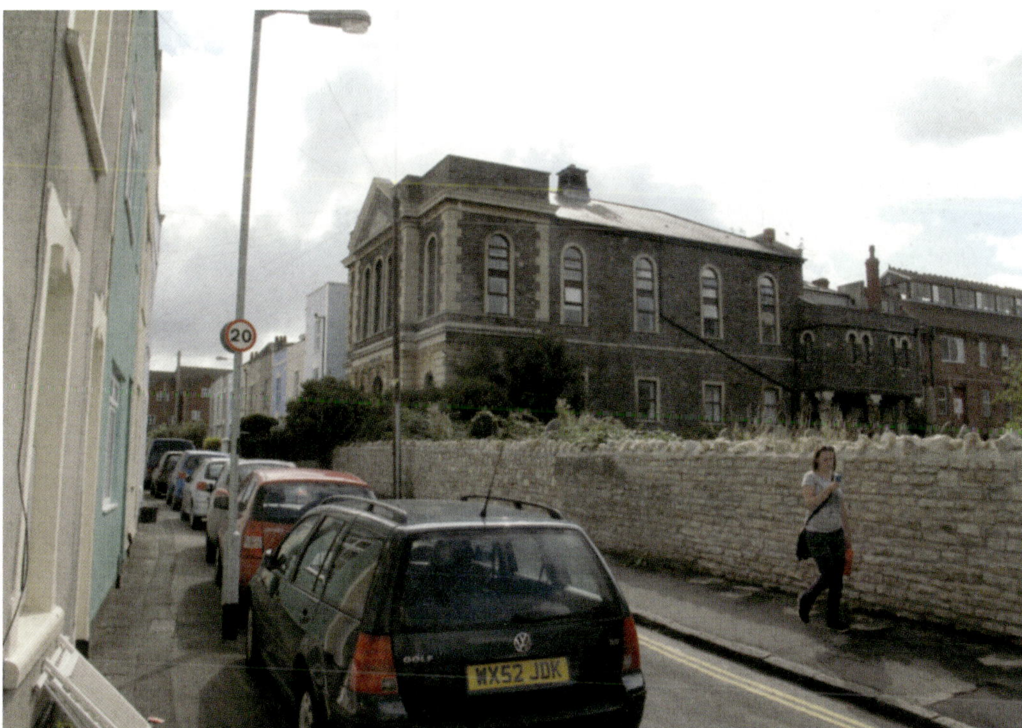

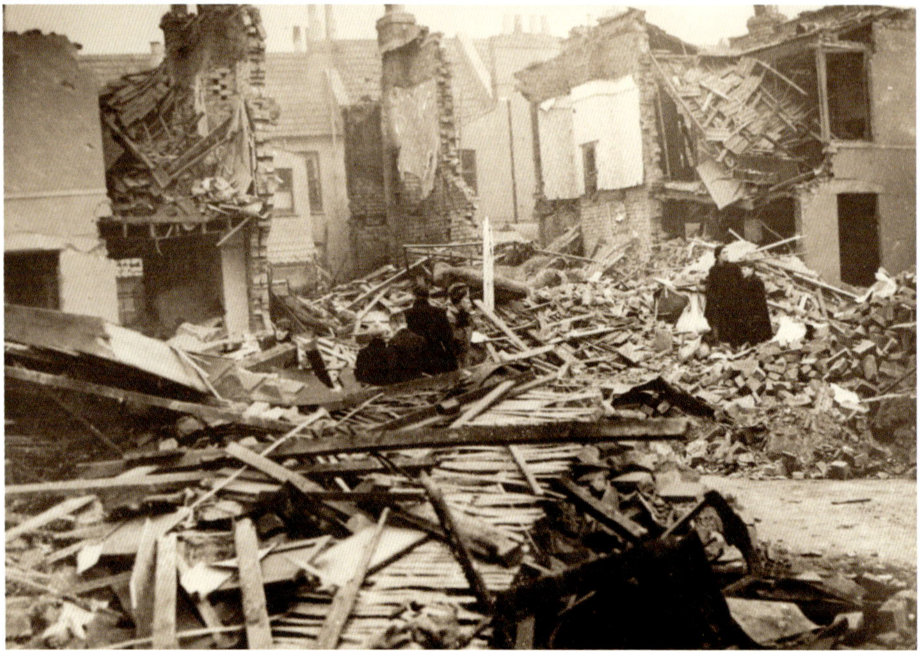

Blitz Damage, Sion Street, Bedminster

The photograph below is taken looking north to North Street. The tower block is Gaywood House, which is on the corner of Sion Street and North Street. The high-rise has sixty-four flats for residents aged over sixty, and is managed by Bristol City Council. The 1880s map shows mainly terraced housing on both sides of the street. Bombs destroyed many on the west side where only eight remain.

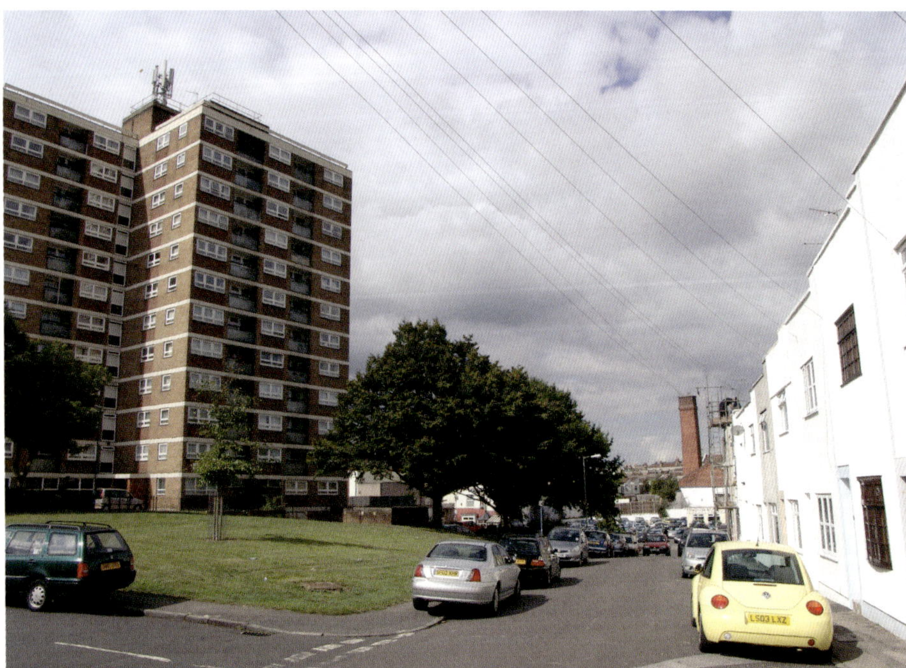

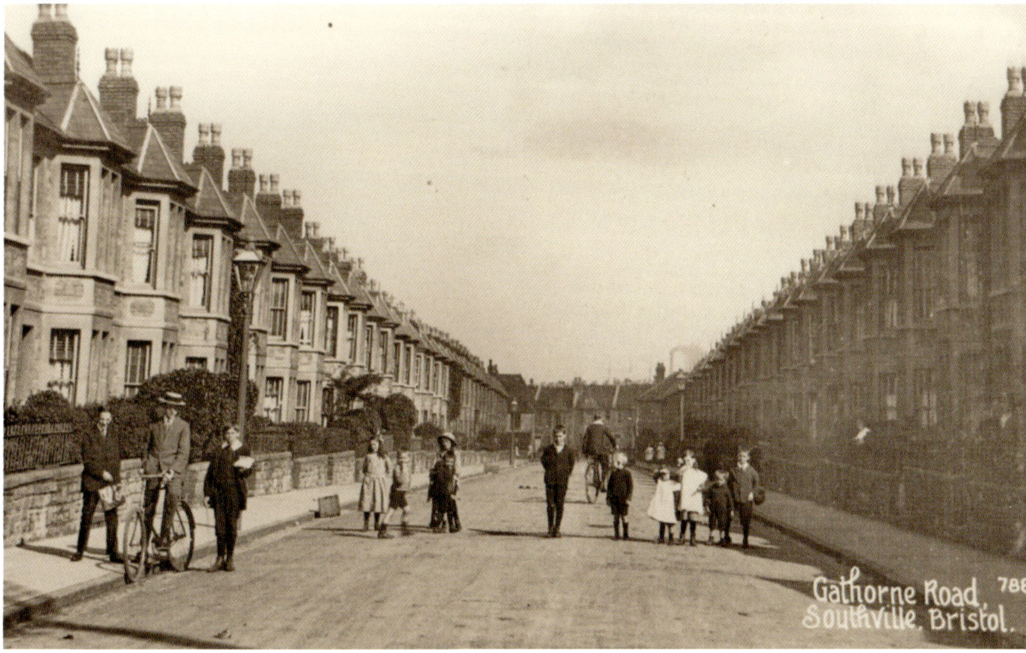

Gathorne Road, Southville, 1910s

This is one of the three straight roads that run north to south between the Tobacco Factory and Greville Road. It was built in the 1890s, when the regular pattern of terraced streets was moving west from Bedminster into Southville. The housing and road have not changed very much, maintaining the bay windows and pitched roofs. Finding a car parking space was clearly less of a problem in the first part of the twentieth century.

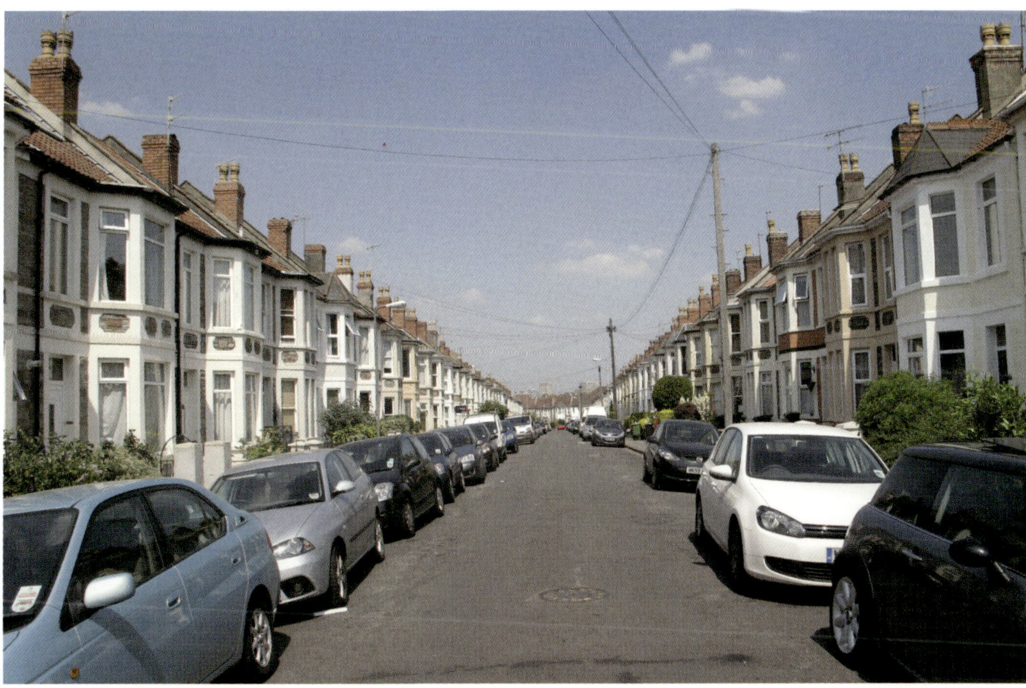

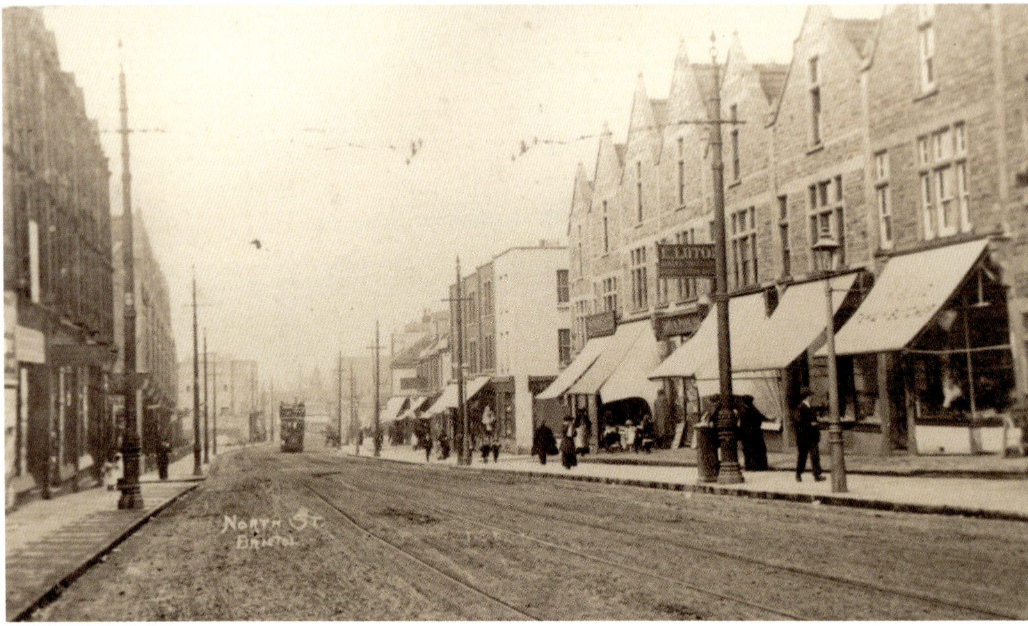

North Street, Bedminster, Early 1900s

Bicycles and cars have replaced the tram that is trundling down this western end of the shopping area of North Street. The modern Tobacco Factory can be seen more or less centrally in the photograph, but the building is absent from the picture above. Most shops on the right side have their awnings up; the north-facing left-hand side was out of the sun at the time the photograph was taken and was awning-free. Today, the street is enhanced with the trees and window boxes at first-floor level further down the street.

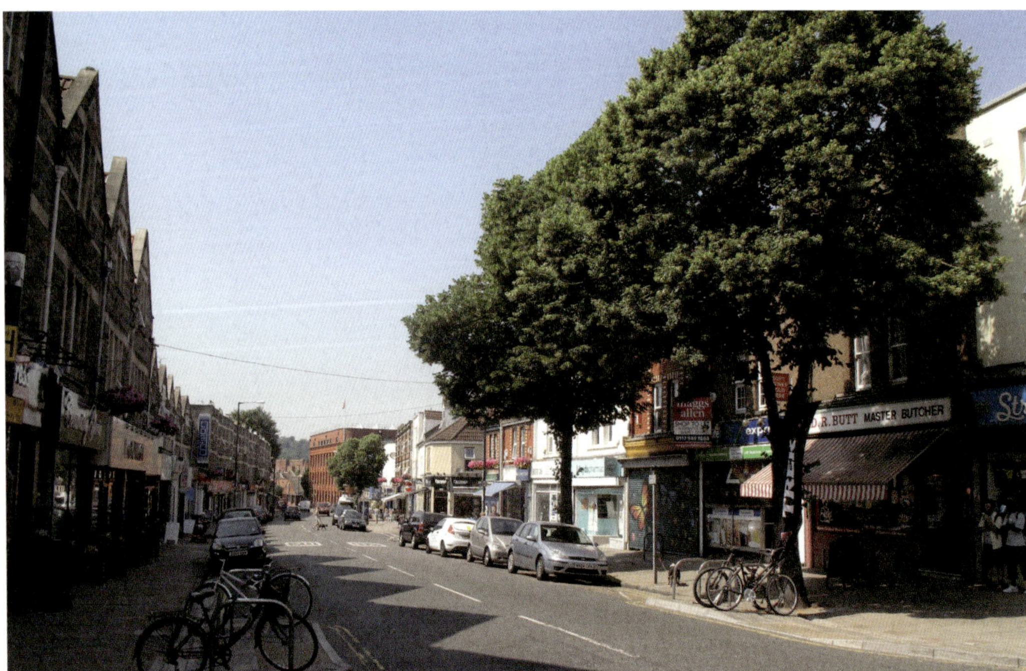

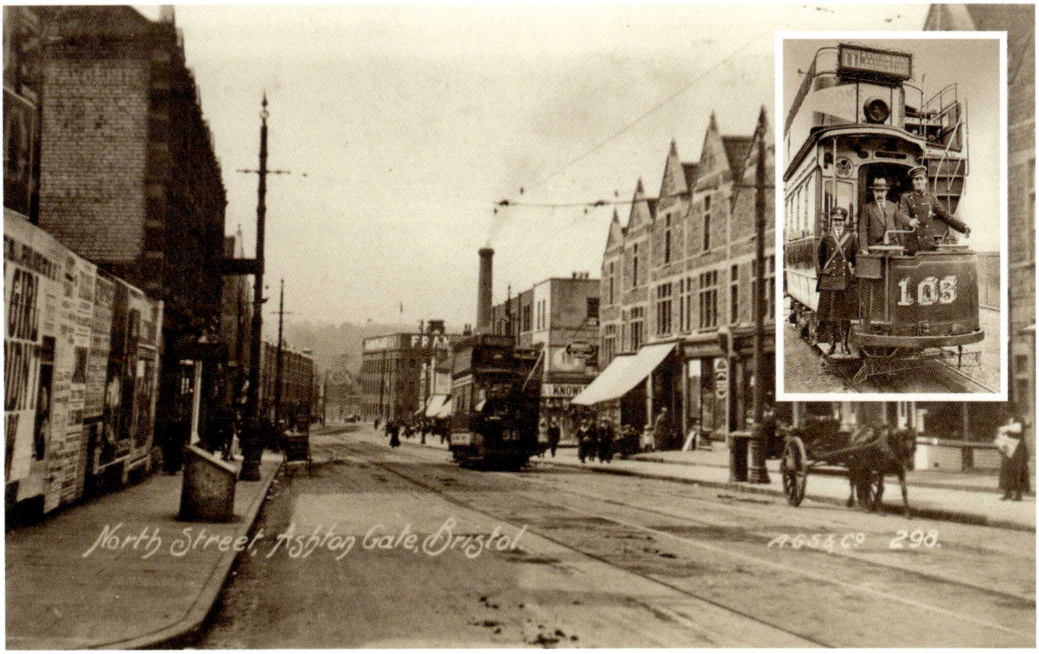

North Street, Bedminster, 1910s

The road surface has improved in the ten years or so that have passed from the image on the previous page. Also, the Franklyn Davey & Co., with its smoking chimney, has appeared. The inset shows a 'clippie' (*left*) in her uniform. Female clippies started working during the First World War due to a shortage of manpower. The tram is running from Ashton Road to Bristol Bridge. The circled '20' painted on the road shows that North Street is one of the Speed Limit Pilot Areas that was set up in May 2010, and which is likely to become city-wide.

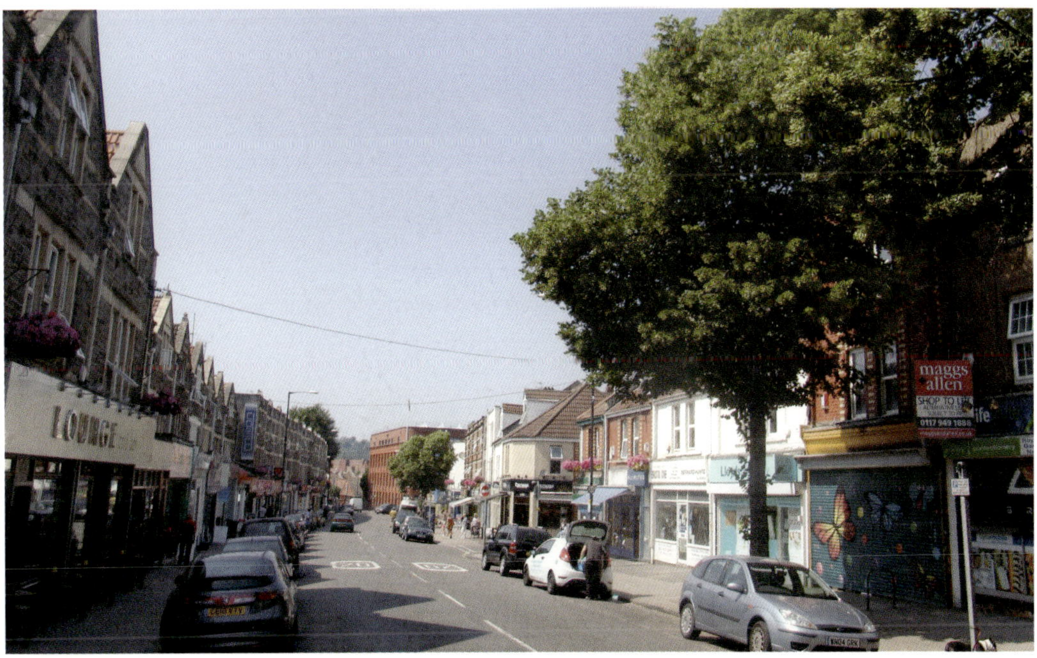

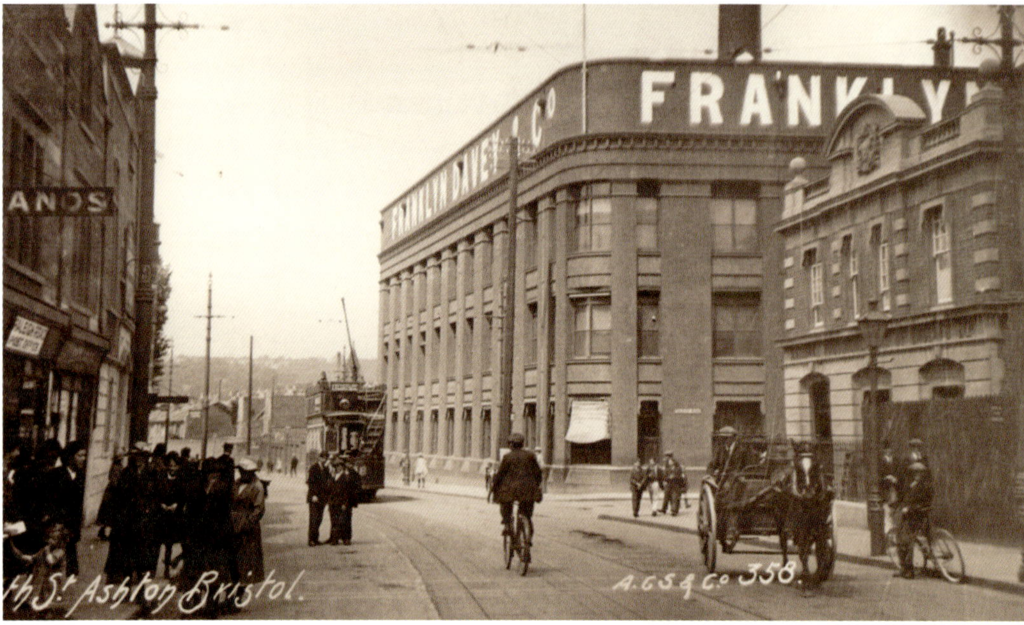

North Street, Bedminster, Postcard Dated 6 March 1920

Franklyn Davey & Co., one of the smaller tobacco companies in Bristol, was taken over by the Imperial Tobacco Company in 1901. These smaller companies kept their names. Frank Wills was the architect of all the twentieth-century brick buildings on the Wills/Imperial sites in East Street and Raleigh Road. In the 1980s, Imperial Tobacco relocated to Hartcliffe and this is the only complete building still standing. The building on the corner of Raleigh Road is the NatWest Bank, formerly the National Provincial, until they merged in 1968.

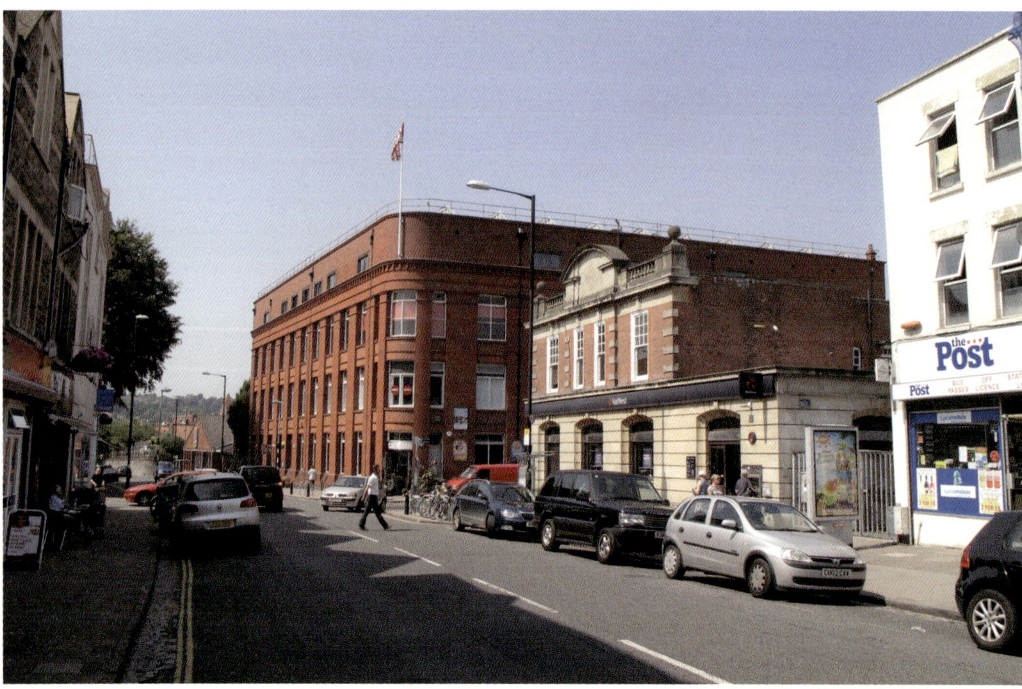

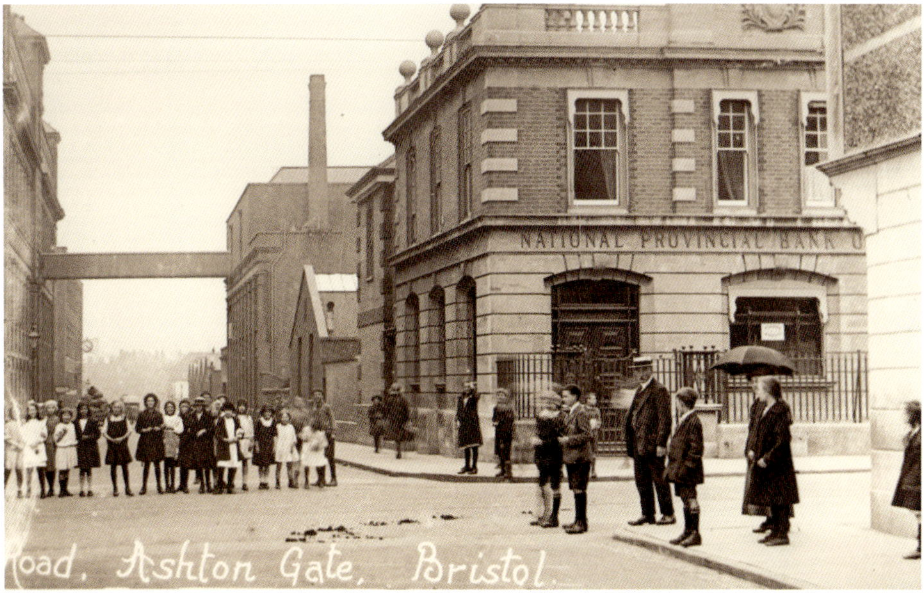

Raleigh Road and North Street, Bedminster, 1910s

These pictures are taken standing in North Street and looking north up Raleigh Road. The industrial bridge links the Wills factory (now demolished) to its extension across the road, which can be seen in the recent photograph with a green roof. The Franklyn Davey factory on the left of the recent photograph was saved from demolition in the 1990s by the architect George Ferguson (later to become first elected mayor of Bristol), and became a model of urban regeneration. His purpose was to encourage independent outlets and businesses to help redress the balance against chain stores trading at the expense of local character and enterprise. It is also a mixed-use cultural space with a café/bar and the nationally acclaimed 250-seat Tobacco Factory Theatre.

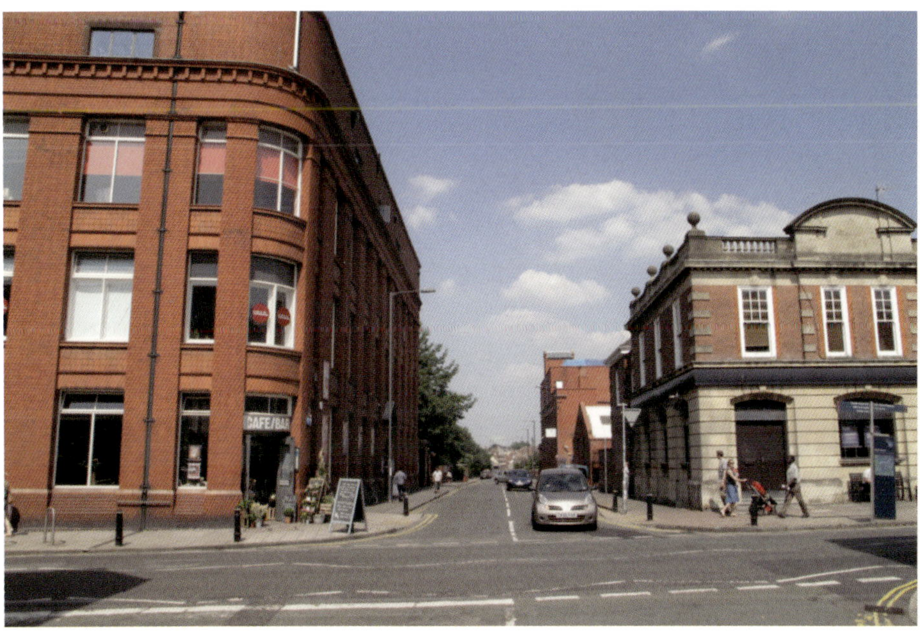

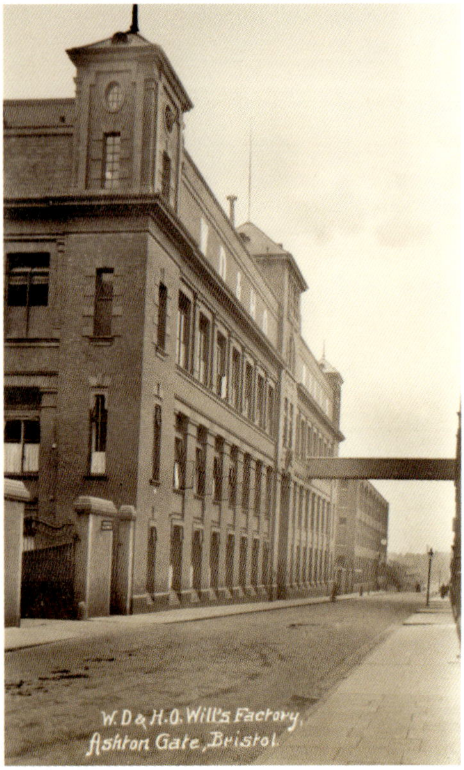

Raleigh Road, Southville, Early 1900s

The monumental Wills factory that covered a large site was demolished after the company's relocation. It is now covered by the Amerind Grove nursing home and the car park for the Aldi supermarket. However, the gateposts remain and are now the entrance to the rear of the Tobacco Factory where various outdoor events are held, including the regular Sunday farmers' market. Just beyond is the exit to the Aldi store, which is sited on past industrial land immediately to the west of the Tobacco Factory. On the right of the present photograph are the buildings that were linked by the industrial bridge. Together with the Tobacco Factory, they are all that remains of this erstwhile industrial site. The insets below show the future George VI and Queen Elizabeth visiting the Wills factory.

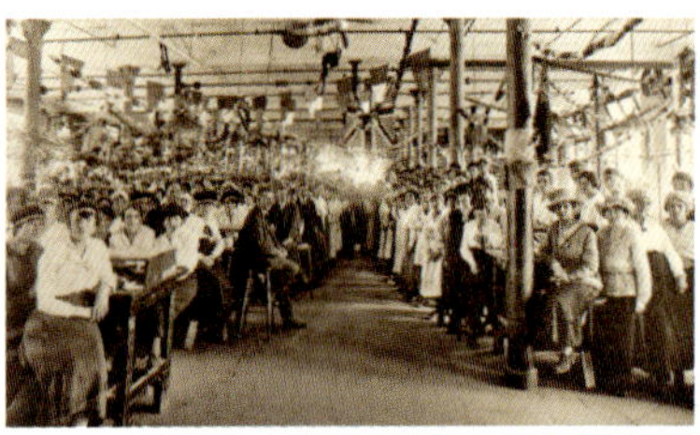

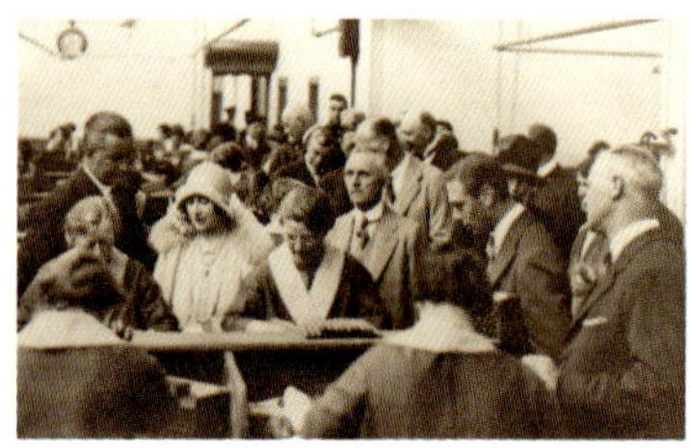

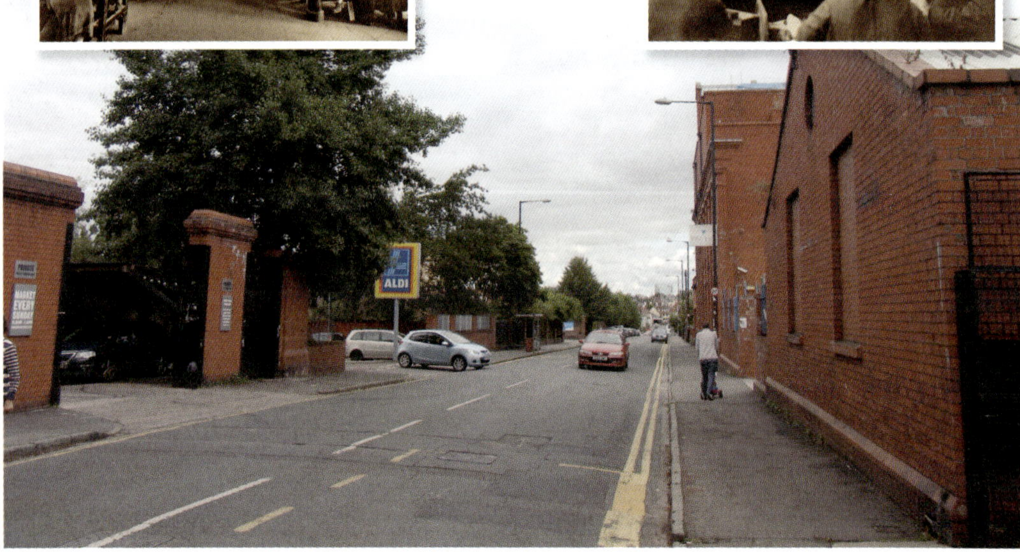

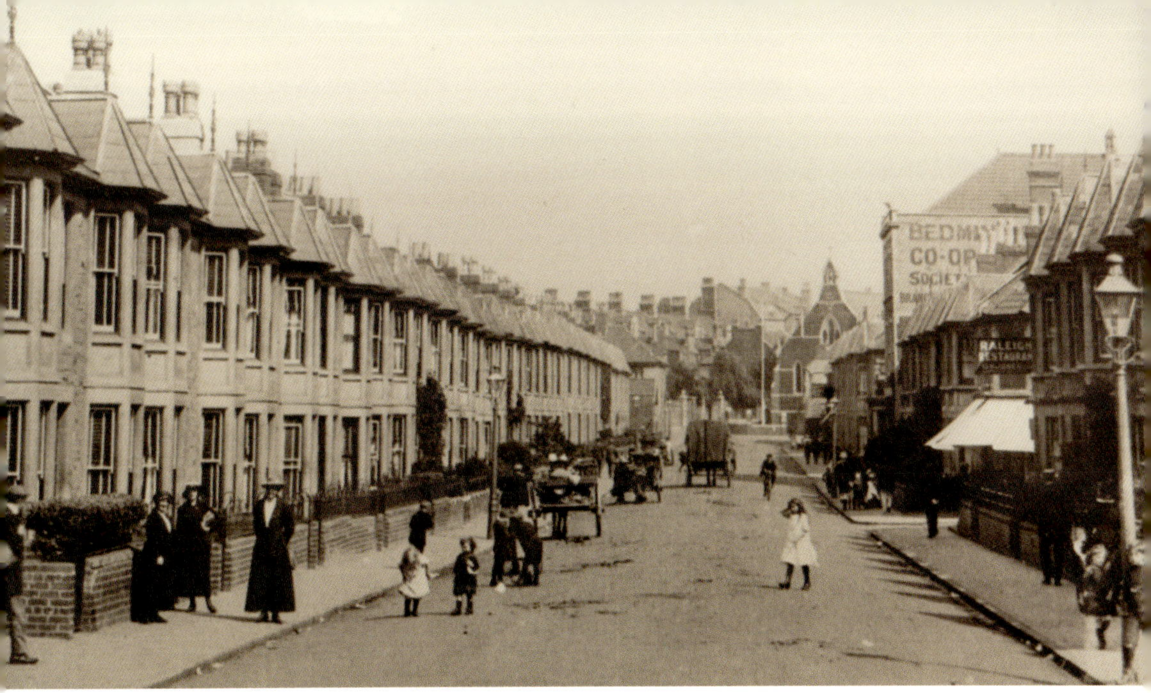

Raleigh Road, Southville, Early 1900s

Running almost from Coronation Road across North Street and on down to Duckmoor Road, Raleigh Road, is now one of the longest predominantly residential roads in the area. But in the central stretch until the 1980s, from North Street to Upton Road, there stood the two large Wills tobacco factories. The pictures are taken at the junction with Upton Road, looking north. The housing has not changed, but children cannot play freely in the road today. The Co-op building is now residential units, and at the end of the street can be seen the former St David's church in Beauley Road.

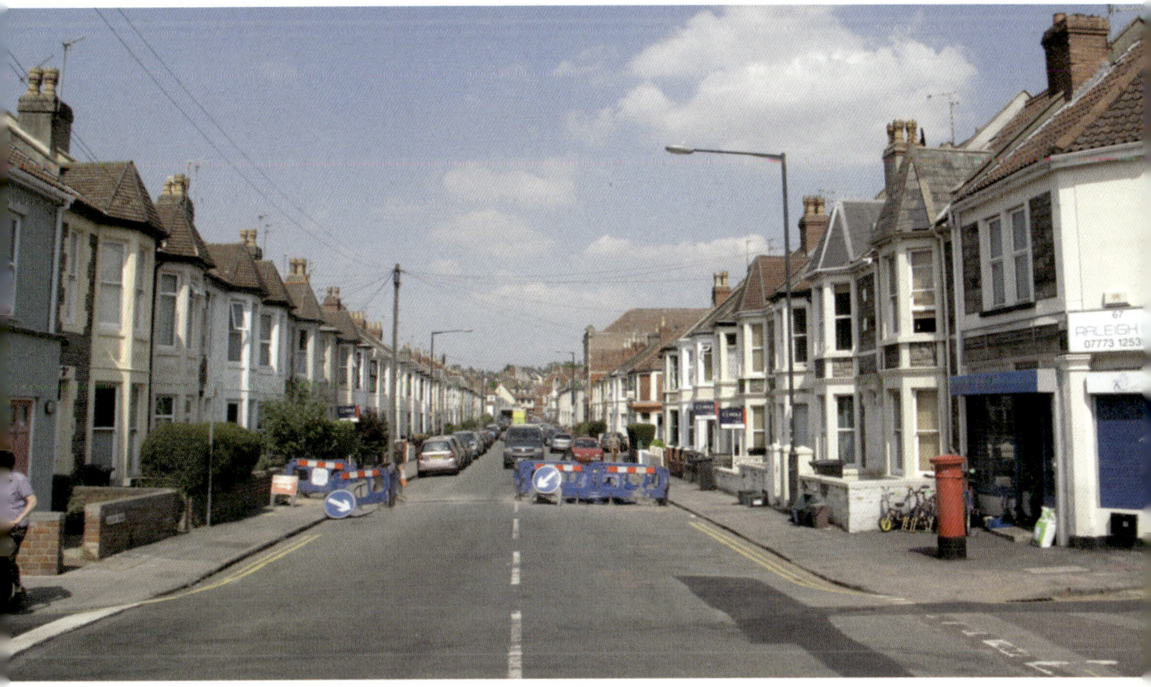

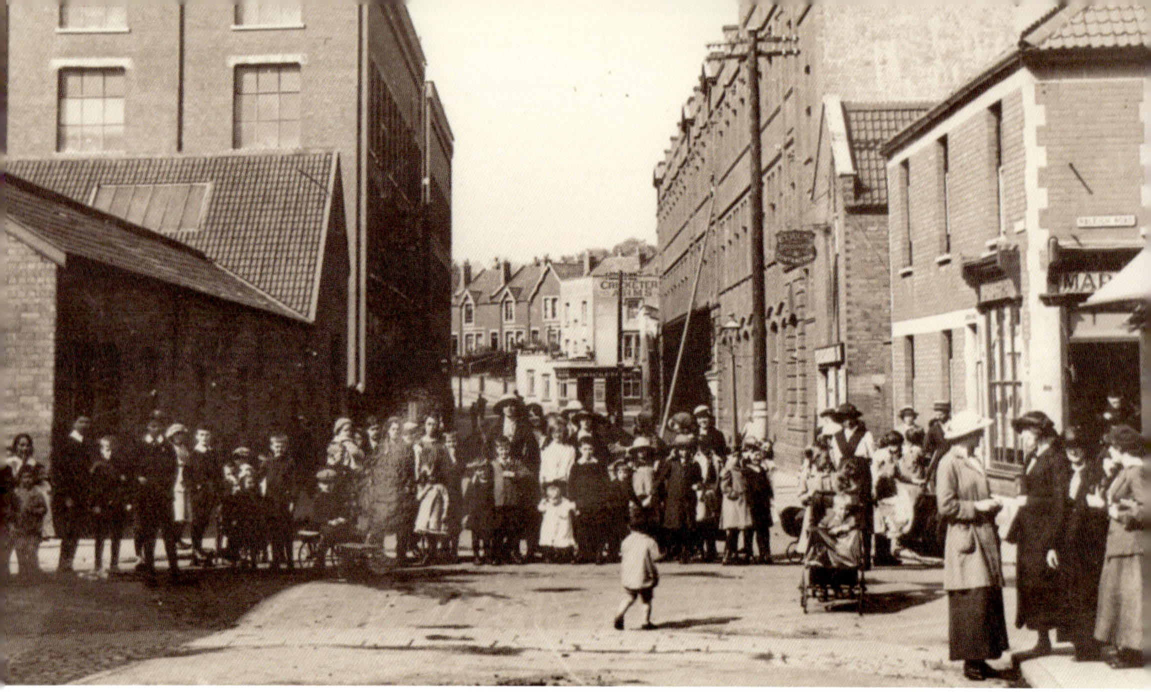

Upton Road, Southville, Early 1900s

These pictures are at the west end of the road where it crosses Raleigh Road. In the old picture, both sides are tobacco factories (the one on the left was the Virginia Cavendish Works). When the tobacco industry moved to Hartcliffe, the building on the right became Imperial Tobacco's global headquarters in Bristol. In April 2013, it was announced that the city council had bought the building, which will become an extension to Ashton Gate Primary School. The Cricketers' Arms pub seen in the old picture was destroyed in the Blitz.

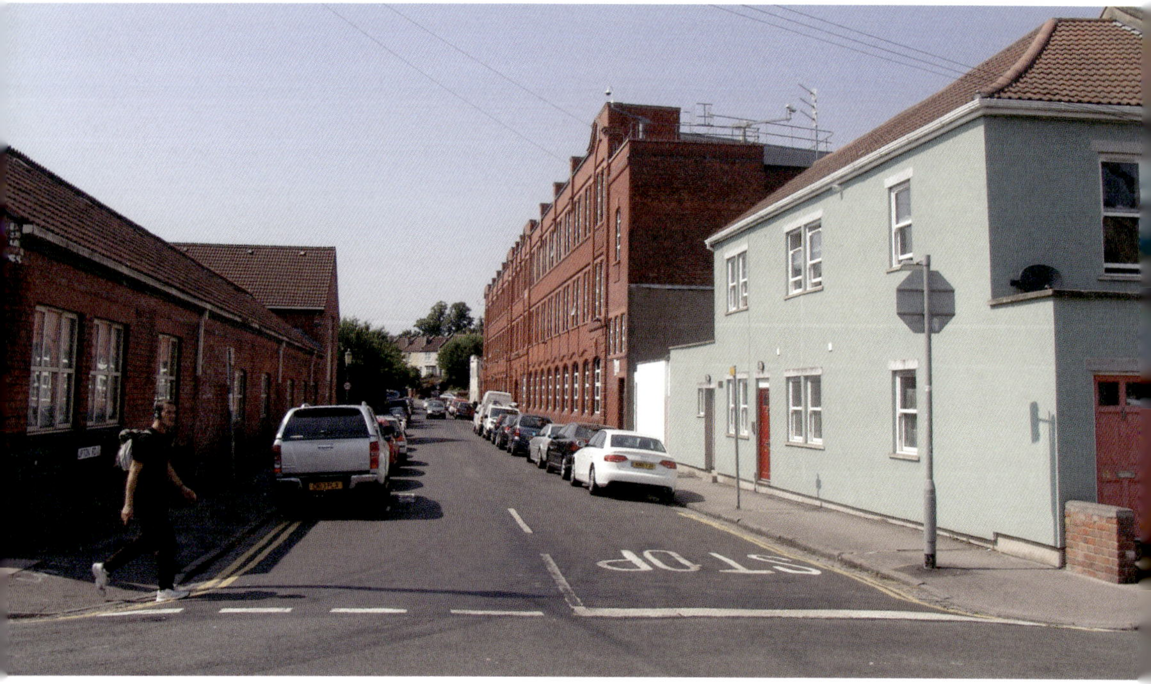

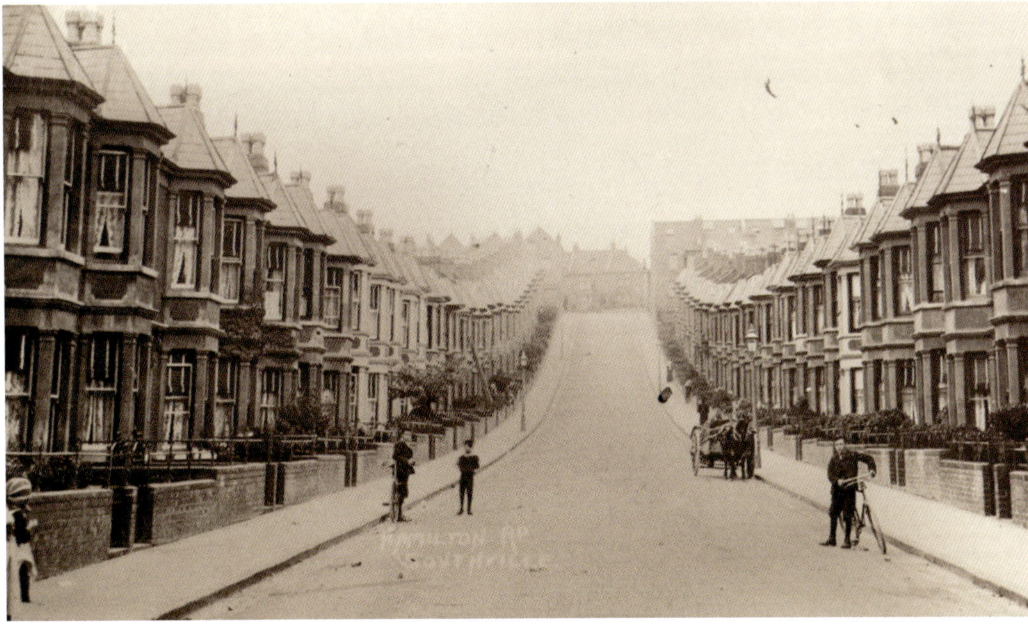

Hamilton Road, Southville, Early 1900s

Hamilton Road is the central one of the five roads that run between Raleigh Road and Stackpool Road. The pictures are taken looking south-east towards Stackpool Road. The terraced houses have slightly ornate bays and in the older picture, pitched roofs over them. The 1880s epoch map shows an undeveloped area bounded by Greville Road, North Street and Greenway Bush Lane; ten years later, Hamilton Road, its neighbouring terraces and the tobacco factories had filled the extensive gap.

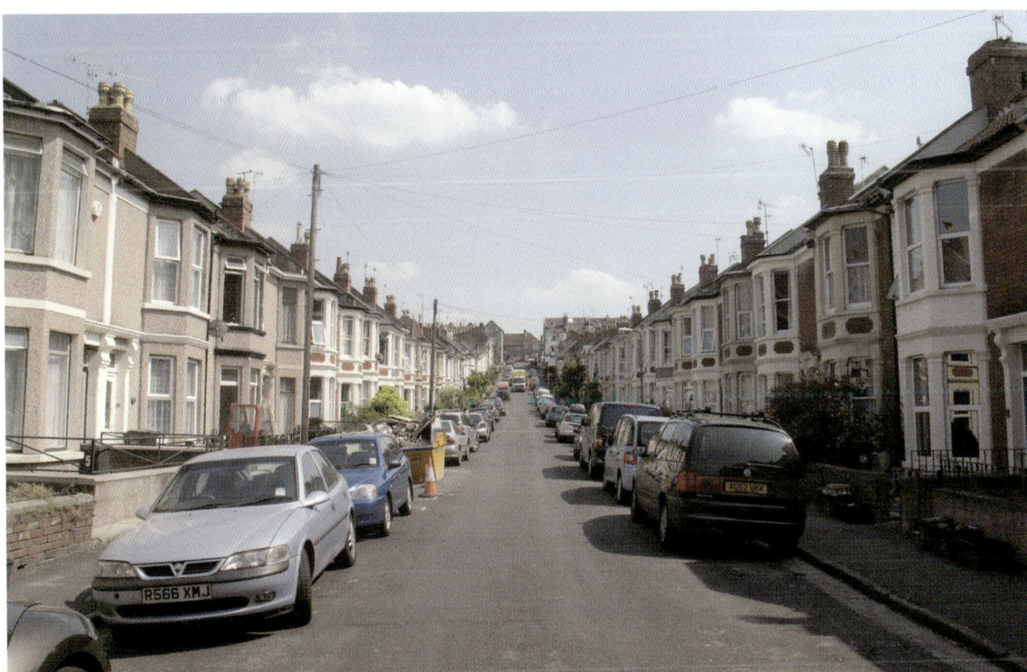

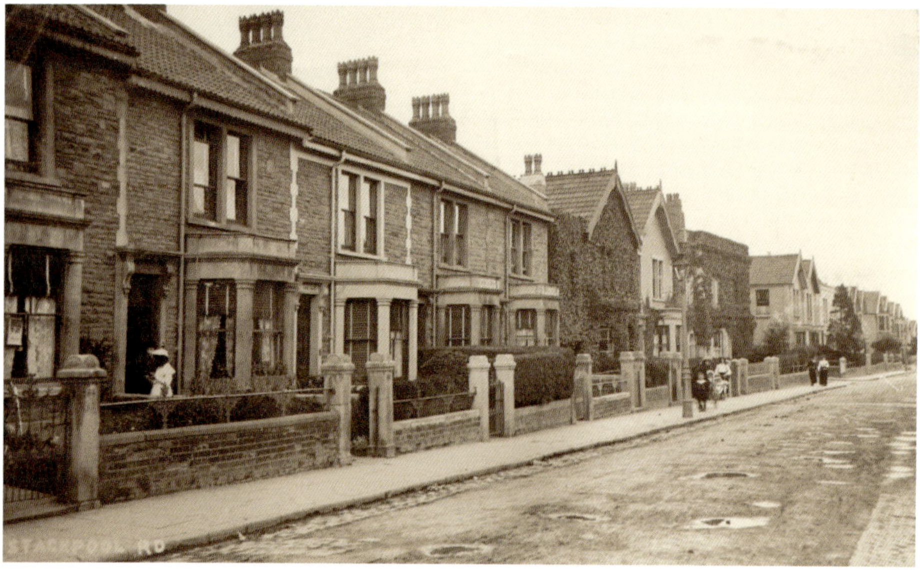

Stackpool Road, Southville, Postcard Dated 10 August 1906

This 1906 picture shows that in this part of Southville there was a variety of styles of housing, and that they were larger houses than the majority of the terraced housing in the area. The distinctive gateposts have been retained. It is clear that potholes are a perennial problem. The 1911 census records that the householders were in the middle income bracket: shop owners, church minister, police inspector, university lecturer and a female elementary schoolteacher. The road markings are for Southville Primary School, which was built on the site of the former Merrywood Hall. There is no apparent reason why the road should be named after the Irish family of that name, unless perhaps they had a hand in developing it.

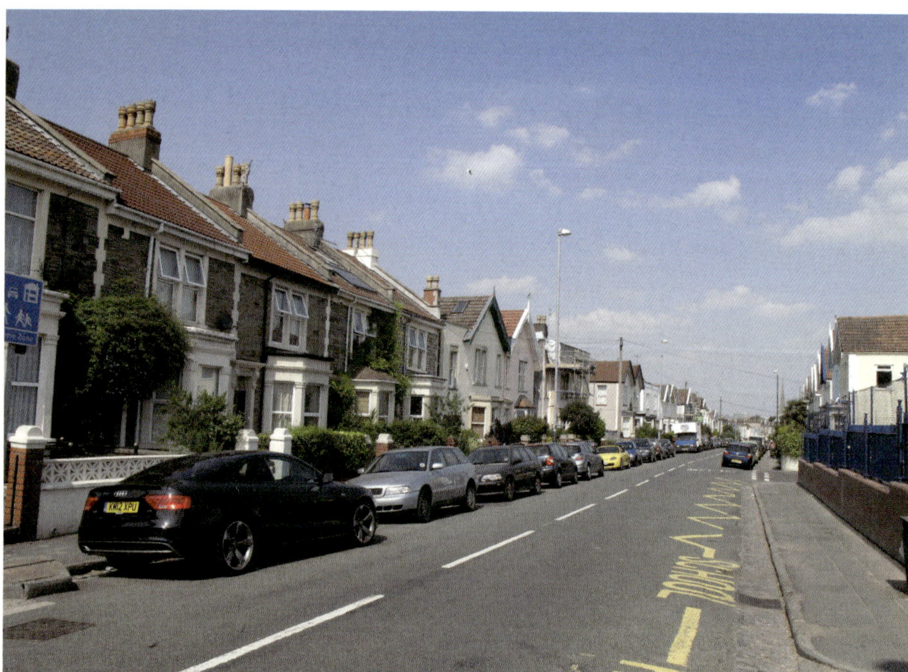

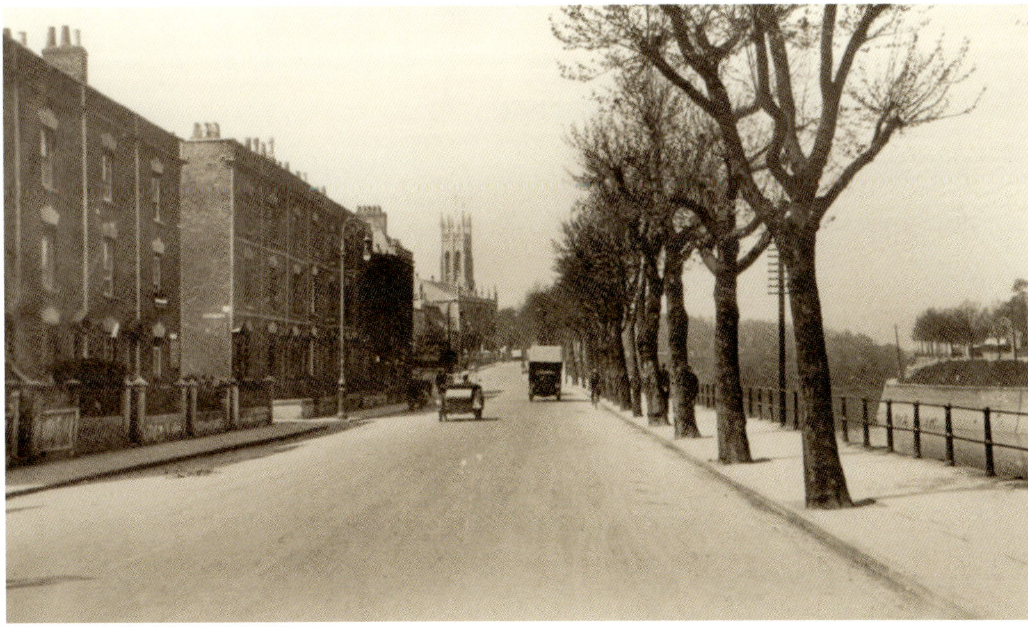

Coronation Road, Southville, Postcard Dated 2 July 1934

These pictures are looking west along Coronation Road with the tower of St Paul's church in the background. Coronation Road runs beside the New Cut for 1.8 miles, from Bedminster Bridge to the Cumberland Basin. Coronation Road dates to just after the digging of the New Cut, and gets its name because it was completed in 1821, the year of the coronation of George IV. Behind the trees on the left and as far along as the white car in the centre of the road, is the Asda car park, on which were four streets of small terraced houses, a timber yard, a sawmill, and a small box factory.

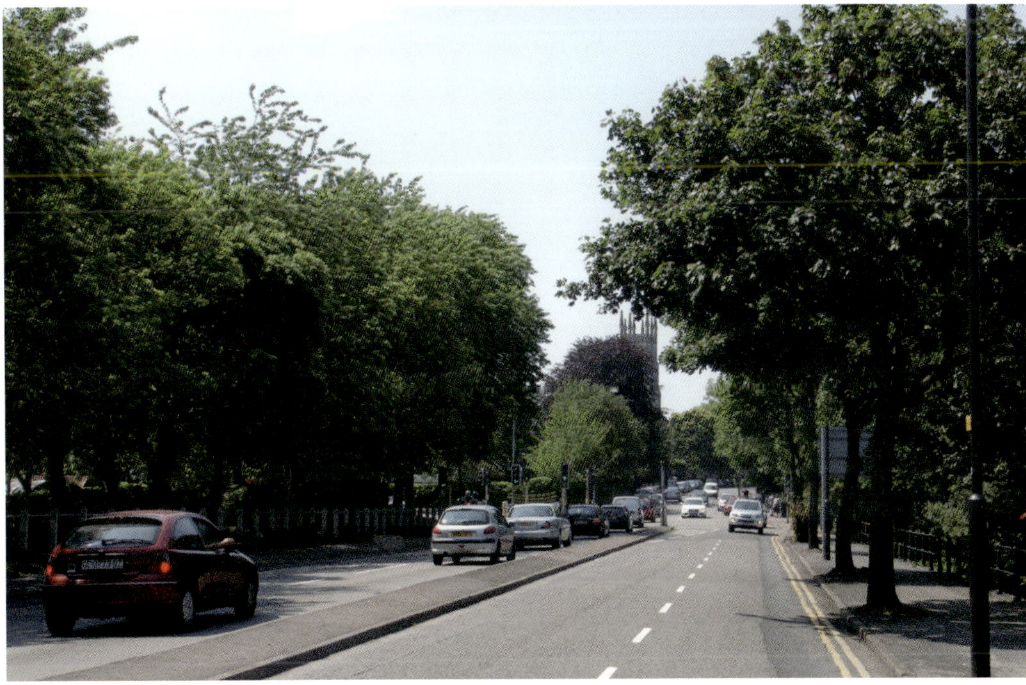

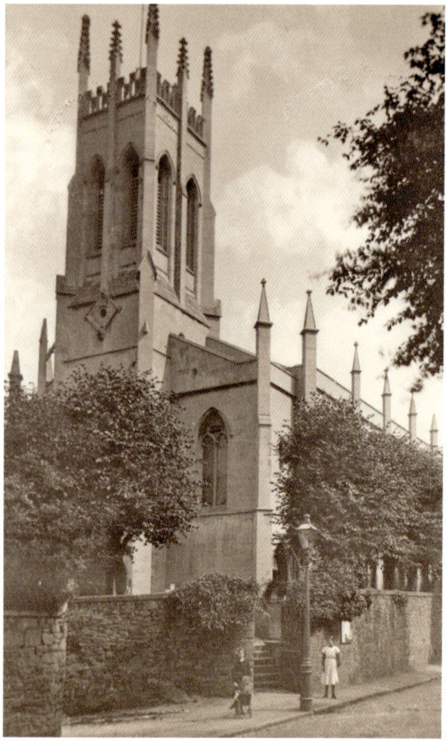

St Paul's Church, Coronation Road, Southville, Early 1900s

St Paul's church dominates the eastern end of Coronation Road. The building was designed in 1829 by the Bristol architect Charles Dyer (probably best known for his later design of the Victoria Rooms in Clifton). He carved his name and the date above the church entrance. The church was badly hit during the Good Friday Blitz in 1941. The photograph taken from Southville Road shows that the reconstructed building was less ornate. It also suffered in 1990 when severe gales hit Bristol. On both occasions, emergency services were conducted in the deconsecrated church of St David in Beauley Road, which had been built as a subsidiary church to St Paul's.

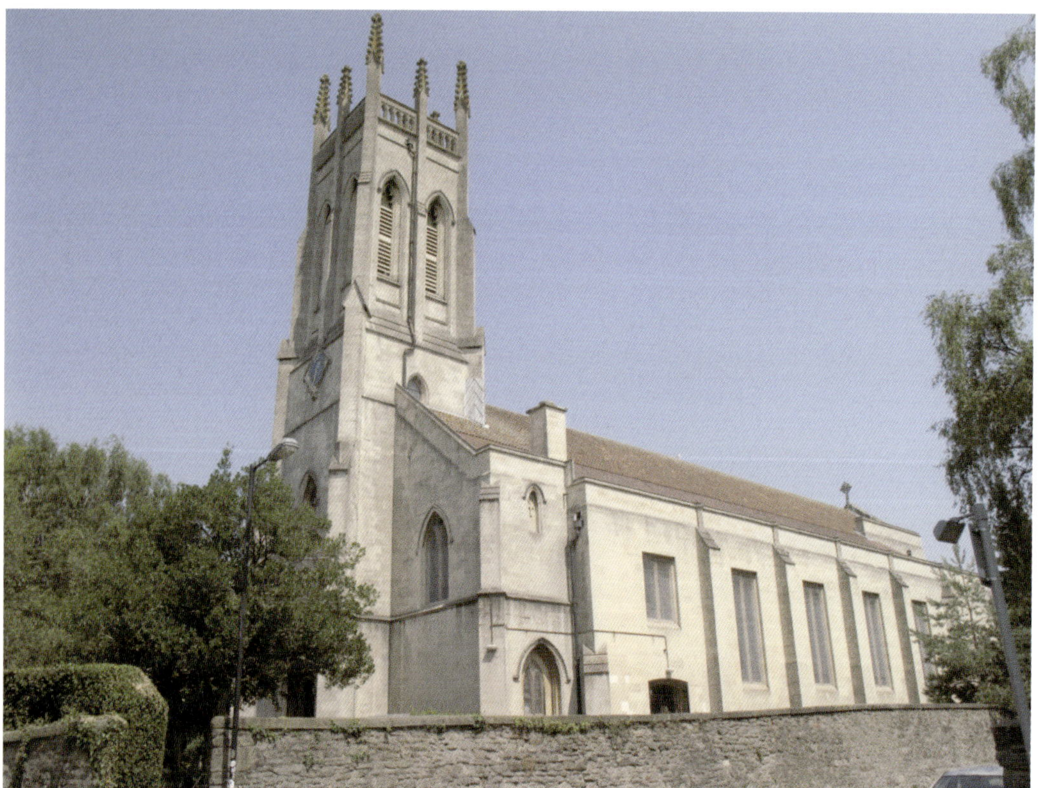

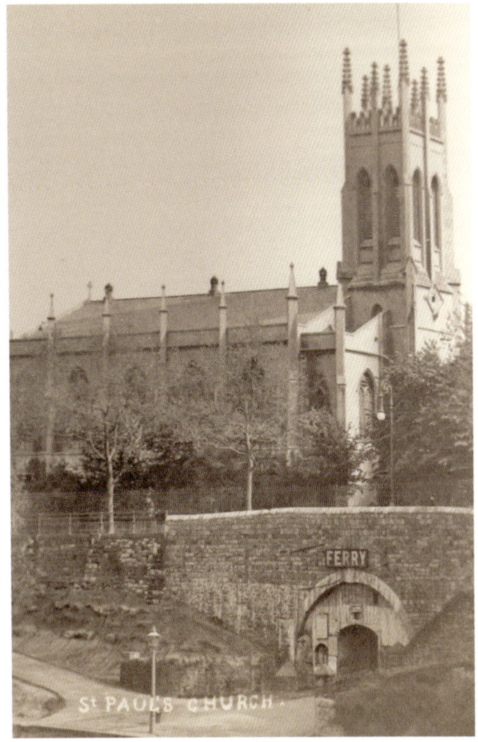

St Paul's Church, Coronation Road, Early 1900s

The old picture clearly shows the point from which the ferry ran. If one walks along the Coronation Road footpath, the slipway can still be seen. The ornate footbridge, which now stands just to the right of the photograph, was built in 1935 by David Rowell & Co. to replace crossing by ferry. The ferry was given various names: on the 1880 and 1900 maps it is called the Coronation Ferry, and it was also known as Gaol Ferry or Wapping Gaol Ferry. In the 1920s, it is recorded as taking at least 10,000 passengers a week for half a penny each straight across to Cumberland Road.

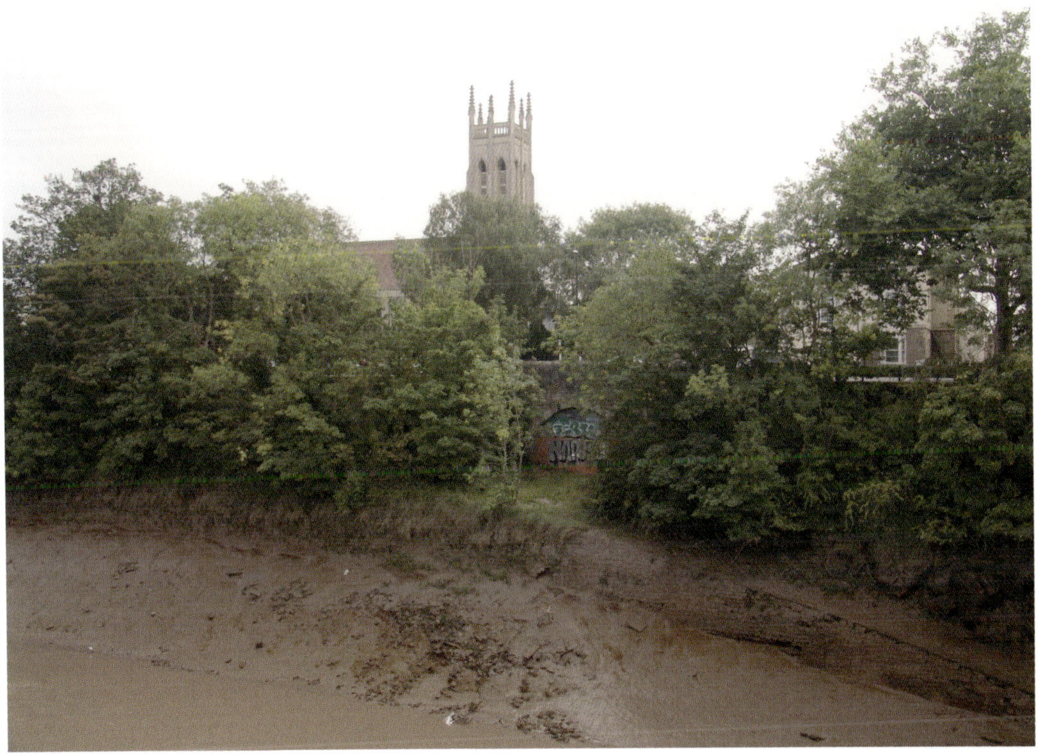

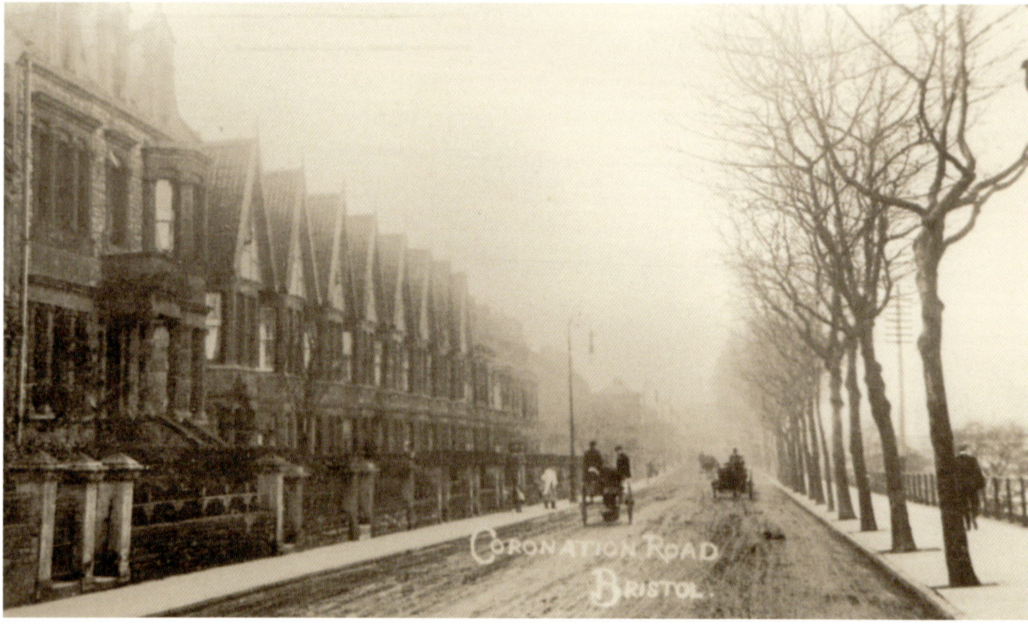

Coronation Road, Southville, Early 1900s

These pictures are looking west along the stretch of Coronation Road between Camden Road and Beauley Road. The prominent white sign is for the Magic Roundabout Nursery at No. 141. The road in the 1900s is in a pretty poor state – typical of the condition of many of Bristol's roads in the days before mass car ownership. The trees on the pavement have gone, replaced by more natural growth on the riverbank behind the railings. The row of eight houses with pitched roofs was built in the early 1900s.

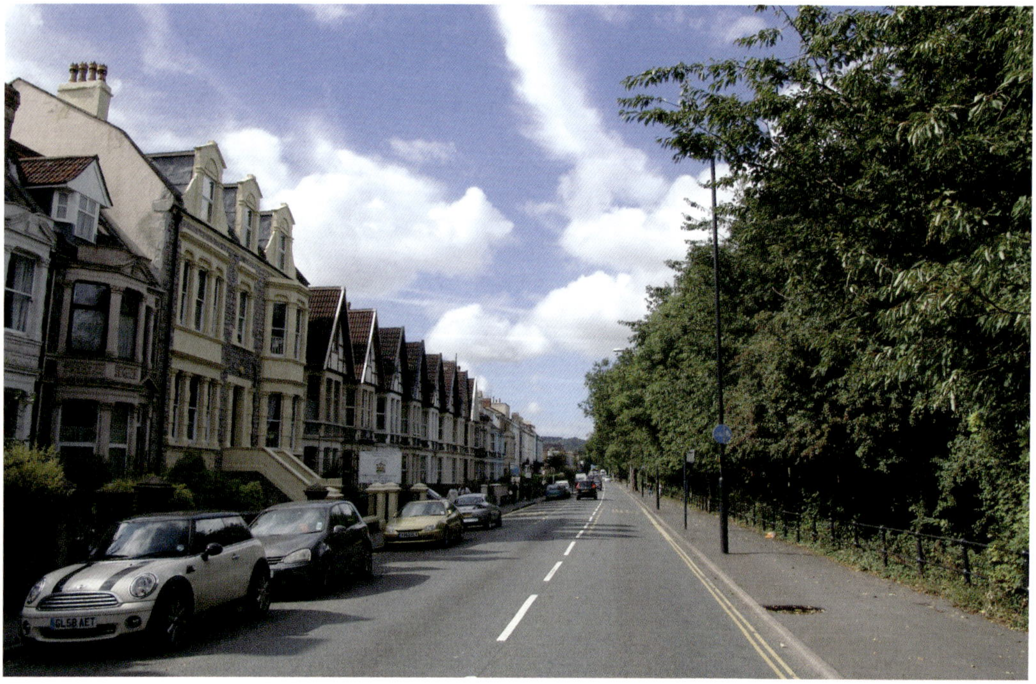

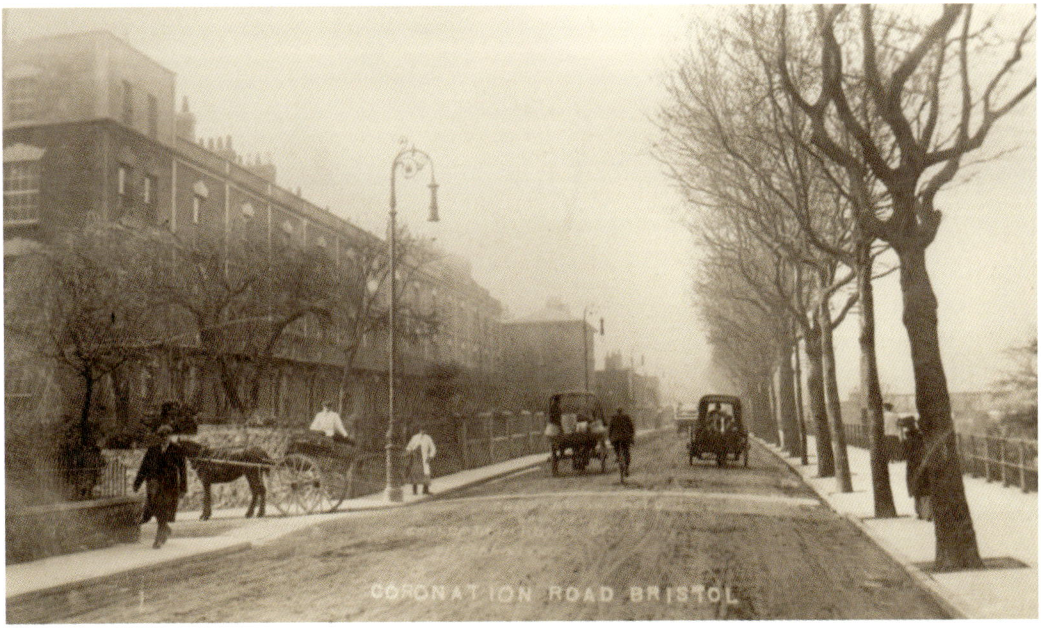

Coronation Road, Southville, Early 1900s

In the modern photograph, the brightly coloured mobile disco van is pulling out of Beauley Road into Coronation Road. Under the fine lamp-post in the old picture, there are white-coated delivery men. The cyclist is overtaking another delivery or collection cart. This section of terraced housing actually predates Coronation Road. On the 1828 Ashmead map, it is called Stroud Terrace and by the 1855 edition, it had become Ashton Terrace. At least one of the trees remains standing in the pavement.

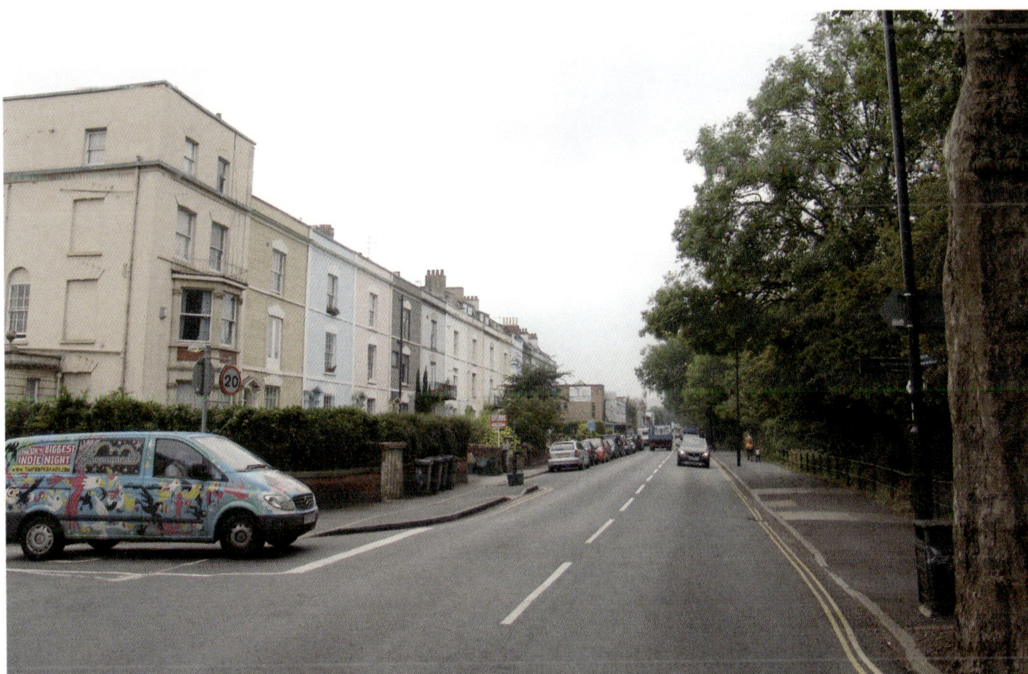

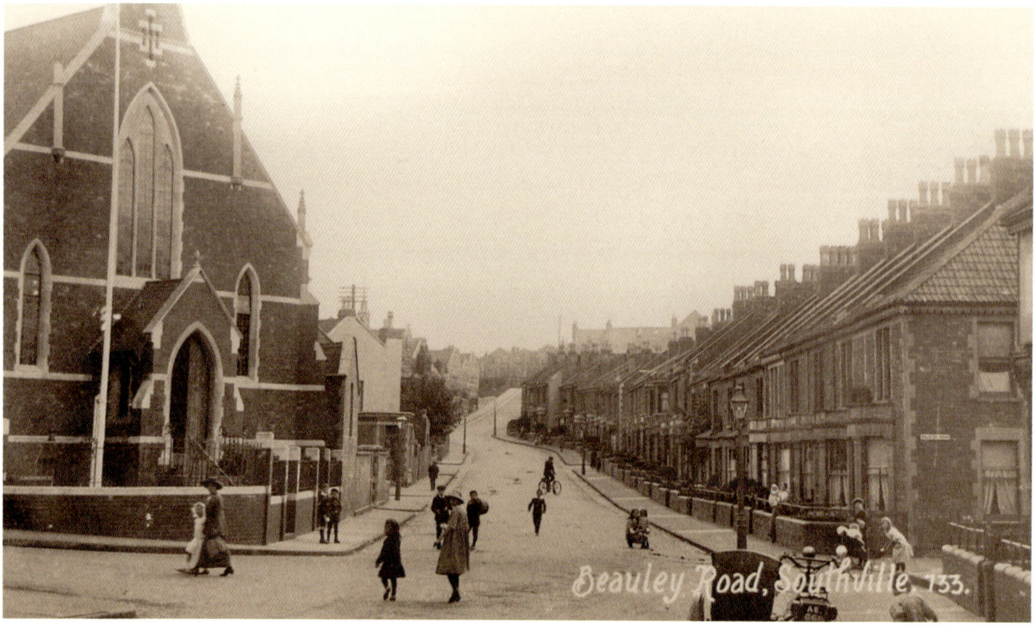

Beauley Road, Southville, Early 1900s

The pictures are taken at the junction with Raleigh Road, and look south down Beauley Road. The church was built to the design of Scammell Son & Perkins in 1908 as a mission church for St Paul and dedicated to St David. It ceased being a church before the Second World War, and became a parish hall. Services were resumed during the Blitz in 1941 and briefly again between 1990 and 1991. Now it is an apartment block (The Parish), which has cleverly made use of some of the original fenestration.

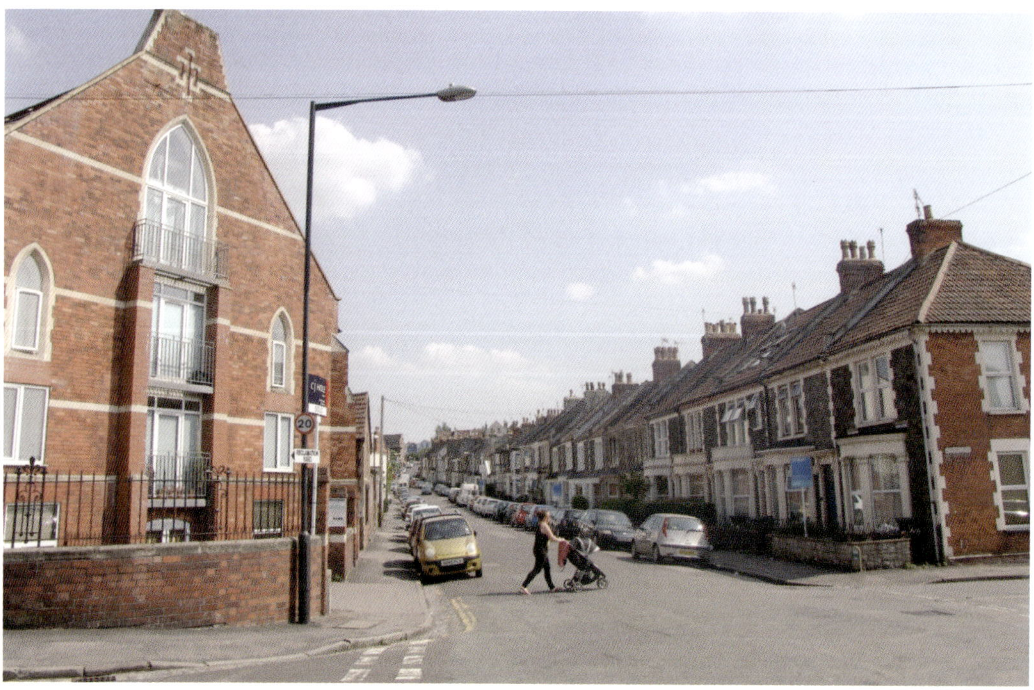

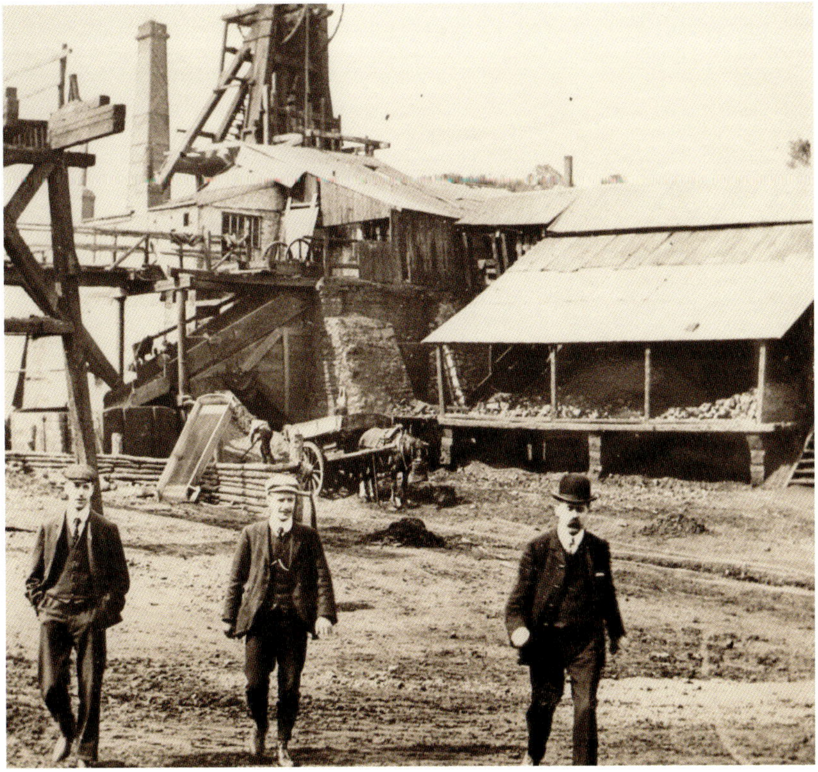

Mining Site, South Liberty Lane, Ashton, Early 1900s

Beneath the modern industrial estate lay what changed Bedminster from being a small market town in the eighteenth century into a high density industrial suburb in the nineteenth century – coal. These pictures are at Liberty Lane colliery, which was the first to open (1745) and the last to close (1925). Because of this available fuel, the area had its own industrial revolution; for example, Capper Pass set up his smelting and refinery factory. An opportunity for paid employment in the pits and factories resulted in a massive influx of people. Many were poor and vulnerable farm labourers, and tellingly an Act of Parliament in 1846 forbade women and girls below the age of ten from working in the pits. Little evidence remains of the collieries themselves.

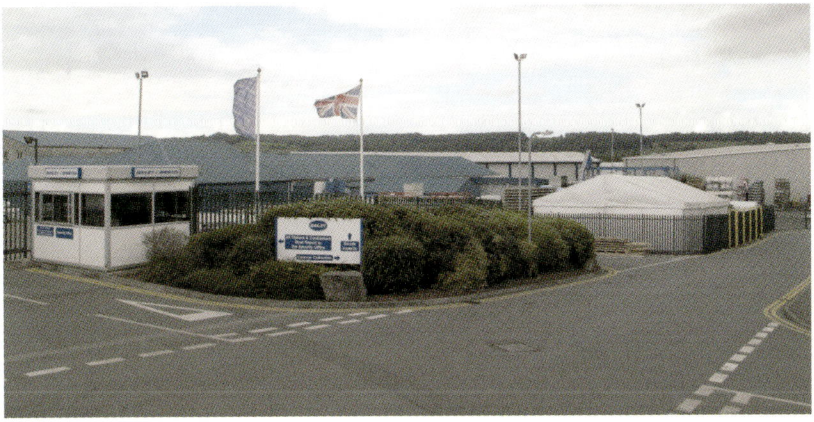

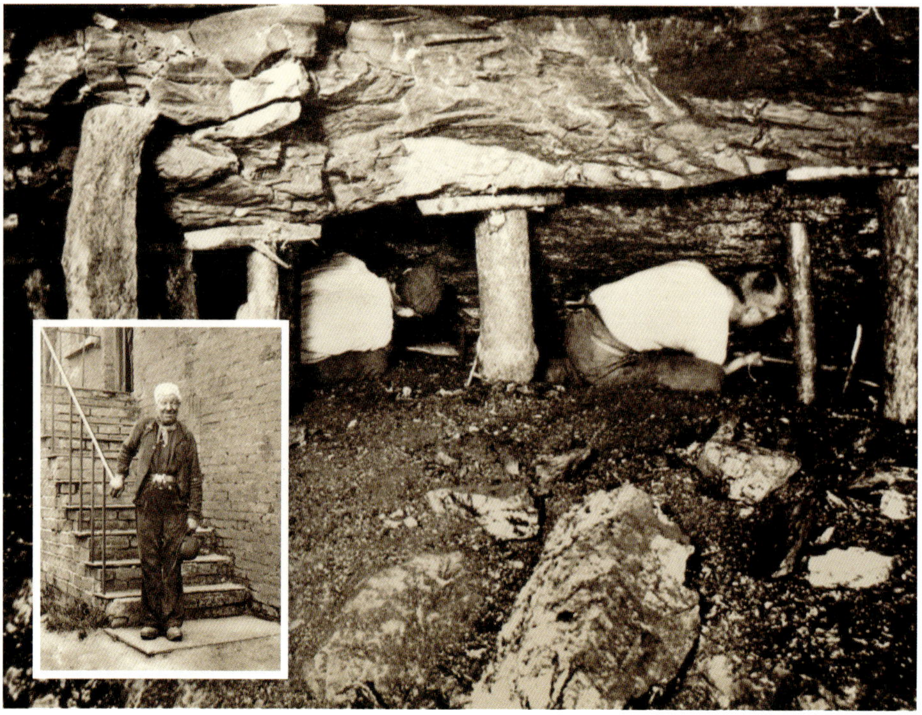

Miners in Early 1900s and Dame Edith Playpark, Bedminster

This skatepark and graffiti wall are part of the Dame Emily Playpark on the site of the Dean Lane pit. Dame Emily was a member of the Smyth family of Ashton Court, who owned the mineral rights to most of the land in the area and received a royalty for every ton mined. When this pit closed in 1906, she gave the land to the city council for a park. Dean Lane was the largest of the pits, with a mainshaft of over 1,000 feet and employing 400 men. One large seam extended to beyond Temple Meads station. The work was cramped, hard and dangerous, with the ever-present danger of rock falls and explosions. The Bedminster mines were also known for 'after damp', which could suffocate. Nevertheless, some miners laboured on into old age, as can be seen in the inset, showing an elderly South Lane worker.

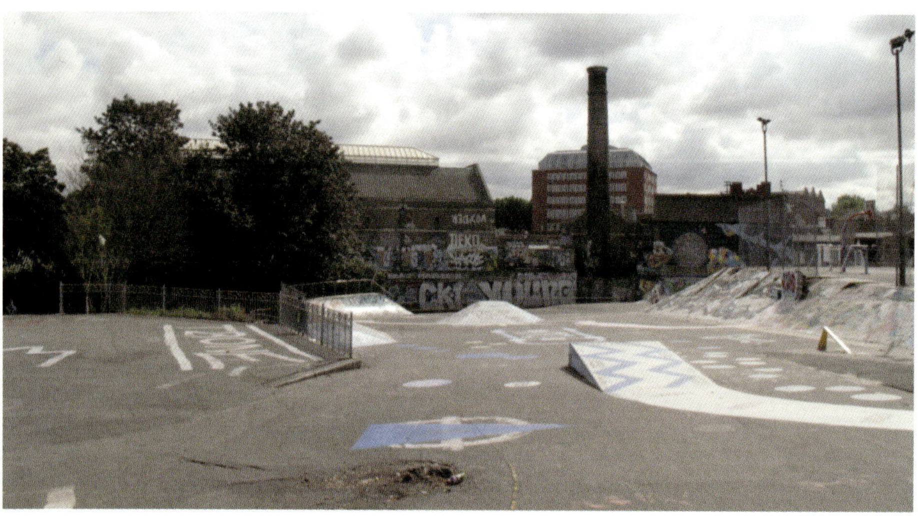

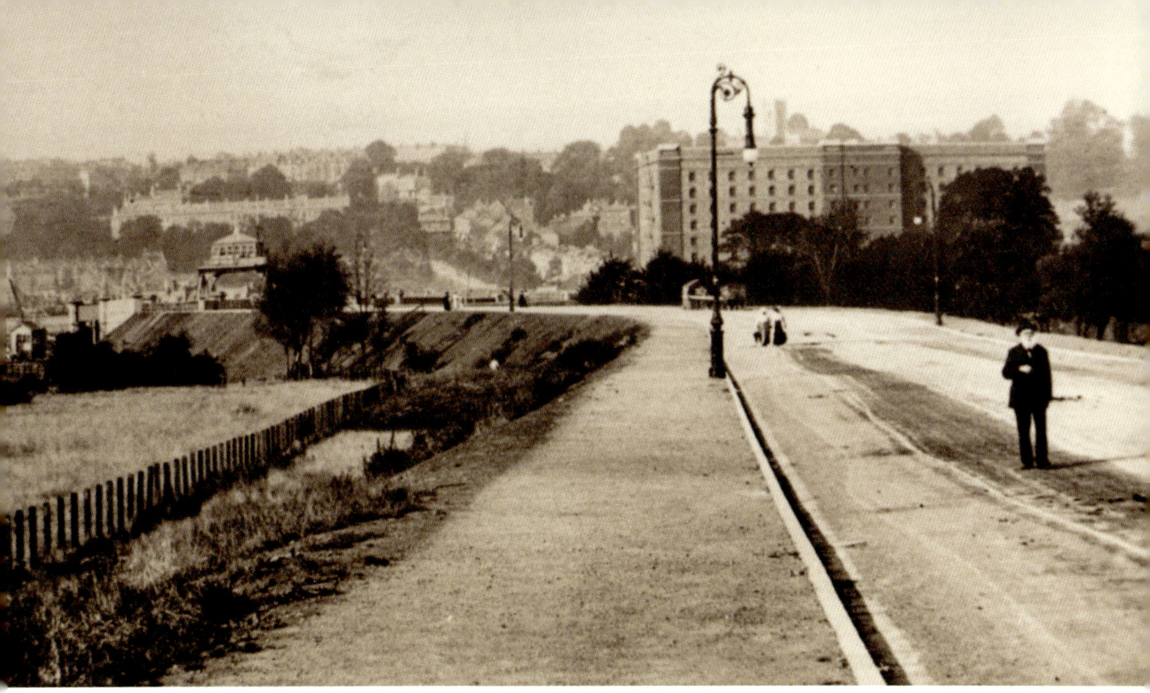

Ashton Avenue, Early 1900s

The old picture shows the road on its embankment heading towards the swing bridge and on into Hotwells. Today, in stark contrast, it is the busy dual carriageway of the A3029 (Brunel Way). The major road alterations were made in the 1960s, when the flyover was built to carry the ever-increasing amount of traffic. Bond House A is on the right, and just above it the tower of St Andrew's church, Clifton, which was bombed in the Blitz and demolished in 1954, is visible. The Cumberland Basin was part of the work in 1804–09 that created the Floating Harbour and diverted the Avon into the New Cut. It was named after the Duke of Cumberland, who visited in 1803 and became a Freeman of the City.

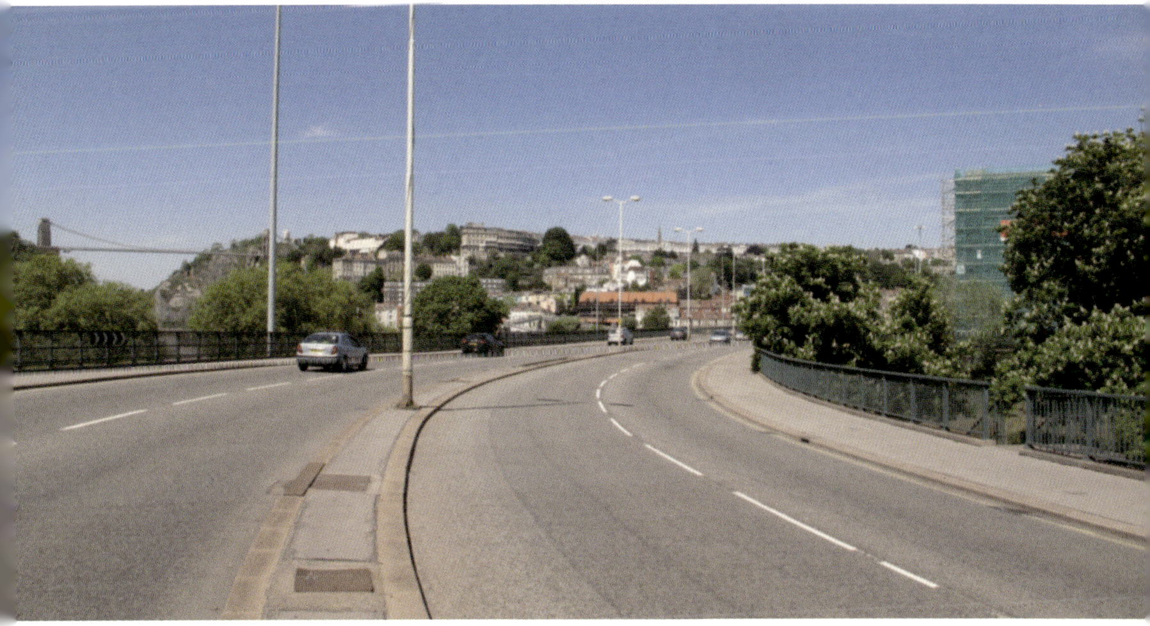

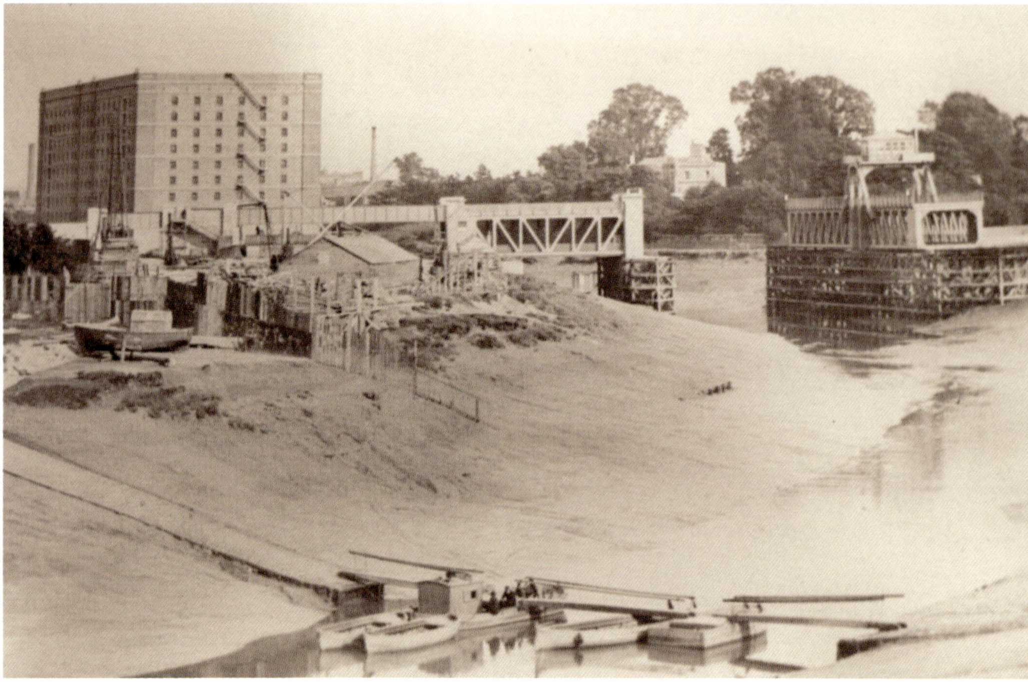

Ashton Swing Bridge, Early 1900s

This shows the New Ashton Swing Bridge, which crossed the Cut under construction. It opened in 1906. In the recent photograph, there are two bond houses: A (1905) on the left and C (1919) on the right. All the bond houses were designed by a dock committee engineer and built by William Cowlin. They were duty-free warehouses for tobacco, wine and spirits. They became Grade II-listed buildings in 1988 and have different uses. The one on the right rents space for storage and the white-roofed building is Riverside Garden Centre. It stands on the site of Clift House, which was the dower house for Ashton Court and, in its final years, a diphtheria hospital. It was replaced in 1919 by the bond house.

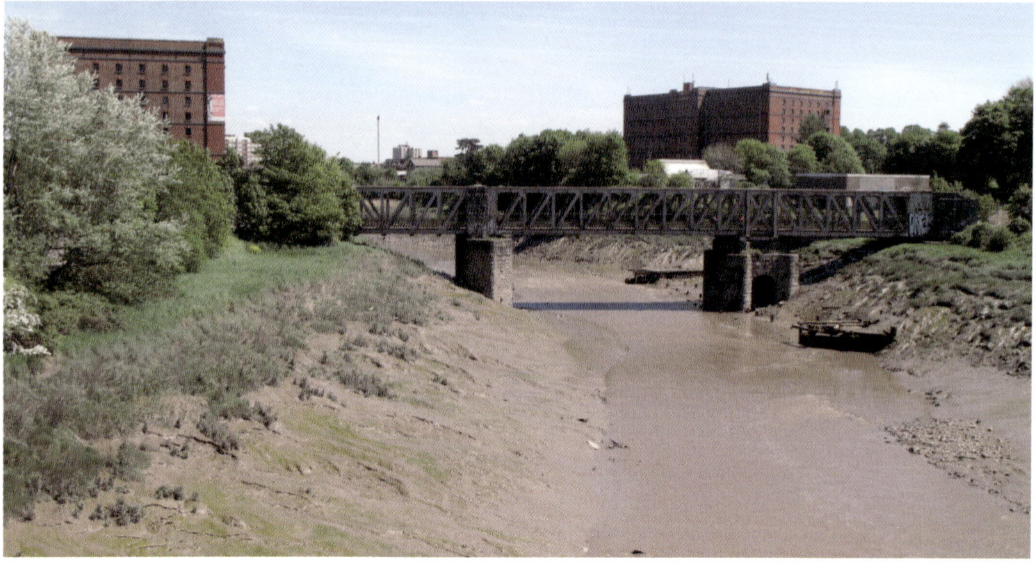

Ashton Swing Bridge, 1930s

The old picture shows the control tower for the bridge in the previous set of pictures. The swing bridges allowed water traffic to move up the river Avon past the Floating Harbour (which had its own swing bridges). The motor cyclist is an AA man (in the 1930s they wore a distinctive uniform and cap but no crash helmet). The recent picture clearly shows the fate of the two layers of the bridge; the road that ran along the top has been removed, and the rail track below is now a pedestrian and cycle way. The bond house on the right is A, and on the left is the corner of B.

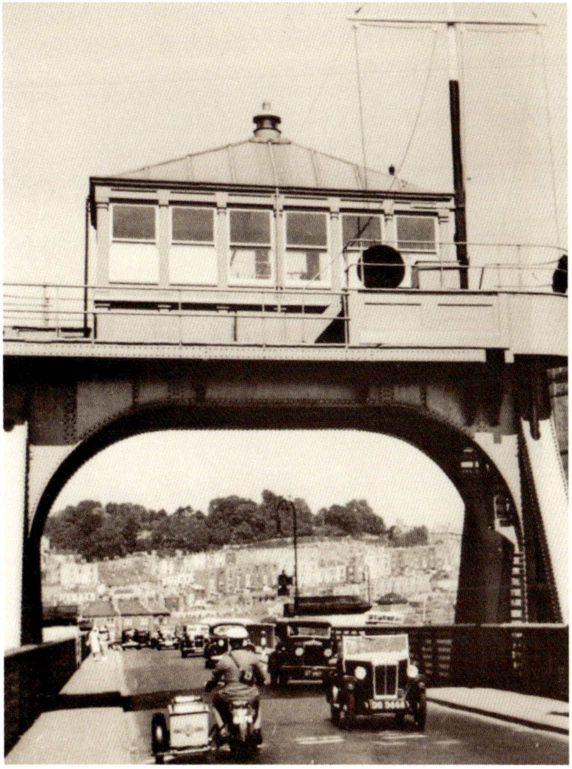

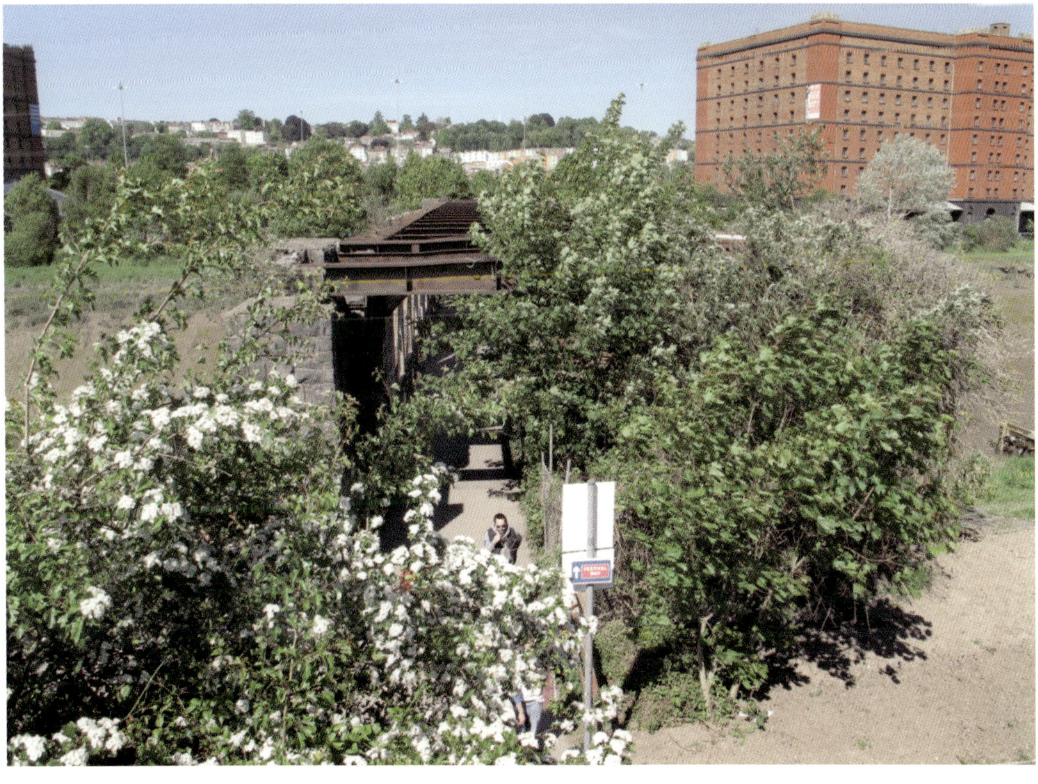

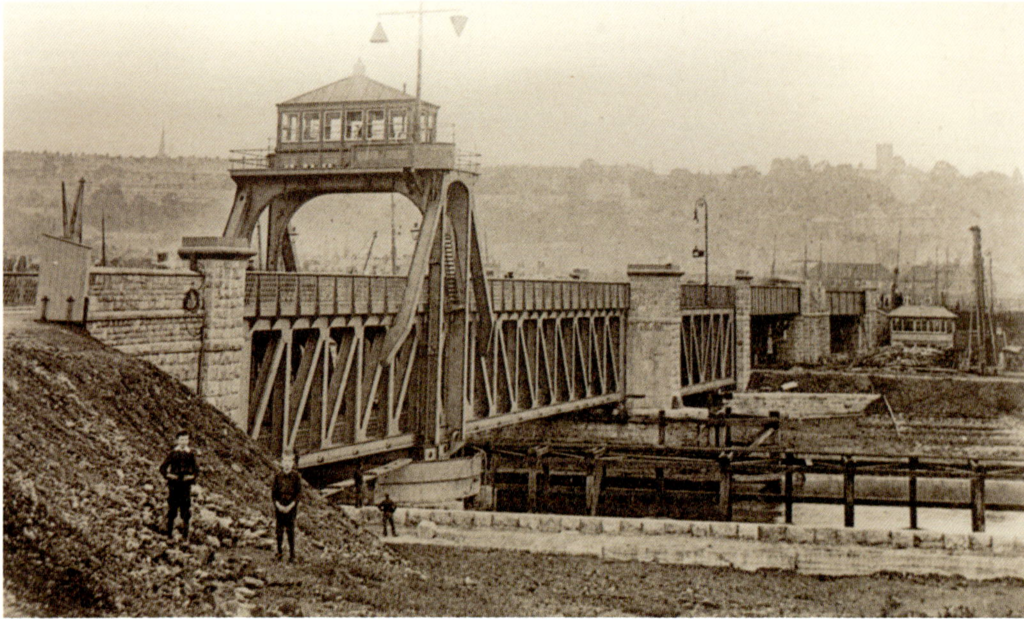

Ashton Swing Bridge, Early 1900s

The old picture shows the fine structure of the bridge with the control tower, the road (which has been raised by the embankment), and the railway underneath. The recent photograph shows what is left of the bridge. Between this and the suspension bridge is the large B Bond House, which was built in 1908. It now houses the Bristol Record Office and the Create Centre, as well as several other organisations working in sustainable development, including Bristol City Council's Sustainability Team.

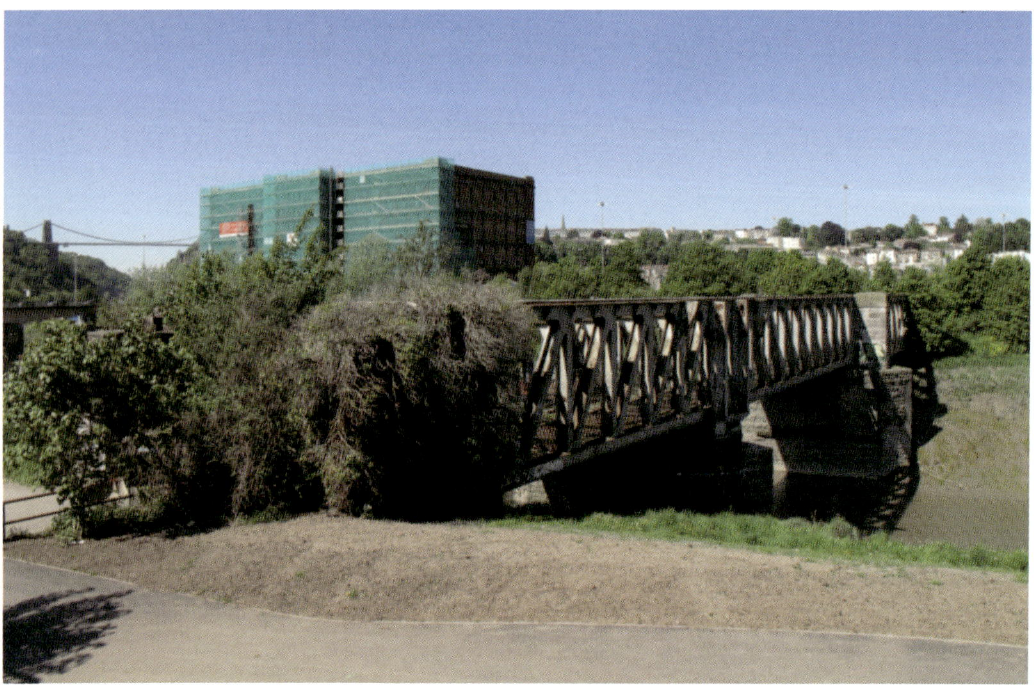

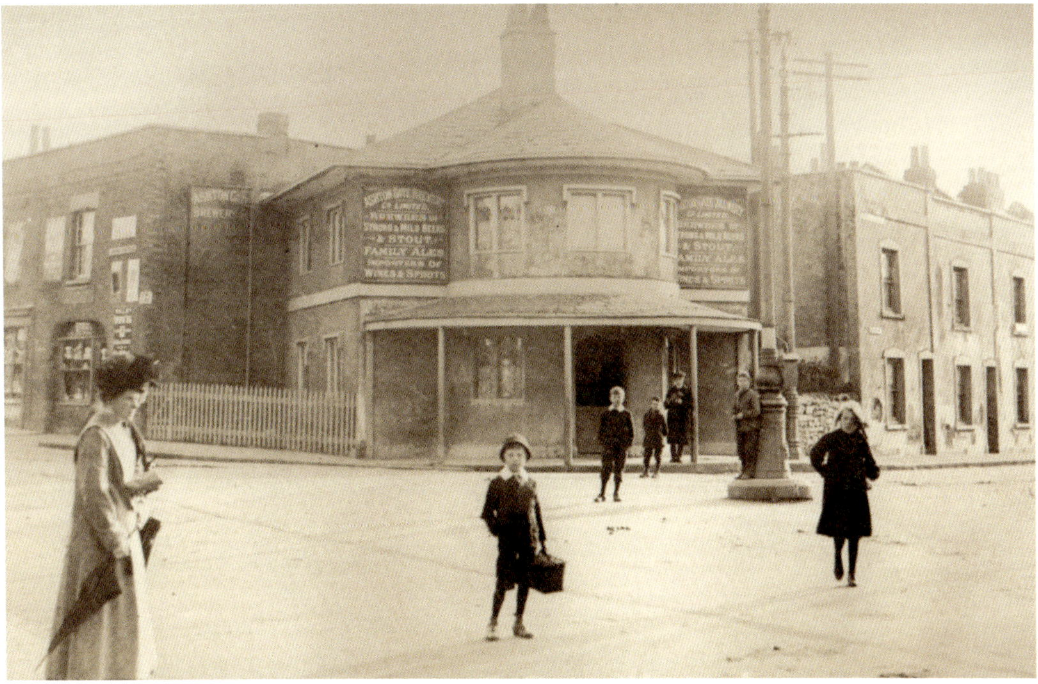

Ashton Gate Toll House, Early 1900s

This stands at the junction of Coronation Road and North Street. The building is a former toll house, built around 1820. The turnpike roads were unpopular because they were an expense for people who brought goods in from the country to the city markets. In 1749, there was a riot here that resulted in damage to the building. The Ashmead 1818 map draws a set of gates across the road, with the house set behind them. The old picture shows big advertising boards for the Ashton Brewery. This was established in 1865. The brewery itself was across the road, just about where the dark tree is in the new photograph. The building has been incorporated into Toll House Court, which is sheltered housing.

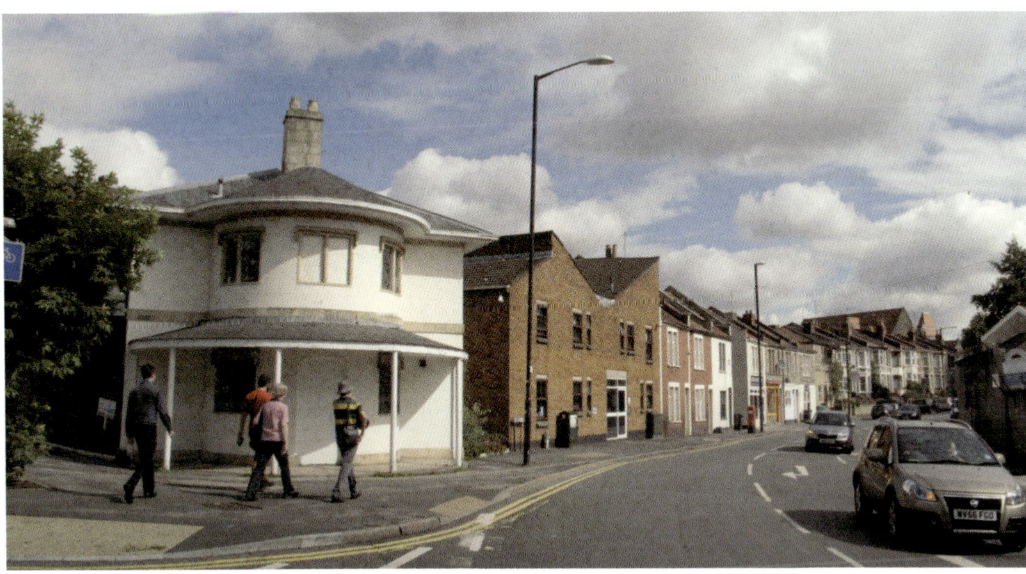

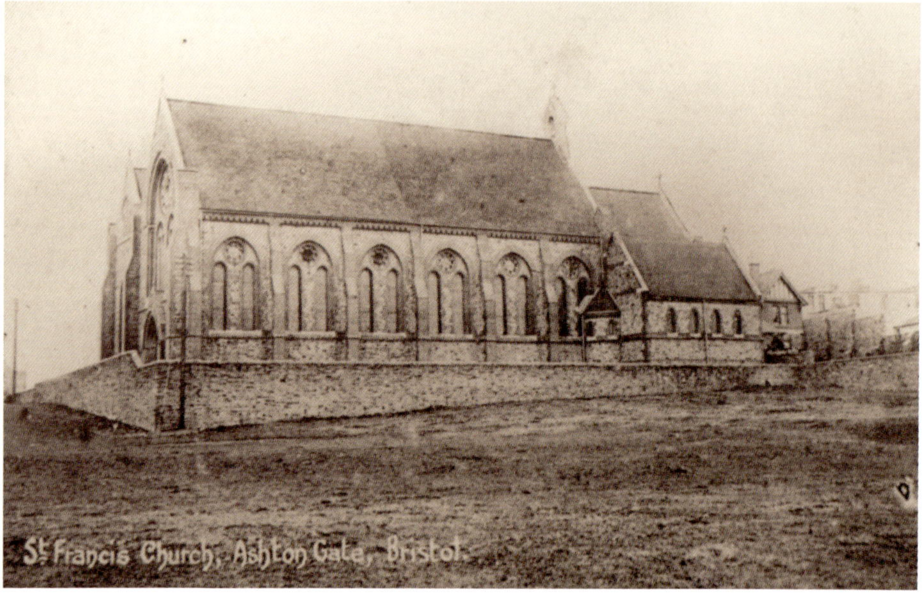

St Francis Church, Ashton Gate, Early 1900s

The first church on this site in North Street was opened in 1873. It was a 'tin tabernacle' built of corrugated iron, and was dedicated to Holy Cross. Plans for a permanent church followed and John Bevan was chosen as architect. The building was constructed in 1886/87, and was one of the largest of Bristol's suburban churches. It was blitzed in December 1940, and parts of the roof were burnt. It was quickly restored, only for the whole interior to be lost in the air raids of Good Friday in 1941. After the Second World War, the ruins were cleared and a new church was built in 1950–53 to the designs of Robert Potter. The foundations of the old nave and north aisle were reused. Its exterior is of yellow brick with Bath stone dressings.

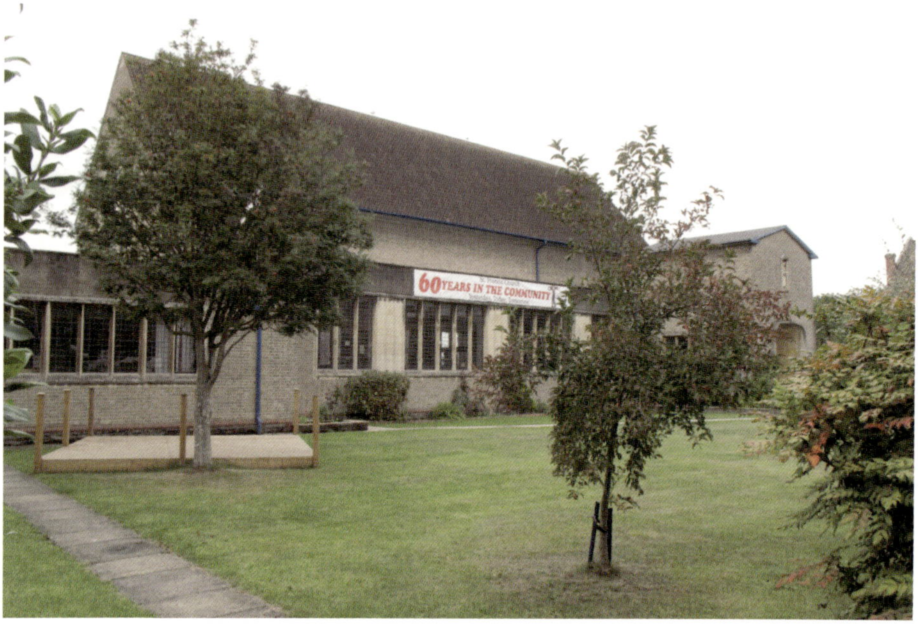

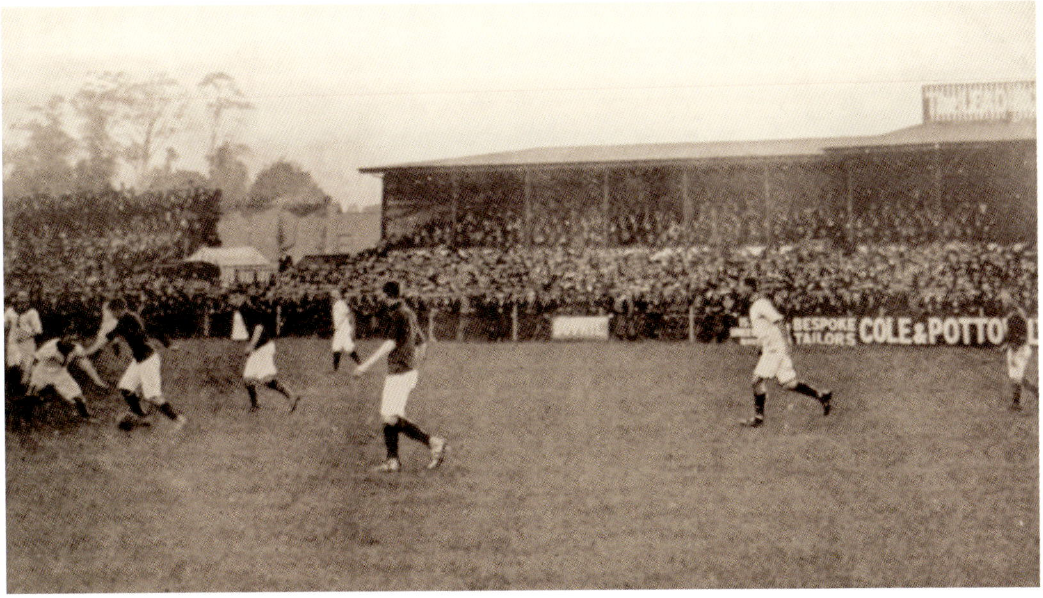

Bristol City, Ashton Gate, Early 1900s

Known locally as 'The Robins', Bristol City Football Club was founded in 1897 when Bristol South End turned professional and changed its name. The team merged with Bedminster in 1900, and joined the Football League a year later. The postcard above can be dated to the pre-First World War period as their opponents, Woolwich Arsenal, moved to their new home at Highbury in 1913, and dropped the 'Woolwich' name the following year. Bristol City's main rivals are the Bristol Rovers, or 'The Gas', who were founded in 1883. Bristol has the dubious record of being the largest metropolitan area never to have won football's top flight! The photograph below shows local fans arriving at the Ashton Gate Stadium entrance opposite the gates to Greville Smyth Park.

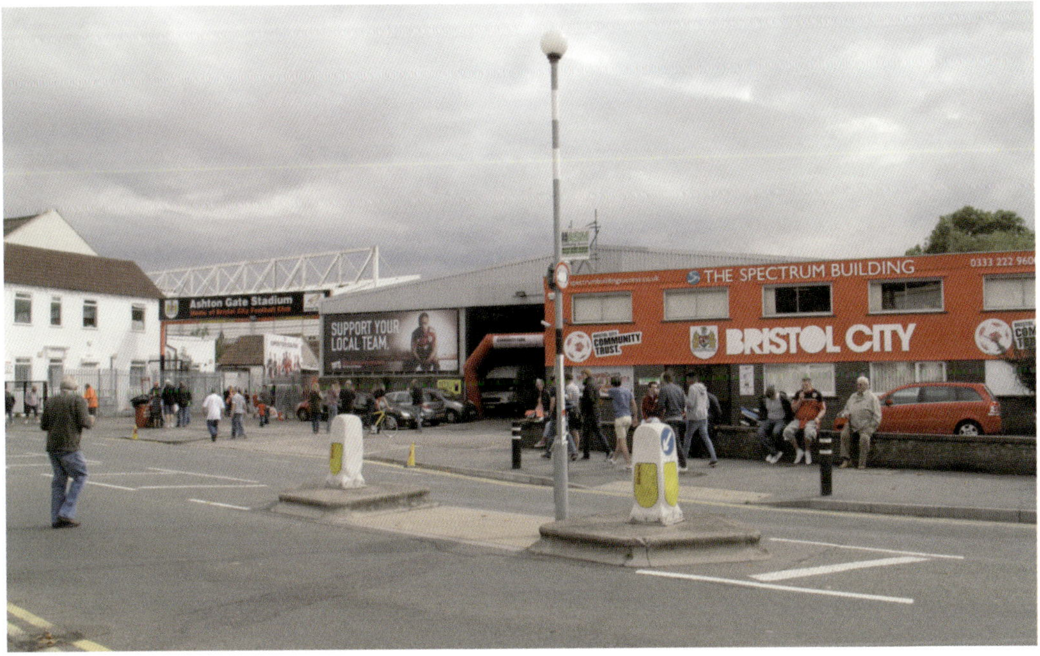

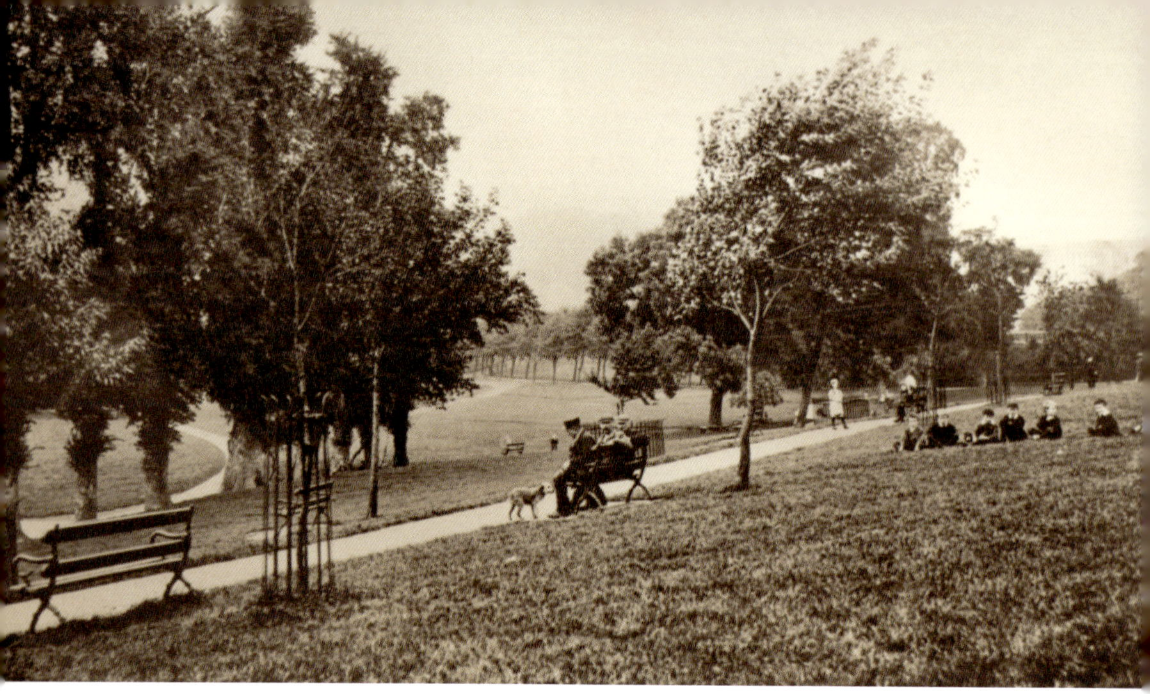

Greville Smyth Park

In 1881, the City of Bristol's Sanitary Committee received a letter from the solicitors of Greville Smyth, owner of Ashton Court, offering 21 acres of land of the Clift House estate at Ashton Gate for the purposes of establishing a 'Public Park or Pleasure ground'. The city happily accepted the generous donation and in the next three years, plans were drawn up for 'The People's park at Bedminster'. The pictures here are looking out towards Ashton Court.

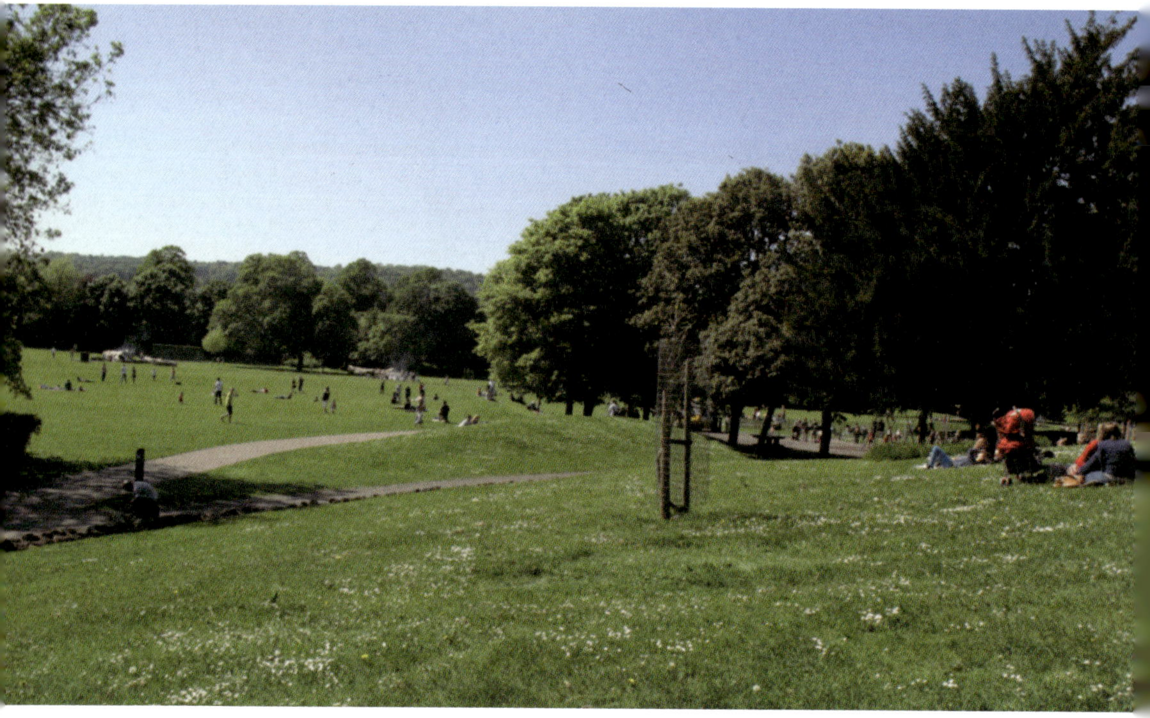

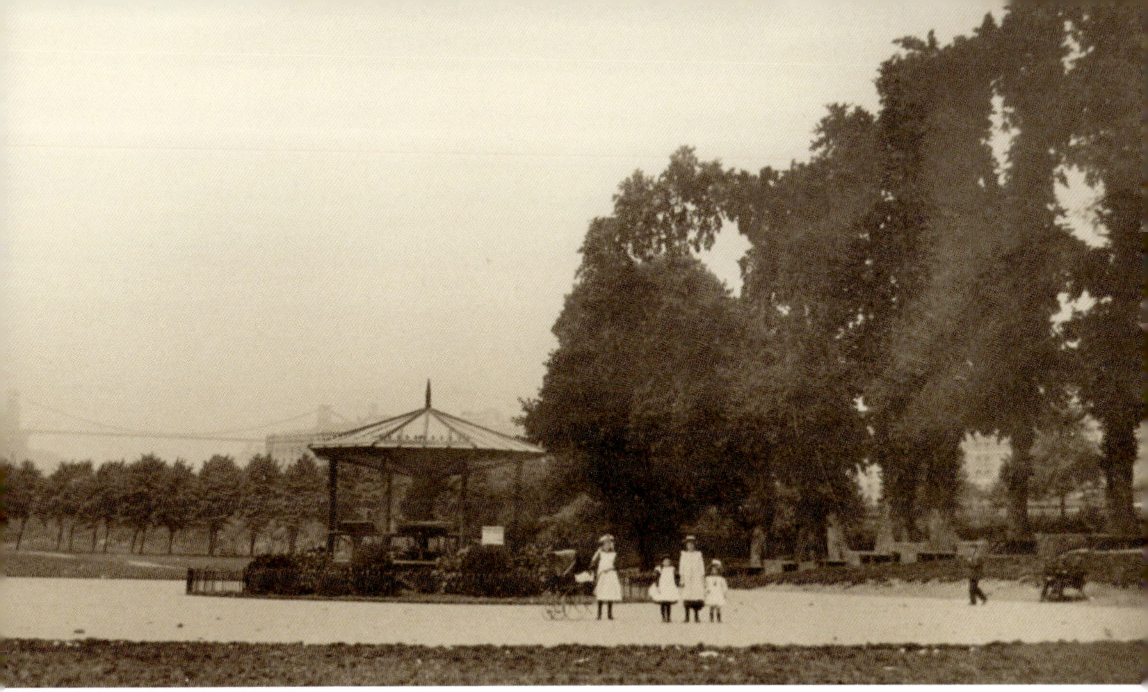

Greville Smyth Park

During the 1880s, paths were laid out, walls, entrance gates, a drinking fountain and two urinals were erected, and trees and shrubs were planted. The bandstand, seen here with the Clifton Suspension Bridge in the background, was built in 1887 to the same design as the one in Cotham Gardens. Sadly, the days of open-air brass band concerts have passed, but the playground that sits on the site of the bandstand is a popular replacement.

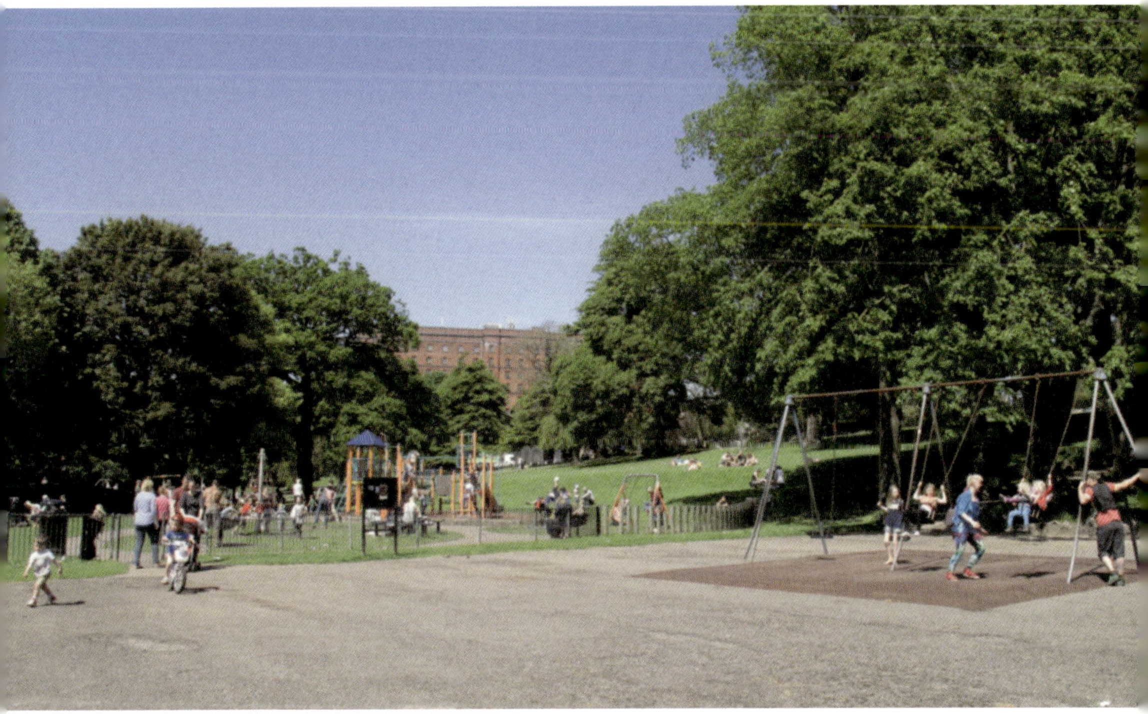

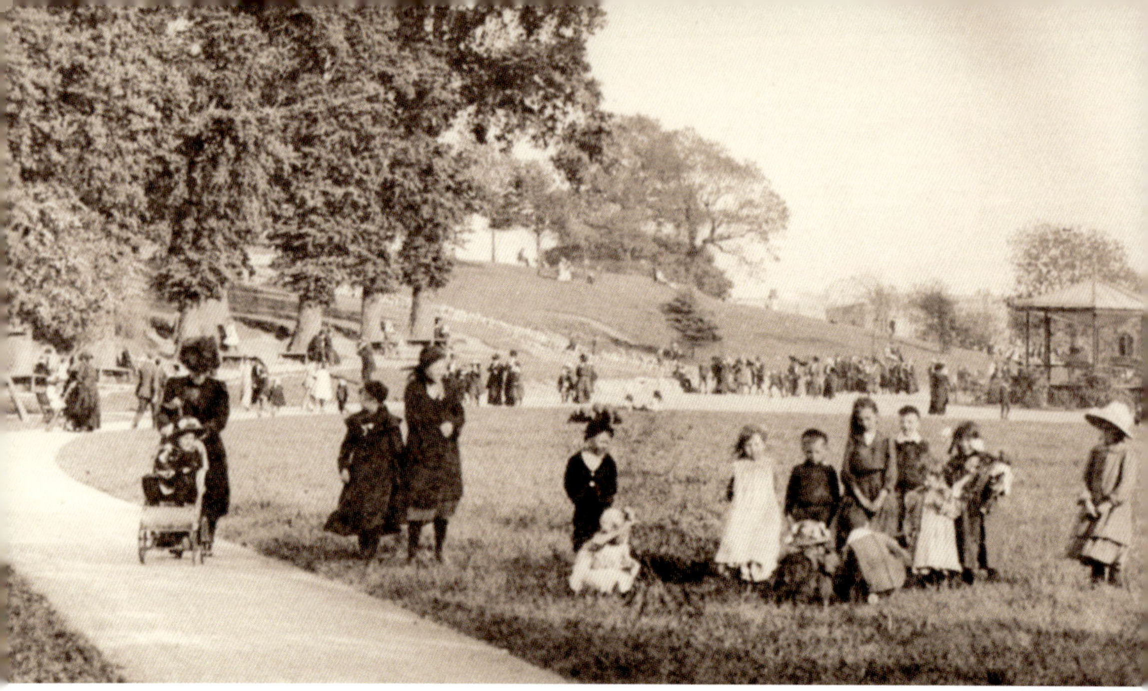

Greville Smyth Park

The general layout of the park has remained pretty much intact, and the sight of young mothers pushing prams along the paths would seem very familiar to our Edwardian ancestors pictured here (although they might be surprised that people no longer dress up to visit the park). The one major difference that marks out the old park from the new is the towering presence of Brunel Way and Clift House Road (which acts as an access point to the ever-busy Cumberland Basin).

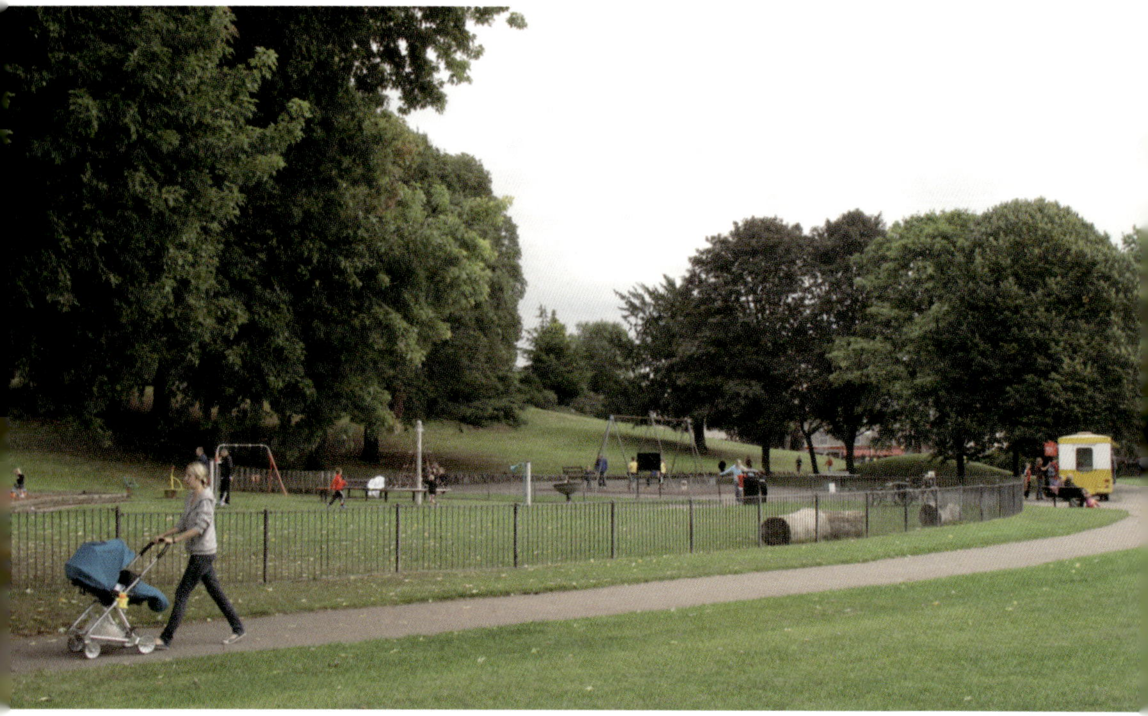

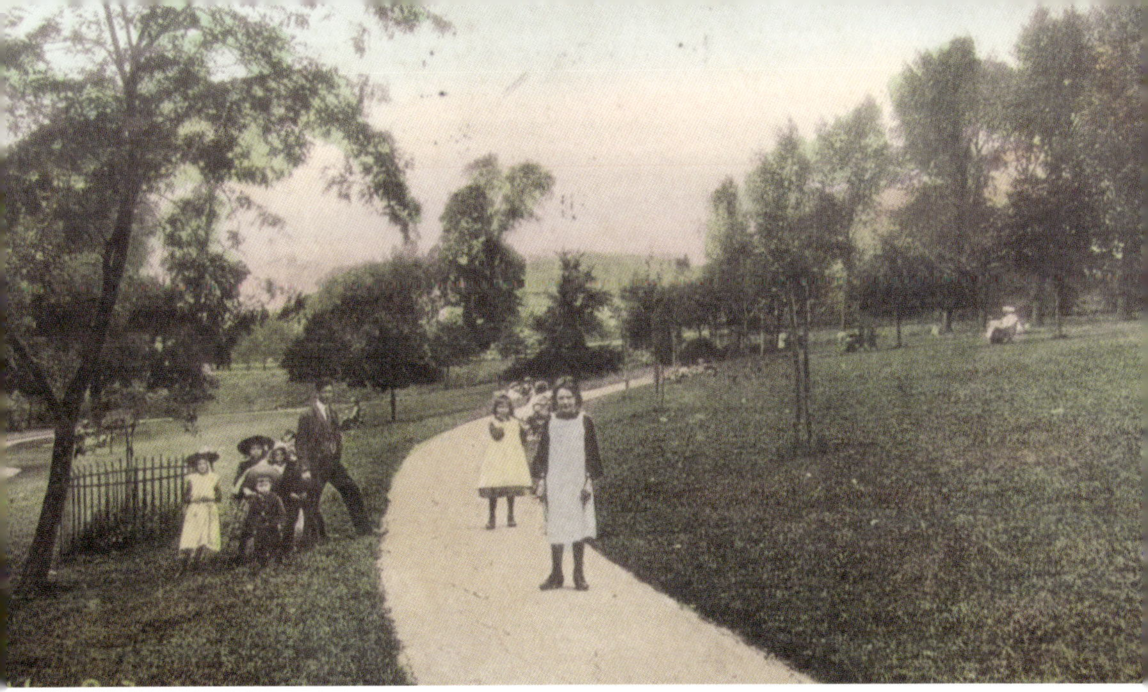

Greville Smyth Park

Previously known as Bedminster Park, and sometimes still referred to as Ashton Park, it was officially named the Greville Smyth Park in June 1902 on the request of Lady Smyth, who donated a further 4 acres at that time. It's a fitting tribute to the original benefactor, whose generosity has provided generations of Bristolians with a place to relax and unwind. Seen here is a group enjoying a barbecue on a sunny spring bank holiday in 2013.

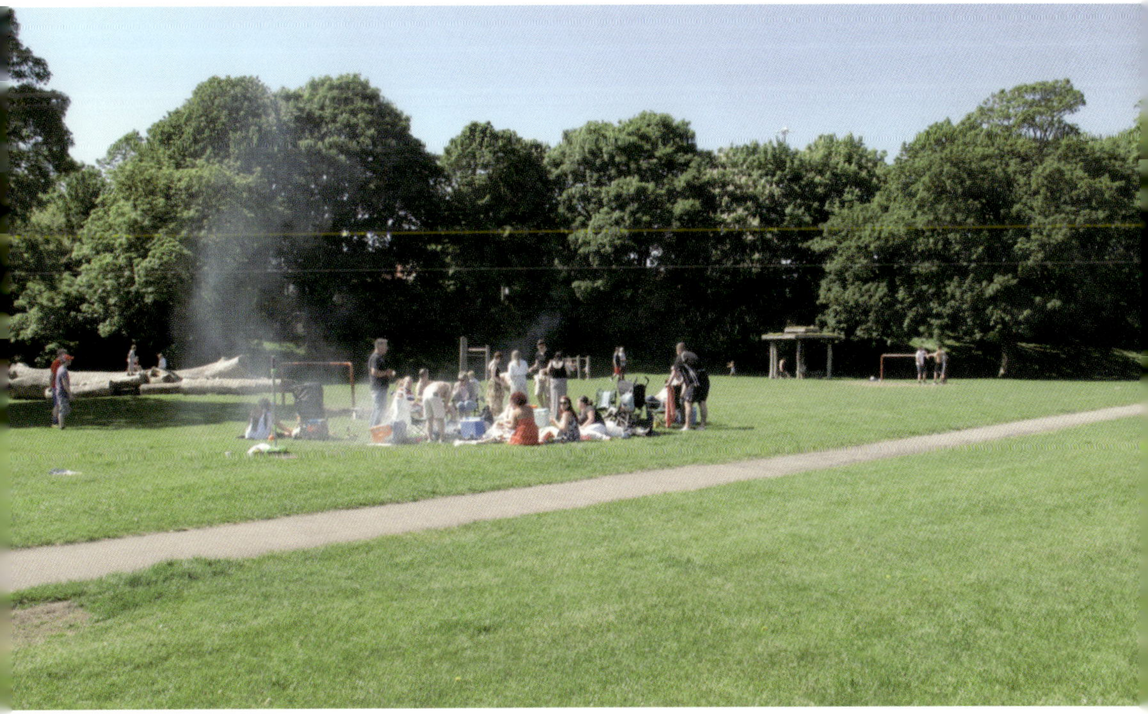

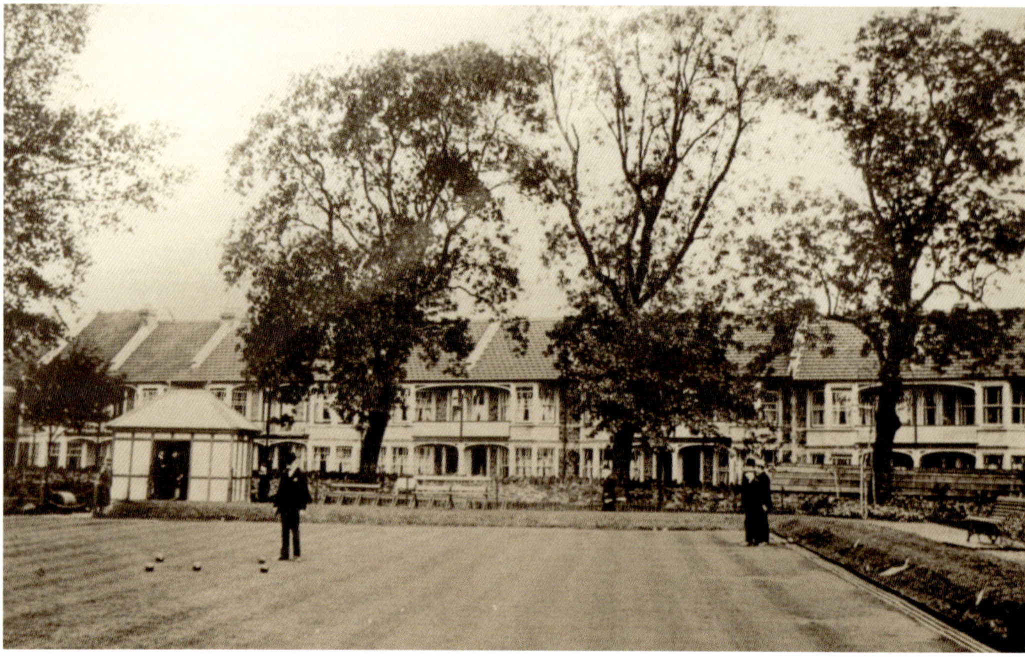

Bowling Green, Greville Smyth Park

As with many other public parks, Greville Smyth Park had a popular bowling green. The original clubhouse was built in 1909. Today's facilities are now surrounded by barbed wire. Sadly, some of the park's other amenities have not survived, and the open-air swimming pool, which was opened in 1905, has gone the same way as Victoria Park's. In the background is Frayne Road; the terraced houses still sport distinctive small balconies.

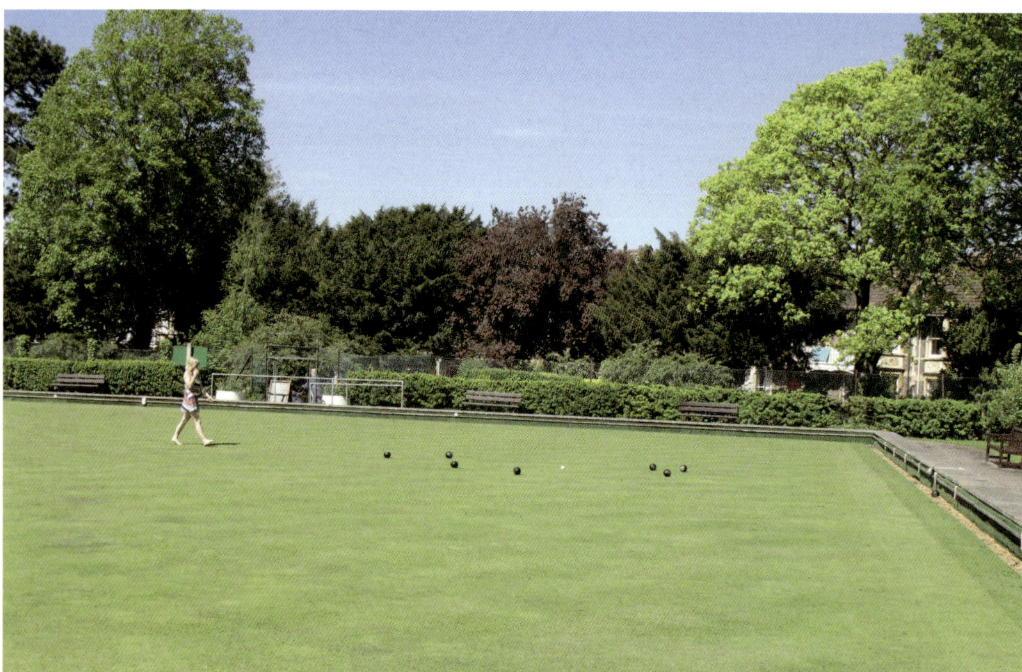

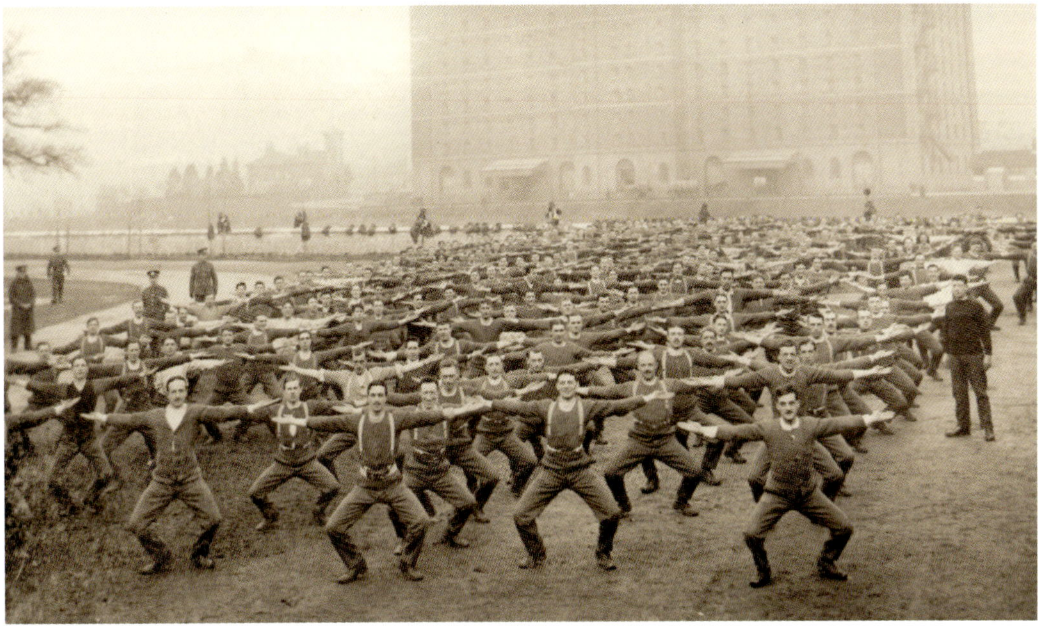

First World War Exercises, Ashton Gate, 1910s

The 12th Battalion, Gloucestershire Regiment, known as 'Bristol's Own', was formed by the Bristol Citizens Recruiting Committee, which was created in 1914. Comprised mainly of miners and farmworkers, the recruits trained in Ashton Court and here at Greville Smyth Park (the B Bond House is in the background), before moving to Yorkshire in June 1915, and then to Salisbury for their final preparation. The regiment arrived in France on 21 November 1915, and went on to be involved in all major battles in the next three years, including the Somme and Passchendaele. The casualty toll was horrific – one third of the original men were killed, and many more were injured. They were disbanded just before Armistice Day, by which time twenty-two battle honours had been awarded to 'Bristol's Own'.

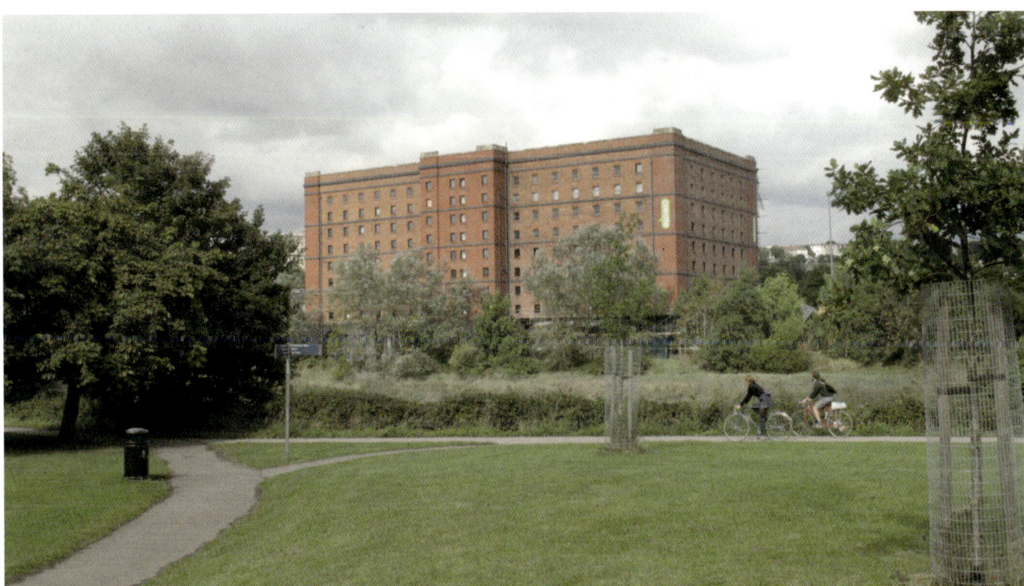

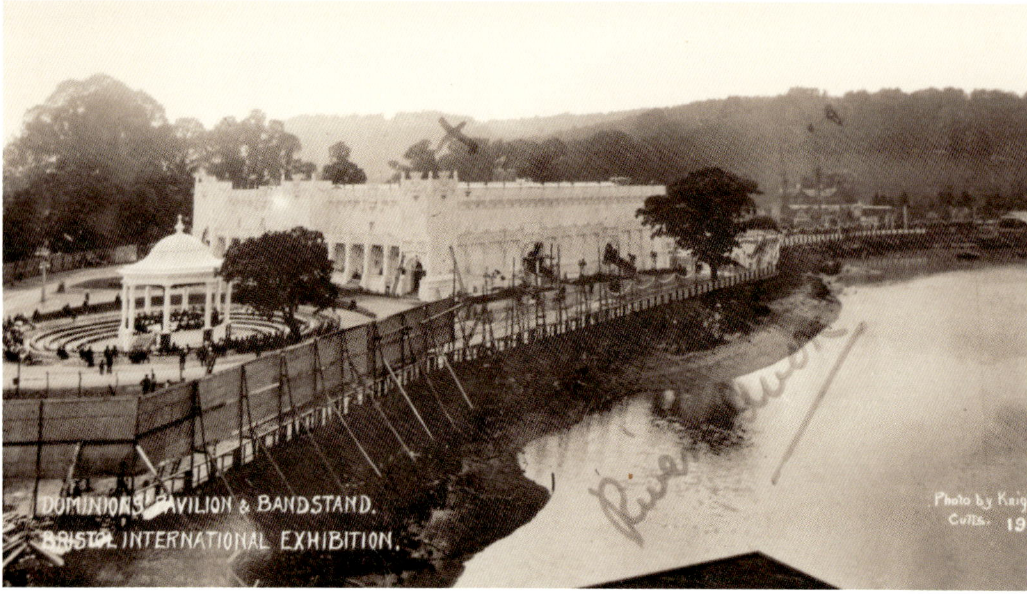

Bristol International Exhibition, Ashton Gate, 1910s

As it says on the old postcard, this is a picture of the Bristol International Exhibition that was held in 1914. It was a huge undertaking that cost £100,000. It covered 32 acres and took 2,000 workers 8 weeks to set it up. It was locally referred to as 'The White City'. The only reminder of this impressive display of Imperial pride are the allotments accessed from Clanage Road, which are called White City Allotments. There is a poignancy about the exhibition; opening on the bank holiday of 28 May 1914, it was due to run until October but on 4 August war was declared. By mid-September, the War Office had acquired the site and converted it into a temporary military facility used as a base for 'Bristol's Own'. Today, it is a nice place to walk, play or cycle beside the river.

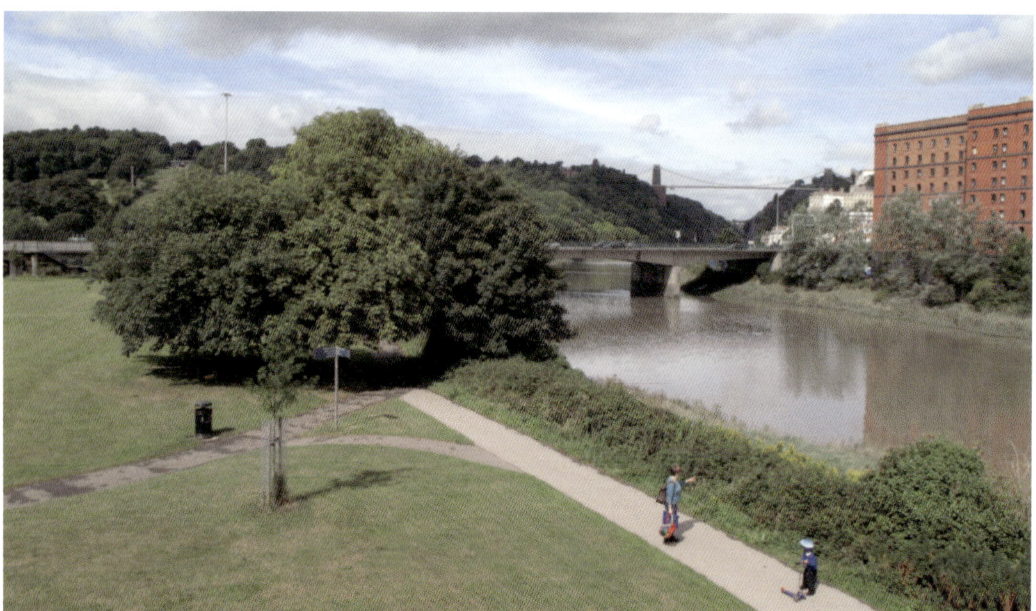

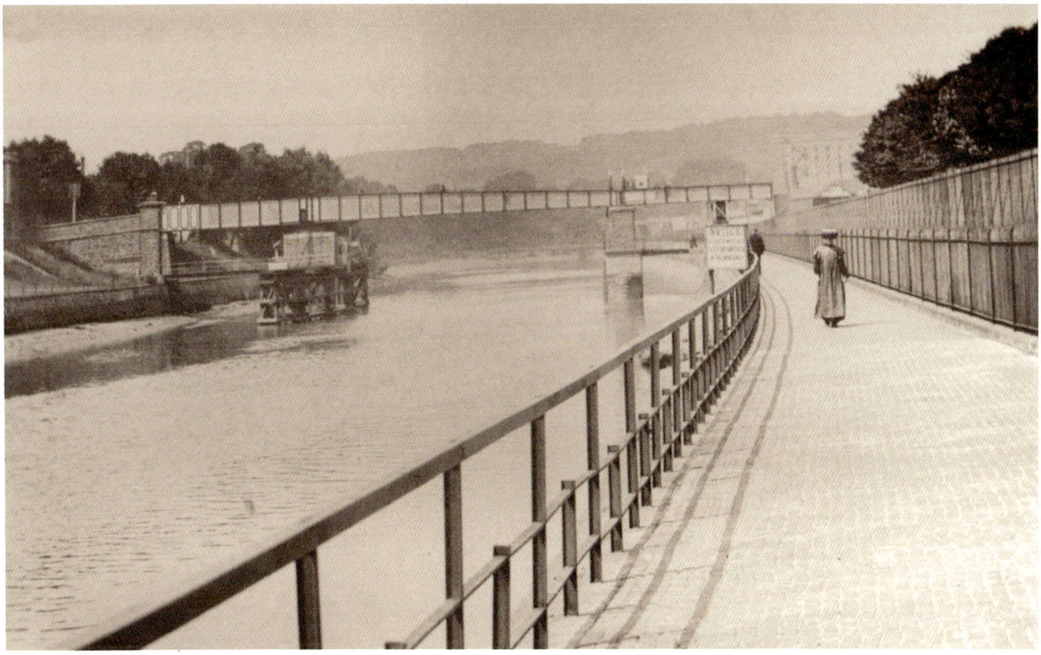

Vauxhall Bridge, Southville, Early 1900s

Built at a cost of £10,000, Vauxhall Bridge was opened by Lady Ashmead with a silver key on 1 June 1900. Originally, it was a swing bridge, linking Southville with Cumberland Road and Spike Island (which was comprised mainly of timber and boatyards and a tannery), but the ending of river traffic along this part of the Avon made the swinging feature redundant and it is now a fixed structure for pedestrians. Carefully hidden on the right of the picture above is the railway line to Temple Meads.

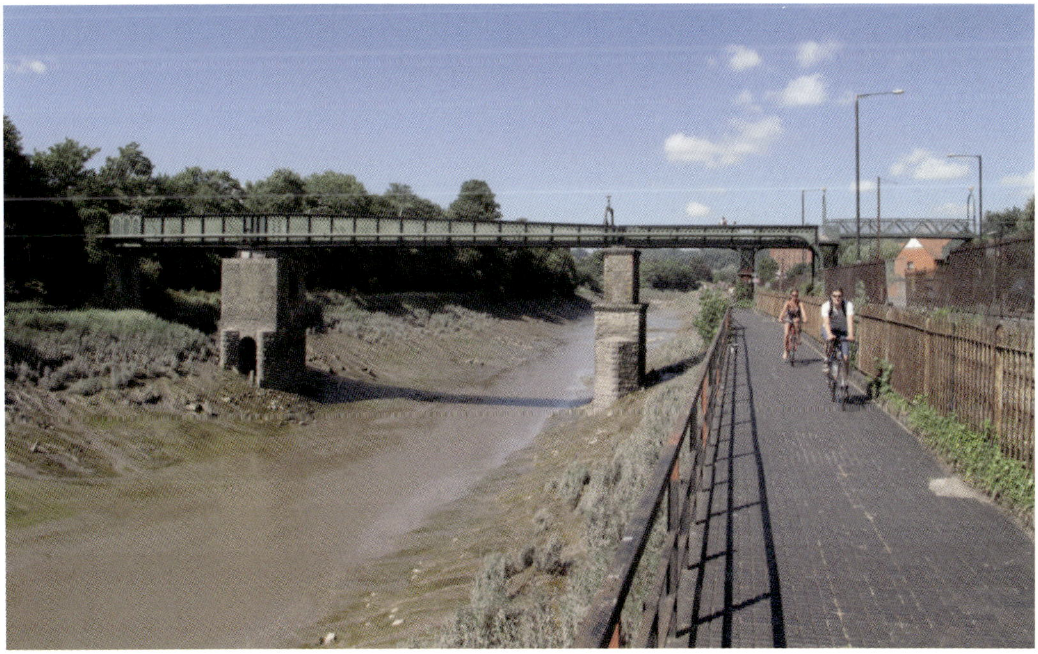

Acknowledgements

The author would like to express his gratitude to the staff at the Bristol Record Office, the staff at the Bristol Reference Library, the volunteer workers at the M-Shed museum, the City and County of Bristol Fire Brigade archivists, Jim Facey, the Malago Society, the late Roy Vaughan, Anton Bantock, David Lambert, Leonard Vear, and the many other authors and historians who have added to the knowledge and appreciation of South Bristol through the years. Finally, I would like to say a special thank you to my mother RoseMary for her patience and encouragement.

The following are the reference numbers for the images reproduced from the Bristol Record Office archives:

BRO43207/8 No. 24; BRO43207/9/5 Nos 53, 56, 57, 58, 59, 60, 92, 162, 163, 228; BRO43207/9/13 Nos 2, 3, 4, 5, 8, 10, 17, 32, 35, 38, 40, 42, 43, 45, 46, 53, 55, 60, 63, 67, 71, 72, 73, 74, 99, 101, 102, 103, 105, 106, 107, 108; BRO43207/9/29/10 Nos 49, 71, 73; BRO43207/21/13 No. 3; BRO43207/25 Nos 14, 17, 18, 20; BRO43207/29/11 Nos 2, 3; BRO43207/37/7 No.1; BROPicBox/2/Bst/74; BROPicBox/3/Blitz/36; BRO41969/1/ Nos 50 and 52.

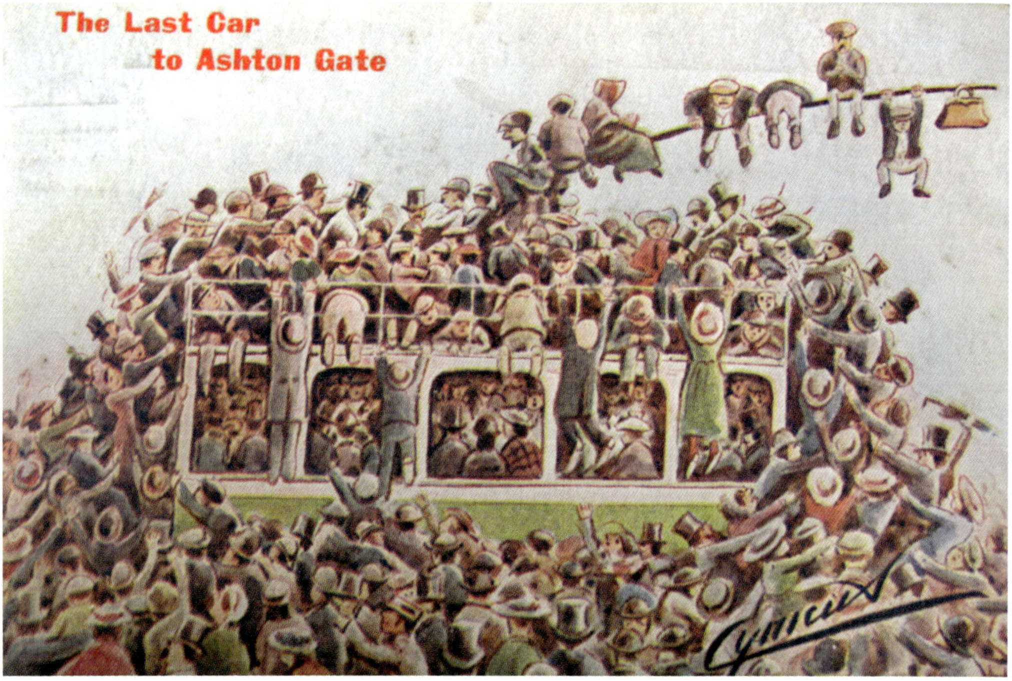

'The Last Car to Ashton Gate'.